The Making of
Nova Southeastern University

The Making of Nova Southeastern University

A Tradition of Innovation, 1964–2014

JULIAN M. PLEASANTS, PHD

Foreword by Ronald G. Assaf
Chairman, Nova Southeastern University Board of Trustees

Nova Southeastern University, Inc.
Fort Lauderdale-Davie

Printed in the United States of America. This book is printed on Glatfelter Natures Book, a paper certified under the standards of the Forestry Stewardship Council (FSC). It is a recycled stock that contains 30 percent post-consumer waste and is acid-free.

This book is also available in an electronic edition.

18 17 16 15 14 13   6 5 4 3 2 1

Library of Congress Cataloging-in-Publication Data

Pleasants, Julian M.
  The making of Nova Southeastern University: a tradition of innovation, 1964–2014 / Julian M. Pleasants; foreword by Ronald G. Assaf.
      p. cm.
  Includes bibliographical references and index.
  Summary: A history of the establishment and growth of Nova Southeastern University in Fort Lauderdale-Davie, Florida.
  ISBN 978-0-9892991-0-7
  1. Nova Southeastern University—History.   2. Universities and colleges—Florida—Fort Lauderdale—History.   3. Private universities and colleges—Florida—Fort Lauderdale—History.   I. Assaf, Ronald G.   II. Title.
  LD4130.P54 2013
  378.759′35—dc23

                                                                        2013018436

Nova Southeastern University, Inc.
3301 College Avenue
Fort Lauderdale-Davie, FL 33314-7796
http://www.nova.edu

NOVA SOUTHEASTERN
UNIVERSITY

Contents

Foreword

It gives me great satisfaction to write the foreword for Dr. Julian Pleasants's *The Making of Nova Southeastern University: A Tradition of Innovation, 1964–2014*.

My professional training was in business, and in 1968 I cofounded Sensormatic Electronics Corporation, expanded it into a New York Stock Exchange company, and in 2001 retired as its chairman of the board. I have had a lifetime commitment to education, having sent to college five of my children and six grandchildren (with more to come). I have established scholarships at three different universities and have served on two other university boards. I believe in the American dream, with education as the critical driving force in making the reality of that dream available to all. Education is a gift that keeps giving over a lifetime, provides opportunity in many directions, and changes lives for the better. After meeting with then board of trustees chair Ray Ferrero Jr., he convinced me that Nova Southeastern University (NSU) would be at the forefront of innovation in developing quality education and delivering education at a time and place not bound by walls, thus making a degree attainable for all potential students. It was an exciting new concept, and I wanted to be part of it.

Elected to the NSU Board of Trustees in 1994, I have served on each of the NSU board's numerous committees. I assumed the duties of chairman of the board in 2005, and I am proud to have been a small part of the tremendous growth the university has enjoyed over these past eleven years.

Distinguished scholar Dr. Julian M. Pleasants is professor emeritus of history at the University of Florida (UF), where he taught for thirty-nine years. Pleasants served as director of the Samuel Proctor Oral History Program at UF from 1996 to 2008. He taught more than 11,000 students in his career at UF and was the recipient of more than a dozen teaching awards. He was chosen for inclusion in *Who's Who Among American Teachers*, *Who's Who in America*, and *Who's Who in the World*. He is the author and editor of eight books and numerous articles in various publications. His books about Florida include *Hanging Chads: The Inside Story of the 2000 Presidential Recount in Florida* (2004), *Orange Journalism: Voices from Florida Newspapers* (2003), *Gator Tales: An Oral History of the University of Florida* (2006), and *Seminole Voices: Reflections on Their Changing Society, 1970–2000* (2010) (with Harry A. Kersey). In 2010, the Florida Humanities Council awarded him the silver medal for nonfiction for his book on the Seminoles.

In 2014, NSU will celebrate its fiftieth anniversary. The State of Florida chartered NSU (then called Nova University of Advanced Technology) in December 1964, when its only office was a storefront on Las Olas Boulevard. NSU's history is one of a series of difficulties and hard-won successes. As this book explains, in the early years the university often struggled for its financial life and survival as an institution. NSU has come a long way since 1964.

The administrative leadership of an organization has two options in the approach to its managerial responsibilities: one is maintaining the system the way it is, and the other is changing the system so that it performs more efficiently and serves its client in a more accountable way. As Dr. Pleasants makes clear in his discourse on the university history, the latter was the NSU way.

There was a popular saying among NSU administrators that "you cannot spell innovate without using the word Nova." Dr. Pleasants illustrates this point by identifying the following themes as common threads throughout the book: a spirit of innovation, an unrelenting entrepreneurial drive, and a tenacity to succeed despite financial adversity. These attitudes and other factors enabled NSU to rise from humble beginnings to become one of the largest and most successful not-for-profit independent universities in the country. To have accomplished this feat in less than fifty years is, to say the least, extraordinary. In fact, many would describe NSU's evolution from a relatively unknown local institution to a worldwide multidimensional university as revolutionary.

The rewards of reading this book are many—and often surprising. The reader's natural curiosity about how NSU got started, which initial colleges were established, and what courses were taught is satisfied, but the book offers much more. Those interested in other topics, such as university personalities, governing bodies, presidents past and current, campus construction, athletics, diversity, international programs, and community outreach, will have their questions answered as well.

Several pivotal events are noted throughout the book. Perhaps most important was the timely merger with New York Institute of Technology. The eventual breakup with this institution due to incompatible goals enabled NSU to pursue its goal as an independent institution. Other significant events include the loss of the research vessel *Gulf Stream* and its crew, the establishment of the law school, the relocation of the Germ-Free Life Research Center from Tampa to the main campus, the innovative programs developed at the University School, the partnership with the Miami Dolphins, the establishing of a private/public joint-use library (the largest library in Florida at the time of this writing), and the important and successful merger with Southeastern University of the Health Sciences.

The early years at NSU were characterized by periods of major organizational changes and educational program reforms. This book describes these changes in detail and their implications for NSU's future. Initially, the university was heavily involved in programs such as science education, ocean sciences, behavioral sciences, and cancer research. This focus has since been expanded to include new offerings in law, business, computer science, psychology, medicine, pharmacy, dentistry, optometry, nursing, physical and family therapy, and allied health. Many of these programs are multidisciplinary in nature.

One of the core principles at NSU is that higher education should not be bound by time or place; instead, it should be an avenue to provide an increasing number of options for students in pursuit of their academic goals. Parallel to this basic philosophy is the view that the traditional classroom approach to education held many aspects that were inefficient for both teachers and students. Education is always an individual experience. The early visionaries felt that in future years, it would be possible to earn an ever-increasing number of credits toward obtaining one's degree on-site, off campus, or in an online classroom environment. Institutions must create a culture that values change.

As one might expect, when these innovative ideas were adopted, other colleges and universities initially opposed the new teaching techniques, and NSU was attacked, criticized, and hampered by a series of lawsuits. Vindication would come in later years, as many of the country's most prestigious universities have implemented a similar approach to teaching. Perhaps this, more than any other event, is evidence of NSU's singular influence in curricular and delivery systems in higher education. As Dr. Pleasants states, "Nova University, which began with the goal of becoming the MIT of the South, now has the satisfaction of seeing one of the best institutions in the country [MIT] adopt the format of off-campus online education that [Nova] pioneered in 1974."

Readers of these pages will learn about innovation and tradition at a very unique academic institution during its formative and later years. The reader, mainly through oral history interviews, will garner insights into the men and women who accomplished this feat, their successes and failures, and their ultimate triumph.

Meticulously researched and written in a straightforward, easy to read style, Dr. Pleasants has given us a thoughtful, balanced, well-written history which will broaden our understanding of what took place during NSU's first 50 years. In addition, all nine chapters have readily free-flowing text, firsthand accounts, biographical data, and illustrative photographs.

What has been accomplished in fifty years is nothing short of remarkable, and only the imagination can tell how great this university can be over the next fifty years.

Ronald G. Assaf
Chairman, Nova Southeastern University Board of Trustees

Preface

I first became involved with Nova Southeastern University (NSU) when Lydia Acosta, vice president for information services and university librarian, called to ask if I would conduct some oral history interviews with the current and former presidents of the university and with some of the founding fathers. I did research on the university's history and found that it had a fascinating past. Several times during its formative years, Nova University of Advanced Technology—the school's original name—had almost gone bankrupt and narrowly avoided closing its doors for good. When I first visited the campus in 2009, I was impressed with the extraordinary progress that Nova Southeastern University made in its less than fifty years of existence. Today, the university has a law school, a medical school, an attractive campus with a student body of some 27,000 students, and an annual budget of $600 million. Nova's evolution began in 1961 with the long-range vision of a group of local businessmen who called themselves the Oatmeal Club. Thus, when Lydia asked me to write a history of NSU, I readily agreed.

I interviewed some thirty individuals, including all of the living presidents, who were part of the founding and development of the university. The administration and staff members of the NSU Archives at the Alvin Sherman Library suggested most of the interviewees. I could have interviewed other important people in NSU's history, but time and funding was a factor, so we selected those who we thought would give us the best chance to discover the details behind the school's success. I am deeply indebted to those who took the time to sit for an interview, and I am grateful for the knowledge and wisdom they imparted.

Dr. Richard Dodge, Dr. Jerry Chermak, Dr. Arnold Melnick, Dr. Brad Williams, John Santulli, Jamie Mayersohn, and Professor Ron Brown were gracious enough to review the section of the book that related to their experiences and saved me from a number of errors.

It is important to note that discrepancies, inaccuracies, and distortions often occur in any oral history. The human memory is not perfect and is often flawed when retracing events that happened many years ago. Other versions of the same event might differ in several specifics from the oral history interviews used in this volume. In a few interviews, some recollections have been clearly disputed by the facts. One member of the board of trustees, for example, remembered that he had voted for a certain merger when the minutes of the board clearly showed that he voted against it.

Each person brings his/her own values and background (gender, age, race, religion, experience) to the interview, and what one person thinks is important, another person might dismiss out of hand. As with a traffic accident viewed by three different people, there are always conflicting and differing views of the same event. I have tried to look at official documents and any other factual material to determine the accuracy of oral presentations. Often there was no supporting evidence and I had to take a person's view as his/her truth. There are serious gaps in the official record, especially in the early years. On some occasions I had to assume facts not in evidence and make the most appropriate conclusions possible without all the necessary information. Frequently, several accounts taken as a whole provided a basic understanding of what happened, and I have tried to accommodate all of the differing opinions as best I could. Nonetheless, these oral history interviews play an important part in understanding the history of the school—these "spoken memories" provide insight into how and why decisions were made, how certain individuals influenced the evolution of the institution, and what events were most significant in the fifty-year history of NSU. In addition, oral histories can provide powerful and evocative accounts of events from people who experienced them firsthand. The NSU interviews personalize events and elicit information lacking in university documents, newspapers, and other more formal sources.

While much of the information on which this book is based came from oral history interviews, the majority of the factual material was gleaned from sources in the NSU Archives. These sources included official documents, such as the minutes of the South Florida Education Center (SFEC) and the Nova Southeastern University Board of Trustees, presidential papers, newspapers and periodicals, university publications and press releases, and outside historical accounts of events in Broward County.

As one might expect, the information obtained from these university sources is uniformly positive in its treatment of the university. Some of the material is outright propaganda, which is part of the responsibility of any publicity office—to make the institution look good. Even the local newspapers, with some exceptions, have reported favorably on NSU. Nonetheless, I have attempted to present an unbiased view of the history of the university, warts and all.

When writing this history on Nova Southeastern University, as is the case with any institution, there was a lack of sufficient and verifiable factual information in the NSU Archives and other sources to support conclusions about specific issues, such as NSU's financial activities, land acquisition, and the designation of money for certain projects. Without all of the necessary information, one had to draw conclusions based to some degree on conjecture.

I have attempted to footnote each reference of importance, but have taken the liberty of putting several sources in one footnote at the end of a lengthy discussion of an issue or event rather than overwhelm the reader with hundreds of separate footnotes. This practice may create some confusion about exactly where one quotation came from, but all of the collective footnotes relate to the subject at hand.

This book is not meant to be a complete academic history of Nova Southeastern University. Rather it is an informal compendium of facts, events, reminiscences, and stories. In writing a history of NSU, I have attempted to enliven facts with personal recollections of faculty, administrators, staff, supporters, and students. I have focused on some of the more interesting situations rather than provide a boring recitation of facts. There have been so many events and personalities in the history of NSU that it would require three volumes to cover all the details of the university's history. The aim of this book is to enable readers, through a tapestry of various events and key personalities, to understand the evolution of NSU from an institution that was barely viable in the 1960s to a thriving and successful university in 2014. Any choice one makes about source materials will necessarily omit some facts that another observer would insist on including. Hopefully, this mix of recollections, official documents, and newspapers will cover all the historical highlights, while explaining how each university president influenced the school and how the academic programs and social activities have changed over the years.

The manuscript could never have been completed without the assistance and support of many people. President George Hanbury endorsed the project and was available with suggestions and recommendations for the manuscript. Frank DePiano, provost and executive vice president for academic affairs, first proposed the idea for a history of NSU and fully supported the project with funding and wise counsel. Lydia Acosta functioned as my liaison with NSU from the beginning. Lydia was very generous with her time and advice during the entire project. Harriett MacDougall, executive director of the Alvin Sherman Library, helped in the review and editing process and supplied valuable information on the construction of the library.

The manuscript could never have been completed in such a short time without the superb assistance from the staff of the NSU Archives in the Alvin Sherman Library. First and foremost, Robert Bogorff, director of the NSU Archives, is a walking encyclopedia of the history of the university. He came to the campus in 1971 and knows most of the players and events during the school's history. He has a deep and sound knowledge of the various collections, and his support and advocacy were invaluable. Cheryl Peltier-Davis, a published author and librarian par excellence, aided the process tremendously with her expertise in technical matters, research, and writing. She accessed fugitive bits of information from the archives with accuracy and dispatch. Cathy Elios, the Archives coordinator, was enormously helpful with a myriad of activities, from obtaining information from university sources to securing necessary material to support the writing of the book. Her advice, as was the case with all of the aforementioned, was almost always on target. Allison Durland, who worked as the student assistant, is a master of the Internet and helped all of us get the information we needed. Piya Chayanuwat, director of library computing services, was both brilliant and patient in helping this technologically challenged writer with computer problems. For readers wishing for more information on NSU history, please contact NSU Archives by visiting http://www.nova.edu/archives/ or calling (954) 262-4642.

I am grateful to the staff of the University Press of Florida; Meredith Morris-Babb, director; Dennis Lloyd, deputy director; Lynn Werts, associate director; and Iris Sutcliffe, copy editor. Their professional expertise has improved the quality of the book and made the entire process much easier.

The help and support of everyone mentioned was valuable, but I alone am responsible for the interpretation, the factual presentation, and the conclusions in this book. Any mistakes and errors are my responsibility.

Julian M. Pleasants
February 19, 2013

The Making of
Nova Southeastern University

1

The Beginning
The Oatmeal Club, Early 1960s

The concept of Nova Southeastern University began in the imagination of a few conservative businessmen in Fort Lauderdale, Florida. It grew from storefront offices on Las Olas Boulevard to what is today the eighth largest not-for-profit private university in the United States, situated on a main campus of over 300 acres, with 27,000 students and a budget of almost $600 million. This is the story of that remarkable achievement.

In the early 1960s, a group of civic-minded pioneer settlers in Broward County, Florida, frequently met for breakfast at Cope's restaurant in downtown Fort Lauderdale. They often discussed the future of the rapidly growing city and of Broward County. They called themselves the Oatmeal Club.

Two of the original group members, Myron L. Ashmore, superintendent of Broward County Schools from 1961 to 1968, and Joe B. Rushing, founding president of the Junior College of Broward County (now Broward College), had long discussed the possibility of expanding educational opportunities in South Florida. Both men had significant experience in secondary and higher education and had pursued inventive and original concepts in learning. Rushing and Ashmore would be two of the most influential members of the original Oatmeal Club in developing a new educational concept.

In the years after World War II, Fort Lauderdale, with its beautiful beaches and warm climate, showed positive signs of rapid growth and developed an active, aggressive business community. The local businessmen who made up the Oatmeal Club understood the unlimited future for the South Florida area and believed that Broward County would eventually need an integrated educational system. Historian Gary Mormino described the dramatic growth of Broward County from the 1950s until 2000. In the 1950s, Broward, "a huge county sprawling over 1,200 square miles," had only 83,933 residents. Most of the local communities, such as Deerfield Beach, Pompano, and Davie, "had one foot in their rural past with the other striding toward a dynamic future." The transformation of these agricultural and rural communities into heavily populated retirement communities and suburban developments was, according to Mormino, "stunning in its size and scope." Broward County's population quadrupled in the 1950s and nearly doubled again in the 1960s. By 1980, Broward County had one million residents; by 2000, the population increased to 1.6 million. During the 1990s, among counties with a population of more than 100,000, Broward was the country's third fastest-growing county at an astonishing rate of 22.3 percent.

The county's growth, however, proved to be somewhat of a mixed blessing. While 750 families moved to Broward County each week in the 1950s, in the 1960s Fort Lauderdale's vital and energetic downtown area, especially Las Olas Boulevard, began to fall prey to the same problem encountered by other large cities—suburbanization. By 1963, more than 125 stores in downtown Fort Lauderdale fell vacant.[1] The population flight—primarily whites—away from the urban center proved beneficial for some smaller towns, such as Davie, the ultimate location of Nova Southeastern University, as it grew rapidly in size and influence.

The Oatmeal Club, aware of the great potential for growth in South Florida, began to contemplate what kind of educational system they would want for Broward County. Robert Ellyson recalled attending a Rotary Club meeting where Stuart Synnestvedt, newly arrived in Fort Lauderdale, made a presentation on education. Synnestvedt, a successful businessman who never completed his university degree, spent much of his life contemplating the importance of education in developing future citizens. Synnestvedt talked about the importance of teaching students not only factual information, but also how to learn. He proposed a unified educational system from kindergarten to PhD—from the womb to the tomb, or the cradle to the grave. He wanted to teach children and adults how to meet the advanced challenges of a new age: "To provide a system of quality education from infancy onward for the common man and also provide a challenge and inspiration for the uncommon man."[2] The original members of the informal Oatmeal Club—Stuart Synnestvedt, Joe Rushing, Charles Forman, Jack Hines, and Myron Ashmore—were impressed and intrigued by the concept of an integrated educational system from kindergarten to graduate school and decided then and there to pursue Synnestvedt's dream.

The group later expanded to include L. Coleman Judd, Henry Perry Sr., Carl A. Hiaasen Sr., James (Jim) Farquhar, George English, and Hamilton Forman. The group envisioned a pioneering type of educational complex where instruction would be provided at all levels and where new ideas in education could be developed, implemented, and evaluated for the benefit of not only the local community, but also society at large. Initially his colleagues were uncertain whether Synnestvedt was "a genius or a crackpot" and knew that the dream would be difficult to achieve, but they decided to push forward anyway. There were already elementary schools and a junior college in the county; to complete the educational complex they needed to create a kindergarten, a middle school, an innovative high school, and a university. All would be part of the Broward County public school system and would be supported by public taxes.[3]

In 1961, the Oatmeal Club incorporated the not-for-profit South Florida Education Center, Inc. (SFEC), with Joe Rushing as president. With the cooperation of the Broward County Board of Public Instruction, the SFEC formed the Nova Educational Complex, which included the Junior College of Broward County, Nova Elementary School, and, on April 5, 1964, Nova High School, an experimental high school that had won national recognition. They chose the name Nova because it is derived from the Latin word novus, meaning new, since they believed that their concept was new and different.[4]

The most unique aspect to this educational experiment was that the idea came full-blown from the local community. The founders did not initially consult with state officials or national experts on education; rather, they discussed the matter and decided to go ahead on their own. It seems almost incredible that these local businessmen, who had no experience in education except for their own schooling, would come up with such an original and challenging concept. A.D. Griffin recalled, "We all pitched in. We had a good group." Hamilton Forman recalled, "Nova University started one night on [my wife's] dining room table when group member and businessman Jack Hines pounded on the table and said, 'We've just got to have a university.'"

Two of the most influential participants in the Nova plan were Charles and Hamilton Forman, members of one of Broward County's pioneer families. In 1910, Hamilton Forman Sr. and his wife, Blanche, left Illinois, lured by the promise of riches to be made in Florida. They built a shack out of hard pine with no electricity or indoor plumbing in what is now Davie, Florida, and in 1917 started the county's first dairy farm. The family braved droughts, mosquitoes, and the horrendous 1926 hurricane but survived and prospered. Charles Forman remembered his mother hoisting a rifle to her shoulder to shoot alligators that came too close to the chicken coops. Charles and his brother learned their can-do individualism from their parents, and by the 1960s the Forman family was one of the most politically powerful families in the county. As Hamilton Forman later acknowledged, the farsighted members of the Oatmeal Club wanted to develop the educational system to benefit the community, but as businessmen, they also hoped that the success of their vision would benefit them as well.[5]

Other key participants in the early planning stages included Tinsley Ellis, an attorney who supervised the incorporation of the university, and James Hartley, the main architect of the Nova University campus. Both men were born to early settlers who relocated to Hollywood and Fort Lauderdale in 1925. Jim Farquhar, a landscape architect, settled in Broward in 1945 and, realizing that no one was producing sod for the huge future home-building industry, bought 500 acres of land and began a prosperous business as a self-described sod farmer. Farquhar described the tiny town of Davie, which was in the boondocks far from downtown Fort Lauderdale, as "cowboy country." Hamilton Forman referred to it as a nice "one-horse town." There was one service station, and the owner spent as much time working with saddles and bridles as he did repairing automobiles. Citizens rode their horses freely around town, and one could often find a horse tied to the hitching post at the local hardware store.[6]

Napoleon Bonaparte Broward, governor of Florida from 1905 to 1909, started the exodus to southern Florida by sponsoring a giant project that drained the Everglades of saltwater and reclaimed millions of acres of valuable land. Governor Broward, after whom the county was named, authorized the selling of large tracts of land for $2 an acre. That money was used to drain and channel the water that frequently covered the land.[7]

Like the Formans, other pioneer families arrived in Davie around 1909. The Griffins came from Kentucky, the Formans from Illinois, others from Michigan. Several were workers returning from the Panama Canal Zone. Since the southern Florida terrain resembled that of Panama, the town's original name was Zona. There were no roads, and the early families were widely scattered, but the pioneer spirit prevailed as the settlers relied on their own survival skills. In 1925, forty-eight residents decided to incorporate the community and drew up an official code for the town of Davie. However, the citizens were unwilling to pay any taxes, so the municipality was dissolved and the town of Davie was not officially chartered until 1960.

By 1980, the town's population was 80,000, but that number was about to explode. With the ocean to the east and the urban population growing along the I-95 corridor, the logical way for Fort Lauderdale to expand was westward toward the Everglades. At one point, western Fort Lauderdale was considered to be west of Highway 441. There had always been a divide between the urban downtown of Fort Lauderdale and its western neighbors. As late as the 1970s, there were people on the east side who considered Davie to be in the hinterlands and never traveled west of Highway 441. Most county citizens were not even aware that there was much going on in such an unsophisticated area, much less the development of a new university. By the 1990s, as the population inexorably grew, the west side was now considered to be west of the Florida Turnpike and Davie was strategically situated right in the middle of Broward County. Davie citizens dreaded the loss of their rural lifestyle with the coming of new roads, more cars, and more people, but by 2000 the town had become a thriving community.

Victoria Wagner in her book, *The History of Davie and Its Dilemma*, tried to capture the essence of the Davie spirit. She concluded that to prosper, the early settlers had to work hard under the most discouraging conditions, such as the severe hurricane of 1926. To survive, they had to help each other, especially in times of distress. The commitment to cooperation, enterprise, and commerce enabled them to succeed.[8] This same entrepreneurial spirit and commitment to succeed exhibited by the citizens of Davie can be applied to the history of Nova University. The founders, especially the Formans and the Griffins, carried on with the same passion, zeal, and can-do attitude in the founding of Nova University.

The South Florida Education Center began its planning very slowly. They primarily wanted to provide the "missing link" in their grandiose plan, a postgraduate university concentrating on science and technology. The need for a technological university in Florida had been a major concern for some time, but the state had failed to establish one. The SFEC was acutely aware that an institution of the caliber of Massachusetts Institute of Technology or California Institute of

Technology was necessary to provide highly trained students for the area's emerging industrial and government entities. A technological research institution was especially needed in South Florida because previous state legislatures had been dominated by legislators from the northern part of the state. These rural legislators had generally ignored the needs of South Florida; consequently, the two major universities at the time, Florida State University and the University of Florida, were located in northern Florida. With the exception of the recently established Florida Atlantic University, there was no other state university in South Florida. The SFEC, however, did not want a state supported university; it wanted a privately endowed institution that would be free of government control and free to set its own policies for research and instruction.[9]

Joe Rushing, the first president of the Junior College of Broward County, in a report to the SFEC, asked that flexibility be the key word in a proposal to educate broad segments of the population from early childhood to adulthood. He wanted the junior college to develop a broad curriculum in general education and to operate year-round. Rushing proposed a top-level administrative position to deal with the complex relationships between the high school, the junior college, and the proposed university.[10]

In February 1962, the SFEC got its project off the ground by raising money to purchase reference books and periodicals for the library of the proposed university. Initially the group proposed three courses of graduate study, later expanded to seven courses. One of the early courses suggested was tutelage in the use of computers. The SFEC thought it could approach the IBM Corporation to furnish top people to teach the course. SFEC's recommendation to offer a computer course was quite novel at the time, as computers were in their infancy and very few universities taught such courses. This idea gave some hint of the innovative approach that would be demonstrated from the very beginning of the planning.[11]

At this juncture, these businessmen, who had no real concept of what a university curriculum should be, were proposing whatever ideas popped into their minds. They finally realized that they needed outside expertise and turned to Palmer Craig, who was in charge of curriculum development for the Broward County schools. Next, the SFEC provided a prospectus for potential new courses to the two state universities, Florida State University and the University of Florida, for the purpose of obtaining their opinion of the type of courses they planned to offer and with the hope of obtaining top-flight instructors to teach the courses. The SFEC also requested information about the mathematics courses required at the University of Florida for its master's degree so it would have some basis for organizing its own math curriculum.

For classrooms, Joe Rushing offered space in the junior college, and Ashmore promised additional classrooms at Fort Lauderdale High School. The SFEC continued to work on purchasing appropriate books and periodicals although it had no idea which books would be appropriate for the proposed technical reference library. The SFEC, shoring up the organization, approved a set of bylaws and began the long-term process of trying to raise donations for the new university. The SFEC set up a committee to expand its membership and chose Stuart Synnestvedt to conduct a public relations campaign for the planned educational complex.[12]

Although the university was still in the very early planning stages and had little support from the county or the city, the SFEC optimistically pushed ahead. The *Fort Lauderdale News* supplied editorial support by urging local businesspeople and industries to donate money for the educational center. The *News* declared that the proposed project was "of vital importance to our future progress." There was an urgent and compelling need for an educational institution in the county that would provide qualified personnel for the burgeoning electronic and space-age companies.[13] The *Miami Herald* thought the idea of a technological university represented farsighted, constructive thinking and would catch the imagination of educators throughout the United States. The paper pointed out that the local citizens organizing the center were pragmatic and rich in talent.[14]

Despite having no money, no approval from the state universities, no charter, and no land on which to build the university, the members of the SFEC were convinced of the ultimate success of their vision. The founders therefore outlined a plan for obtaining an architect's drawings for the university, worked on the design of a university to be built and run by the corporation, and selected a committee to develop a more specific and suitable curriculum.[15] The SFEC continued to emphasize that the university had to be innovative and would be designed to invent, implement, evaluate, and disseminate new educational practices. The planned institution would concentrate on providing a type of manpower and knowledge that was not being produced in a systematic way in any other institution.

To accomplish its objective, the SFEC obviously needed land for the campus. Without a designated physical location for the university, it seemed pointless to get too far ahead with the planning. During World War II, the Forman family donated what became known as Forman Field to the U.S. Navy for pilots to practice landings and takeoffs. Once the war ended, the federal government declared the naval base to be surplus property and planned to sell it.

Hamilton and Charles Forman thought that 220 of the 550 acres on the Forman Field property would be perfect for their proposed university. After consulting with the Broward County Board of Public Instruction, Hamilton Forman went to Washington, DC, to lobby for the land. To bolster their case, Ashmore asked Thomas D. Bailey, the state superintendent of public instruction, to write a letter to the Government Services Administration (GSA) on behalf of the state board of education requesting that the remaining acreage of Forman Field be held for educational purposes.[16]

At this juncture, Jim Farquhar, who would be a key figure in the development of the university, became fully committed to the dream. "I guess I'm a visionary," he declared many years later, "and to be a visionary you have to be a little stupid." Farquhar knew that many detractors thought the idea had no chance, but he accepted the SFEC presidency with the primary goal of obtaining property for the educational complex.[17] Farquhar's willingness to commit his time and money was a monumental event in the history of Nova University. Without his gift of 100 acres of land adjacent to Forman Field— valued in excess of $500,000—the SFEC would not have had the funds to put up the first buildings. It is hard to imagine that the university would have ever come to fruition without his leadership and guidance. On several occasions, just when the undertaking was about to fail, he came to the rescue. He was later recognized as "Mr. Nova" for his efforts.

Farquhar agreed with the Formans about the viability of the naval air station. He encouraged Hamilton Forman to use his influence in Washington to get the land.[18] Hamilton Forman again went to Washington, DC, to meet with Senators George Smathers and Spessard Holland and Congressman Paul Rogers to do some groundwork on the proposal for the educational complex. Forman reported that both senators and Congressman Rogers were "quite enthusiastic" about the idea and that Florida governor Cecil Farris Bryant was eager to back the proposal. Forman also met with Abraham Ribicoff, the secretary of the U.S. Department of Health, Education, and Welfare (HEW). Ribicoff promised that HEW would try to work with the SFEC.

Figure 1.1 James "Mr. Nova" Farquhar, chairman of the board of trustees for both the South Florida Education Center (SFEC) and Nova University of Advanced Technology. (By permission of Nova Southeastern University Archives, Fort Lauderdale, Florida.)

During his visit to Washington, DC, Hamilton Forman tried to enlist the help of Senator George Smathers to persuade the federal government to give the Forman Field land to Broward County. The secretaries of HEW and the GSA balked and kept defeating the proposal. They opposed the deal primarily because if the land were to be used for educational purposes, the best the Broward County School Board could offer, since they lacked the funds to do more, was to build a portable elementary school. The government did not want the land to be used for an educational center of such limited scope.

Also, the GSA and HEW were aware that the Nova University idea was merely in its formative stage, and since Nova was to be a private entity, the government was unwilling to turn over public land for such an institution. The GSA stated that it would not negotiate with any public agency for the sale of the land and announced it would offer the land at a public sale to the highest bidder. Senator George Smathers asked the SFEC to get the State Board of Education to submit a request to GSA to refrain from any immediate disposition of the property and to ask that this property be preserved for higher-education purposes. Thomas Bailey did make such a request, but the GSA was unmoved.

Senator Smathers, a close friend of President John F. Kennedy, went into action. Hamilton Forman reported that when Senator Smathers was discussing the Forman property disposition with an HEW representative, the bureaucrat refused to accommodate any request from Smathers. Eventually, Smathers lost his temper and yelled at the HEW representative, "Now, you either sit down and be cooperative and help us, or, if you don't want to do that, then sit down and shut your mouth, or, if you don't want to do that, then get the hell out of this office." The bureaucrat angrily removed himself from the room, but soon meekly returned with a much-changed attitude. In the end, the deal was consummated.[19] The Broward County Board of Public Instruction obtained a 325-acre grant for the elementary, middle, and high schools. One hundred acres were designated for an agricultural experiment station operated by the University of Florida, and eventually 125 acres of the 325 acres were specifically designated for Nova University.

In the pursuit of land, Nova's future depended on the skills and influence of Senator Smathers and the Forman brothers. Without them, it would have been exceedingly difficult, if not impossible, to obtain the land from the federal government. Hamilton Forman noted that his brother Charles worked diligently with the Oatmeal Club; he

(Hamilton) did not know much about education or what they wanted to do. Hamilton recalled, "My expertise in this thing was in getting permits and seeing that the right things happened from a political standpoint. . . . I knew what they were planning to do was going to be great and wonderful for the people . . . , but that was not my forte. I was kind of a shadowy figure behind the scenes."[20] In other words, Charles was the planner and Hamilton was the fixer.

By the spring of 1962, very little of significance had been achieved except that the first course of instruction would be electrical engineering. The SFEC had little success in raising funds from individual donors. It worked on trying to hire qualified instructors with PhDs and agreed that more specific and pertinent information about its plans should be disseminated to the public, since very few people knew what the SFEC was doing.

One member realized that the group was not accomplishing much. The SFEC was floundering around trying to raise money, hire faculty, and work on a curriculum without an overall, specific plan. He recommended that it was time for the organization to determine the exact goals of the university, select a strong, dynamic president, and set up an advisory board of nationally known people. The SFEC board acted quickly on these astute recommendations and chose a name for its new university: the Florida Institute of Technology, later changed to Nova University of Advanced Technology.[21]

Throughout the early history of Nova University, the most vexing problem was the inability to raise the necessary funds to move the project forward. Abraham (A.L.) Mailman, who would later become a generous donor and staunch supporter of Nova, suggested that the most effective way to obtain funds quickly was to offer donors membership into the "Founders Club" with a contribution of $1,000. A good idea, but many of the SFEC board members did not meet their obligations. In search of students and faculty, Stuart Synnestvedt reported a positive response when he went to the University of Miami and found two highly qualified potential teachers and some fifteen possible students.[22] The SFEC finally realized it was not qualified to devise an appropriate curriculum and decided it needed expert advice. It asked that university-level consultants be brought in immediately.

While concentrating on the university's development, the SFEC went ahead with plans for an all-encompassing, comprehensive educational center by breaking ground for Nova High School on October 23, 1962. A large crowd attended the dedication of the completed school on April 5, 1964. That same month, Nova High School achieved national recognition when *National School Magazine* chose it as school of the month. The high school billed itself as a space-age school—its primary purpose was to utilize scientific learning methods in a scientific age. The key words were flexibility, self-motivation, and understanding. Nova High School's curriculum taught students the "how" and "why" as well as the "what."

By 1965, one elementary school, the Nova Blanche Forman Elementary School, and the University of Florida (UF) Agricultural Experimental Station had come on line; the junior college had been expanded; and a kindergarten was in the planning stage. The second elementary school, Nova Eisenhower, was unveiled in 1967. It was not until 1977 that Nova Middle School opened its doors to seventh- and eighth-grade students. Sixth-grade students shifted to the middle school the following year. By 1967, all of these facilities were tax-funded.[23]

On November 13, 1962, the South Florida Education Center, Inc. (SFEC), became incorporated as a 501(c)(3) not-for-profit organization.[24] One of the earliest tasks of the newly incorporated organization was to send letters to top educators nationwide requesting recommendations for the best-qualified person to serve as president and to plan and develop the new graduate university. The SFEC received an important boost when Stuart Synnestvedt reported on his meeting with the distinguished scientist James Killian, president of Massachusetts Institute of Technology (MIT). Killian expressed a great interest in the SFEC's objectives and asked to visit the center in Fort Lauderdale. It was just the kind of national attention the SFEC needed.

Killian arrived in March 1965 and spent a day and a half conferring with the trustees. The purpose of his visit was to offer aid in strengthening the university's concept, philosophy, and objectives. The support and approbation of a distinguished scientist like Killian's in those crucial first years confirmed the founders' belief that Nova University would become an outstanding center of technological education and research.[25]

As late as 1963, the SFEC still had not secured formal accession of the land it needed. The board of trustees contacted Anthony J. Celebrezze, then secretary of the Department of Health, Education, and Welfare (HEW), in hopes of immediately acquiring from the GSA the 125 acres at Forman Field that had been designated as the official site for the proposed university. The SFEC printed a brochure for use in soliciting funds for the down payment on the Forman Field acreage.[26] The SFEC then set up a corporate account with Merrill Lynch to deposit donations to the Land Acquisition Fund. Charles Forman chastised the members of the board of trustees for not contributing enough money for the center and complained that there had been significant difficulty in collecting the $1,000 pledges from members of the Founder's Club.[27]

After much wrangling and many starts and stops, the federal government finally and officially decided that 125 acres of Forman Field was surplus land and agreed to sell it to the Broward County Board of Public Instruction for $375,000, which in turn would donate the land to the SFEC. If the SFEC failed to make the payments, then the land would revert to the school board. A document dated July 29, 1963, shows that the SFEC made the initial down payment of $75,000, payable to the GSA. The remaining portion of the sale price, $300,000, would be paid in forty consecutive quarter-annual payments of $7,500 each. Interest on the unpaid balance was at the rate of 5 percent per annum, to be paid with each principal installment.[28]

It took the SFEC a long time to collect the $75,000 down payment. Tinsley Ellis said, "It was the hardest money we ever raised," because so many people were skeptical about the entire concept and thought it would never get off the ground. Ellis recalled that they were still $5,000 short of the $75,000 when A.L. Mailman stepped up and provided the needed sum[29]—yet another example of a civic-minded citizen saving the university at a critical time. With the down payment now in hand, the SFEC issued a $75,000 check to the Broward County Board of Public Instruction.

A.L. Mailman became one of the most important contributors to the new university and later had one of the earliest buildings on campus, the Mailman-Hollywood Building, named after him. A highly successful industrialist, banker, and property developer, Mailman moved to Hollywood, Florida, in 1950 and created the city of Miramar to provide affordable homes for working people and to serve as a bedroom community for Fort Lauderdale and Miami. A.L. and his brother Joseph established the Mailman Foundation and used their assets for philanthropy in South Florida, giving substantial donations to the Mailman Center for Child Development at the University of Miami and the A.L. Mailman Family Center at Nova University. After A.L. Mailman's death in 1980, a new foundation, the A.L. Mailman Family Foundation, was established.

Hamilton Forman recalled that, at the time, even members of the SFEC feared they were "crazy" in trying to create a university for

$75,000 when they had trouble raising even that limited sum. How could an intelligent group of businessmen expect to start a university with almost no money? Forman recalled, "Nobody could believe that we were going to start a university for $75,000, with no buildings, no money, no alumni, no heritage, no nothing." Forman believed the SFEC succeeded in creating an independent, non-tax-supported university with a piece of land and capitalization of $75,000 because everyone in the group believed in the dream and was invested in the outcome because they all contributed land, money, and time.[30] Robert Ellyson said, "We were businessmen, but we were all dreamers. Synnestvedt pressed the right button with us, and we all said, 'You know, this might be doable. Let's give it a shot.'"[31]

Even at this early stage of the planning, several members realized that a PhD university, although badly needed in South Florida, would probably not work since there was little public support for a graduate university that would have only a limited number of students.[32] Beginning with a graduate university was just not a practical operation since there would be very little income from tuition with so few students. The SFEC would have been better advised to begin a university at the junior year, with the Junior College of Broward County providing the educational experience for the first two years.

With the land acquired, the trustees knew that the next and most important step was to hire a president. They needed to raise an additional $150,000 for the first three years of the new president's salary, and they recognized the necessity of hiring professional fund-raisers since they had such great difficulty raising just $75,000.

Stuart Synnestvedt reported that some of the top educators and scientific personnel in the country had promised their help in finding the right person for the job. After contacting the National Aeronautics and Space Administration (NASA), the U.S. Commissioner of Education, the National Science Foundation, and others for advice, the board of trustees recommended hiring Henry M. Brickell, an educational consultant at Columbia University, as the new president.[33] As it turned out, Brickell was not hired, but the SFEC recognized the urgency of hiring a president as soon as possible.

The original SFEC Board of Trustees, as described by Tinsley Ellis, included Jim Farquhar as chairman; W. Howard Allen, head of the First National Bank of Fort Lauderdale; Robert O. Barber, CEO of Unisys Corporation, an optical company; Robert C. Ellyson, a certified public accountant who was very active in the SFEC's early finances; Henry Kinney, one of the editors of the *Miami Herald*;

Henry D. Perry, a dairyman who later formed a bank; John J. Hines, an industrialist; William C. Mather, a Hollywood attorney; L.C. Judd, a prominent real estate developer; W. Tinsley Ellis, the attorney who drew up the articles of incorporation and one of the four original Oatmeal Club members; Robert Ferris; Charles Forman, who was on the local school board and also served on the Florida Board of Control, the agency that oversaw the state university system; Myron Ashmore, superintendent of schools; and Stuart Synnestvedt.[34]

In early 1964, the trustees' search for a president focused on Warren J. Winstead, then the director of the U.S. Army's 510,000-student education program for servicemen and their dependents in Europe. Winstead had been highly recommended by Edward Meade, a program officer at the Ford Foundation. Although Winstead was not a scientist and had never worked in higher education, Meade thought his administrative experience with the U.S. Army might make him a good fit. In February 1964, Stuart Synnestvedt learned that Winstead would be in the United States sometime between April 15 and May 1 of that year and suggested that he should be invited to Fort Lauderdale for an interview before he returned to Europe.[35] Although there is no specific reference in the SFEC minutes to such an interview, it must have gone well since the SFEC offered Winstead the job.

The trustees initially hired Winstead as the director of university programs for the SFEC and offered him a three-year contract, beginning July 1, 1964, with an annual salary of $25,000. The contract directed Winstead to perform any tasks that the SFEC asked of him and to give his full time and attention to his duties. In specific terms, Winstead would initiate a program for the creation and development of the master plan for the educational complex envisioned by the SFEC. Winstead was tasked to coordinate the overall plan for the institute of technology, raise funds, and hire faculty and staff. Winstead thus had the responsibility of coordinating all of the various institutions in the educational complex, as well as beginning the planning for the technological university.[36]

Warren J. Winstead was born on November 10, 1927, in Washington, DC. He obtained his BA and MS degrees from the University of Richmond, and an EdD in education from Harvard University in 1958. He taught at the University of Heidelberg, the University of Richmond, and the University of Virginia.[37] He appeared to be highly qualified for the position as director of the SFEC complex, and the trustees felt fortunate in attracting a person with such good credentials. Abraham (Abe) Fischler, who would later serve as Nova's second

Figure 1.2 Warren J. Winstead, EdD, president, 1964–1969. (By permission of Nova Southeastern University Archives, Fort Lauderdale, Florida.)

president, recalled that in 1964, since there was no university and only a barren field without any buildings, not many highly qualified applicants would even consider the post.[38]

One of the new director's first assignments was to perform a study and make recommendations about the type of university Nova should become. Winstead's next task was to establish the SFEC's executive offices in leased space at 232 East Las Olas Boulevard in Fort Lauderdale. The board authorized Winstead to hire two assistants. His first hire was Colonel Duval S. Adams as his administrative assistant. The proposed budget for the year ending June 30, 1965, was $127,000,

Figure 1.3 Nova Southeastern University's first location for its administrative offices was a storefront on East Las Olas Boulevard in Fort Lauderdale. From left to right: Abraham Fischler, Mary McCahill, and James "Jim" Farquhar. (By permission of Nova Southeastern University Archives, Fort Lauderdale, Florida.)

which included funds to be applied toward the ongoing payments for the 125 acres. The board authorized Winstead to administer the new budget and to approve expenditures up to $500 without approval of the trustees.

Helen Graham, one of the earliest employees at Nova, remembered the rather spartan interior of the executive offices on Las Olas. There were old oak desks donated by the county school board, and venetian blinds and old carpeting donated by the banks. "Nothing quite fit," she said. The staff had to refinish the furniture as well as cut the blinds and carpeting to fit. Graham described the early days of organizing a new university with a limited staff as "an effort of total dedication."[39]

On July 22, 1964, Jim Farquhar provided a significant boost to the fledgling university when he announced that he would donate an additional five acres of land for faculty housing. Even more significant was the gift of 100 acres in what is now Pembroke Pines from William Mather, the attorney for the Bailey Foundation, with the stipulation that a "bona fide" university be established within three years or the land would revert to the donor. Apparently, the board of trustees eventually sold 100 acres for $400,000; this sale provided most of the funds to build and operate the university in the formative period. Another early gift of $15,000 came from the Robert O. Law Foundation to help with the cost of organizing the new university.[40]

A very significant and unexpected contribution came about in a most unusual way. In November 1965, a rather undistinguished-looking man named Louis W. Parker walked unannounced into the headquarters on Las Olas and handed an envelope to a staff member. The back of the envelope read: "I hereby pledge one million dollars to Nova University." No one in the office knew who Parker was or believed he intended to contribute $1 million; everyone dismissed his offer, but Parker kept his pledge.[41]

Louis Parker was born and educated in Hungary. He came to the United States and became a naturalized citizen in 1932. After learning English, he studied at City College of New York and then became a prolific inventor. During World War II, Parker designed and manufactured portable radio transmitters for military use and established his own company, Parker Instrument Corporation. NASA chose his company to furnish instruments for the manned Apollo flights to the moon. His most successful invention was the intercarrier sound system—the modern basis for coordinating sound and pictures, and a part that is still used in every television set. He developed the first color television system using vertical color lines. Parker had more than 250 patents for electronic equipment devices, including radio direction finders for airplanes and an electric car.[42] Parker's inventions made him quite wealthy, and he was looking for opportunities to give his money away. He had no connection with the university but had read about it in the newspaper and wanted to help. Most of his $1 million gift was used to construct what became the Louis W. Parker Physical Sciences Center, always known as the Parker Building. Nova University honored Parker for his generosity in 1970 with an honorary doctor of science degree. Louis Parker died in 1993 at age 87.[43]

The ultimate success of Nova University was due to unexpected and absolutely essential gifts of land and money, such as Parker's $1 million donation, and from the SFEC's shrewd planning and perseverance. Tinsley Ellis revealed that the original board of trustees for the SFEC consisted of conservative Republicans who had no experience in organizing or running a university, but they remained committed to their design despite local sniping that the concept was not doable.[44]

By mid-July 1964, Winstead reported that planning for the new university was going well and, despite the doubters, he emphatically insisted that the university would be established within three years. Winstead agreed with the trustees' original concept for the university and thought it should be founded as only a graduate school. "You can start a graduate school with one student and one professor if you have to. Aim high—at the highest degree of academic excellence. Let your university strive for the excellence of MIT or Caltech and industry will help you. PhDs in research represents brainpower, and industry follows brainpower." Winstead stated that Nova was not designed to be a sprawling "multiversity," attempting to meet the diverse needs of great masses of young people. He envisioned that the student population would never exceed 1,500, and 1,000 of them would be graduate students.

According to Winstead, the primary emphasis would always be on advanced research in science. Nova intended to limit itself to a few narrow fields and would serve those fields better than "any other institution anywhere is serving them." Instead of starting with relatively cheap undergraduate instruction and gradually acquiring expensive graduate specialists, Winstead planned to lure top scholars from prestigious universities by offering generous salaries and complete freedom to research and teach only in their graduate-level specialties. He argued that "serious graduate students could not care less about the name of the school. They want to study under specific professors. The name, Nova didn't have; the professors, it could get." The new president, insisting that the school also offer educational training and liberal arts subjects, said, "You can't separate the technologies from the humanities in the world of today." He wanted to integrate the arts, humanities, and natural sciences. "The technical and theoretical, the aesthetic and the scientific, the factual and the valuable, the creative and the inventive must be recognized as merely facets of one single, cultural core."[45]

Winstead clearly overstated the potential for the new university—it would certainly never become another MIT—and he raised expectations that could not be met, but at the time the excitement about creating a graduate school in science from the ground up appealed to the board of trustees and generated enthusiasm from the community and important scientists across the United States.

Although the trustees had changed the name of the new university from Florida Institute of Technology to Nova University of Advanced Technology, they needed to make the name formal and official. The SFEC wanted to continue using the name Nova (although that was the name of the high school) because it reflected the new idea of a unique institution. The board finally agreed upon Nova University of Advanced Technology, Inc. Tinsley Ellis and Warren Winstead were appointed to come up with a charter of incorporation for the university.[46]

James Hartley fortuitously offered to act as architectural consultant for the university to assist in the initial planning. Hartley agreed to work without a fee, but the board agreed to pay Hartley's out-of-pocket expenses.[47] Hartley had been the architect for Nova elementary schools, Nova Middle School, and Nova High School, and the Ford Foundation considered him to be an excellent educational architect. As Hartley later remembered, "Since I had done schools my entire practice, working with Nova was a labor of love. I got so involved in it, I couldn't have let go if I'd wanted to. I was bound and determined to see it through to its fruition."[48] Nova eventually succeeded because of the skills and determination of early founders like Hartley, the Formans, and Farquhar who were willing to make personal contributions of time and money, forego payments for services, and do whatever it took to succeed despite daunting barriers and little community support.

The most troubling problem continued to be raising funds to get the project off the ground. The trustees decided to invite a fund-raising firm, Tamblyn and Brown, based in New York City, to advise them on the best way to increase contributions. A.C. Barnett, of Tamblyn and

Brown, said that before formal solicitations began, the group should determine how much could be logically raised and the most effective way to raise the money. After Barnett's presentation, the trustees hired the firm to conduct a preliminary survey about how to raise the funds. The preliminary report indicated that adequate financial resources existed in Broward County and that the climate seemed favorable for a local fund drive. Tamblyn and Brown recommended immediately initiating a fund drive with a goal of $5 million to be raised in two years. The SFEC board retained the firm to conduct the campaign.[49]

Winstead, in an attempt to get advice on curriculum and how to structure the new university's administration, went on a fact-finding trip to Caltech and the University of California at Los Angeles (UCLA) with limited results. The board of trustees was short on funds, but they were encouraged by Winstead's progress and gave him permission to hire some key staff members: a vice president for academic affairs, a vice president for finance, a librarian, a dean of the management center, a dean of the education center, and a dean of the school of engineering.[50] Winstead, however, did not fill all of these positions at that time.

Winstead also began recruiting an advisory board that would include a distinguished group of leaders in American science and business. The first four members were James R. Killian Jr., president of MIT in Cambridge; Paul F. Brandwein, assistant to the president of Harcourt Brace and World in New York City; Robert B. Gilmore, vice president for business affairs and treasurer at Caltech; and Ernest V. Hollis, director of college and university administration in the division of higher education at the U.S. Office of Education in Washington, DC. This original group had representatives from two of the most prestigious universities in the country, Caltech and MIT. Killian was one of the most admired and successful administrators in the country. Robert Gilmore had experience in running the business affairs of Caltech, and there was a representative from a major publishing house and a key official in the federal government.[51]

The advisory board was later expanded to include another group of eminent educators. Johannes Hans Jensen, a Nobel Laureate in physics and director of the Institute of Theoretical Physics at the University of Heidelberg, Germany; Richard Folsom, president of Rensselaer Polytechnic Institute; Abram Sachar, president of Brandeis University; Emilio G. Segre, a Nobel Laureate in physics and professor of physics at the University of California, Berkeley; Frederick Seitz, president of the National Academy of Sciences; and Athelstan Spilhaus, dean of the

Institute of Technology at the University of Minnesota. This outstanding board of advisors gave Nova instant national credibility. Warren Winstead accomplished this remarkable feat thanks to his charisma and unbridled enthusiasm for the concept of a graduate university in science. A great salesman, he persuaded some of the most acclaimed scientists in the country, including two Nobel Laureates, to sign on to a project that had not yet broken ground for its first building and did not yet have enough money to develop a university.

Winstead also decided to form a national founders council. This group was just as impressive as the advisory board and included Pierre Bedard, chairman of the executive committee of Cartier and advisor to the John F. Kennedy Center for the Performing Arts; General Lucius D. Clay, a senior partner at Lehman Brothers; Thomas C. Fogarty, chairman of the board of Continental Can Company; Admiral David L. McDonald, chief of naval operations for the U.S. Navy; and W. Homer Turner, vice president and executive director of United States Steel Foundation.[52] All of these illustrious names gave Nova national recognition and may well have swayed some donors, but their relationship with Nova was superficial. The Nova administrators, all academic amateurs, did not know how to take advantage of these important contacts. With the exception of Brandwein's work in developing Nova High School and Killian's favorable remarks about Nova's future, history does not record any special contributions to Nova from these gentlemen.[53]

As President Winstead requested, university architect James Hartley outlined to the board the proposed building sequence for the new campus. He discussed the siting of buildings and the estimated cost of a four-phase construction program scheduled to be implemented in the spring of 1965. Hartley divided his conceptual plan into two phases. The first was the master plan, which completely developed the site and tentatively located the building groups, walks, and drives that would comprise the university in its final stage. The second phase consisted of designing, developing, and supervising the construction of the first buildings. Hartley described the site as a flat, irregular shape—an abandoned airport without any natural landscape and with some of the runways removed prior to construction. He planned to create an independent community of learning, leaving to the town of Davie the responsibility of supplying food, commercial goods, and utilities.

The campus architect divided the campus into four areas: administrative, cultural, academic, and housing and social. Each area would have its own identity yet would be integrated with the other areas via pedestrian walks, malls, and vehicular drives. Hartley placed the areas in such a manner as to allow for maximum flexibility and sufficient room for expansion so that the complete campus could be developed in stages without destroying the spatial relationship. Vehicular drives and parking were confined to the periphery "to prevent the invasion of the automobile into the center of the campus with the resulting congestion and confusion."

The buildings were to be grouped around open courts where students would congregate before and after class. Malls would connect the courts, and a profusion of trees would protect them from the heat and sun. Hartley envisioned significant landscaping with palm trees, shrubbery, and colorful flowers, but the fledgling institution would not have the funds to spend on landscaping until many years later. Several artificial lakes would provide the campus with fill material for site conditioning, improve storm drainage, and add color and texture to the scenery. Hartley was careful to insist that the master plan's unity be maintained throughout the various stages of construction, "especially since there will be a long span of time between the first and last buildings of the completed campus."[54]

With the assistance of developer A.D. Griffin, owner of Griffin Brothers Company, primarily a landscaping and paving business, the trustees authorized planting a few trees and some grass. Since the SFEC had limited landscaping funds, Griffin started by taking trees "out of people's yards and taking them out of nurseries, making people give me their trees" until they had at least a modicum of landscaping.[55]

While President Winstead met in Washington with the GSA and the HEW in an attempt to secure the final release of the land designated for the university, Tinsley Ellis worked on a draft of the proposed university's charter. As Ellis later reported, he had never incorporated a university, so he went to see Tommy Thomas, associate counsel for the University of Miami, and asked for a copy of that school's charter. Ellis recalled that the charter for Nova University of Advanced Technology was essentially a copy of the University of Miami's charter with the names and dates changed. Ellis presented the document to the board on October 1, 1963, and the board quickly approved it.

Now that the SFEC had a charter, it could move ahead and get official authorization and recognition from the State of Florida. On December 4, 1964, five months after Winstead became president, the State of Florida approved Nova University of Advanced Technology,

Inc., under the laws of the state as a private, not-for-profit, degree-granting institution. Although chartered as a separate institution of higher learning, the SFEC trustees indicated that the university remained an integral part of the overall South Florida educational complex and declared that the SFEC would retain financial control of the university.[56]

By November 5, 1964, the SFEC belatedly recognized the reality that very few people in Broward County, let alone the state of Florida and the rest of the country, had ever heard of Nova University. Desperate to get some recognition and publicity to help with fund raising, the SFEC hired Jack Drury and Associates to do publicity and conduct a public relations program. Drury proposed a comprehensive and carefully coordinated program designed to create a favorable public image for the university. Drury expected to start in Broward County, using local media, and then expand as rapidly as possible to state and national scope.

The SFEC's fund-raising effort went very slowly. Because the SFEC had limited assets and no campus buildings, it was unable to persuade local banks to establish a line of credit, nor would any bank lend it money without sufficient collateral. The founders hoped for a more favorable response from the banks when the Mather land gift cleared. At the time, the university had assets of only $115,000. When the Mather land grant became official and was combined with the value of the Forman Field land, the university would have assets valued at $750,000. As would be the case through the first twenty years, the fiscal situation was dire, and the university lacked the money to meet the November 1964 payroll. Tinsley Ellis offered a $1,500 loan; and when Jim Farquhar gave another five acres, the school took out a $10,000 loan against that land. These were merely stopgap measures, and the trustees realized that they had to step up the fund raising or the university would never become a reality.

More promising news came when President Winstead reported on a trip to Washington, DC, New York, and Boston. Winstead explained that the U.S. Office of Education would put Nova on a priority list to receive grants, and that NASA would consider Nova for grants as soon as the university was able to execute such grants. The National Science Foundation and the Ford Foundation continued to provide advice and assistance, and Harvard University faculty promised to help with recruiting faculty and students.[57]

While fund raising remained a top priority, Winstead proceeded with hiring the first faculty and administrative staff. Charles Gauss became the assistant to the president for academic affairs. Abraham S.

Fischler came from the University of California, Berkeley to be dean of the Hollywood Education Center. William S. Richardson, employed to head the physical oceanography unit, brought major research contracts with him. Raymond Pepinsky, with a grant of $35,000, was appointed as the Robert O. Law Professor of Physics. Winstead selected Arthur W. Wishart as head of Nova's planning and development functions. Duval S. Adams served as business manager, and Henry E. Kinney was placed in charge of public relations.[58]

Nova's attempt to get national recognition received an important assist when Winstead journeyed to New York to publicize the school on NBC's *Today* show with Barbara Walters. On January 21, 1965, in a follow-up, the *Today* show came to Fort Lauderdale. The SFEC expected that the *Today* show would concentrate on publicity for Nova University and explain the Nova concept as a cooperative community undertaking. The *Today* show producers, however, focused on Nova High School and only reluctantly mentioned Nova University.[59]

Although Winstead had managed to hire his initial faculty, money remained in short supply. If the SFEC were ever to fulfill the founders' ambitious plans, it needed a massive infusion of cash as soon as possible. Robert Ellyson, vice president for finance for the SFEC, reported that the cash shortage was such that after having just enough money to pay November's bills, the school could barely meet the December payroll. Ellyson anticipated that the following month would end in a deficit unless something was done immediately. Farquhar, recognizing a significant crisis, implored SFEC members to provide additional financial support. Farquhar reminded his colleagues that the board had to show its faith in the project with personal contributions before it could expect outsiders to make substantial donations.[60]

A financial study by Miami firm Hunter Moss and Company became the rationale for a renewed fund-raising effort. The thirty-four-page research report concluded that Broward County citizens would receive a great return on their investment as Nova University grew in size and influence. The study indicated that Nova University would be a huge financial boon for the county and that the economic outflow from the establishment of Nova University would provide a beneficial effect for business, industry, and ordinary citizens. Hunter Moss predicted that by 1975 the university would have constructed twenty-five buildings at a total cost of approximately $27 million. The report claimed that in specific terms, the university would attract high-tech industry to Fort Lauderdale and by 1980 would add 25,000 skilled jobs and 35,000 service workers, (a total of more than 60,000 new positions), and a payroll of $630 million. Hunter Moss concluded that Nova, combined with the research facilities that would be attracted to it, would represent one of the largest industries in Broward County.[61]

The Hunter Moss study of Nova University was flawed in factual content, promotional in tone, and overly optimistic. Despite its extravagant forecasts, the study did reflect the optimism and zest with which Broward County's civic leaders joined the new Nova president in planning the new university. The predicted economic impact was certainly premature, especially in regard to the pace of building construction, but would eventually prove to be more accurate as Nova expanded and prospered. Winstead and the SFEC effectively used this financial study to persuade donors to come to the aid of the fledgling university.

In some ways, the time and place were propitious for establishing an innovative, interdisciplinary, elite graduate research center for advanced technology. In the early 1960s, the federal government was investing more funds into scientific research and exploration and had an increased interest in oceanographic studies. The rapidly growing Broward area had a strong economic base, and the state of Florida would see a population explosion in the 1960s and 1970s. Trained graduates would be needed for the expanding technology markets, and Nova could supply those scientists and inventors.

As the SFEC increased its efforts to obtain more money, they sponsored fund-raising events of every conceivable kind. Cocktail receptions and dinners were frequent but garnered limited results. The SFEC created a newsletter and a fact sheet to explain the university's goals and financial needs. Brochures were sent out to newspapers and possible donors to elicit more interest in and support for Nova. Winstead persuaded the state legislature to extend Broward County's racing season by one day, and then wheedled the pari-mutuel track operators and jai alai frontons into using the extra day as "Nova Day," with all proceeds going to Nova University. These funds netted Nova $153,000 in the first year, but, while helpful, did not provide enough income to establish a new university. One of Nova's early supporters, James Donn Sr., was an honorary member of the board of trustees and a member of the Gold Key Club. The Donn family had established Gulfstream Park as one of the East Coast's most important and best-managed racetracks. James Donn made the Derby Ball and the Nova University Days at the Races annual charitable events; both benefits eventually grossed more than $300,000.

Donn also provided funds for the James Donn Sr. Chair of Science Education.[62]

Winstead kept up his constant search for new sources of income. He managed to get a $1,100,000 federal loan to build married-student housing and a $552,000 HEW grant for an educational center. He talked social activists in nearby Hollywood, Florida, into donating the proceeds of their annual Derby Ball to Nova and picked up another $47,000. He asked local merchants to donate outdated merchandise that was not selling. Nova held a sale of these items and netted $8,000. He managed to convince seven local millionaire yachtsmen that there were tax advantages to giving their old yachts to Nova. One of the donations was the famous racing ketch *The Ticonderoga*, holder of more sailing records than any other craft of its kind. By chartering or reselling the yachts, the university made $100,000. Earl Vettel made a splendid and badly needed donation of fifty acres of land contiguous to the university, and then promised another fifty acres under a life income trust agreement.

From the very beginning, as it would be throughout its history, Nova University demonstrated an entrepreneurial drive in raising funds and establishing the university. Whether selling yachts or outdated merchandise, Nova took advantage of whatever opportunities were presented and figured out new and innovative ways to raise funds. Tinsley Ellis praised Winstead for doing a great job as the "front man" for the university, for persuading the advisory board members to sign on, and for his fund-raising: "He was very charismatic. He had a wonderful personality."[63]

To increase participation from the community's more affluent members, President Winstead set up two special organizations: the Gold Key Society of Nova University, whose fifty members agreed to give $1,000 every year to the university, and the Royal Dames of Nova, whose members pledged $2,500 for a lifetime membership. The Royal Dames solicited funds for cancer research through the Germ-Free Life Research Center, later renamed the Leo Goodwin Institute for Cancer Research. The Royal Dames was a highly selective organization whose membership was chosen to reflect a broad spectrum of talent, leadership, and creativity.[64]

The fund-raising efforts, while picking up significant sums of money, did not attract the very large donors necessary for survival. Most of the local citizenry simply were not interested in making sizeable contributions to such an iffy proposition. After all, there was no physical presence in the community—there were no buildings on campus, no students, no faculty. Many still saw Nova as an unattainable pipe dream. As would be the case throughout the early history of the institution, just when it appeared the plan would fail for lack of money, a white knight, often Jim Farquhar, would come up with money or a land donation. Nova University came very close to never opening at all, and when it did so, it came close to failing on several occasions. In retrospect it seems a miracle that the institution survived, but it did so because of the courage, ingenuity, resourcefulness, and commitment of those who truly believed in the dream.

To provide more information about the university's activities to the general public, the SFEC started a four-page bimonthly pamphlet called *NovaTech*. In 1965, this publication became the monthly *Nova University News*. The Gold Key Club had its own board of directors and its own monthly publication, the *NOVACRAT*, which kept the public informed about fund-raising.[65]

The founders, now ready to begin construction on the first building, asked architect Hartley to explain the sequence of events and the funding requirements. Hartley announced that the first construction would be for the student center, which would cost $1,317,000. He estimated that it would take approximately one year to complete the building. Hartley told the board that as the architect, he had gone as far as he could and now they needed to hire structural, mechanical, and electrical engineers to proceed. Hartley cautioned the finance committee that they must know exactly where all the money was coming from before they entered into any construction agreement. Winstead, Hartley, and Farquhar reported that they had visited several universities and colleges on the East and West Coasts, and that they intended to incorporate the best architecture and structural designs from these institutions into the planning of Nova University.[66]

The development of the administrative structure for the governance of the new university proceeded slowly. At the February 4, 1965, meeting, Winstead asked the SFEC to restrict the new board of trustees for Nova University of Advanced Technology to a small group of dedicated and active individuals rather than a large and unwieldy group, which might find coming to a consensus on issues difficult. The SFEC decided that Nova's Board of Trustees would consist of twenty-five members—the thirteen members of the SFEC executive committee, the university president, and eleven others to be selected by the initial thirteen board members for staggered three-year terms.

For the time being, however, trusteeship of the university continued to be vested in the SFEC executive committee. This small group of dedicated individuals wanted to remain engaged in the constant and strenuous effort of making the university a reality. The SFEC had to continue the planning and organization since Nova University had not yet received its tax-exempt status and thus could not raise money or take over assets held by the SFEC. Shortly thereafter, however, Nova University received its tax-exempt status, and on July 1, 1965, the trustees of the South Florida Education Center signed over all of the assets, including land, all funds save for $1,000, and all liabilities to the not-for-profit corporation known as Nova University of Advanced Technology, Inc., which would "develop and operate the university contemplated by the SFEC."[67] Nova University was now an independent entity. It was on its own. As the first technical university established in the United States in twenty years and with a prominent advisory board, Nova was under extreme pressure to secure formal accreditation. In short, Nova had to become a first-class institution with a superior faculty and qualified students in a very short time.

Nova University of Advanced Technology

First and foremost for Nova would be obtaining the academic accreditation it so badly needed. Warren Winstead visited Gordon Sweet, executive director of the Southern Association of Colleges and Schools (SACS), the accrediting agency, based in Atlanta. Sweet, who would prove to be a loyal friend and staunch supporter, revealed that Nova should have no trouble getting accredited during its first two years of existence. Sweet and the SACS inspection team visited Nova University and found its development on track. Based on SACS's favorable report, the U.S. Office of Education, on October 4, 1965, certified the university's eligibility to receive grants and loans under federal programs—a huge step forward.

Everywhere the new administration looked, they saw that they needed more money for salaries and operating expenses. They needed a physical sciences building, which would cost $2 million, but only $1 million was available. The much-desired administration building was projected to cost $1,400,000. The university had $400,000 from the sale of land, but it had trouble raising additional funds. Despite the lack of money, on December 11, 1965, the university decided to hold a site dedication ceremony for the first building. Having overcome many barriers, Nova was finally beginning construction on its new campus.[68]

The first building was the Edwin M. and Ester L. Rosenthal Student Center. Groundbreaking ceremonies for the Rosenthal edifice were held on June 2, 1966. Edwin Rosenthal, a pioneer resident of Hollywood, Florida, made his fortune in South Florida real estate. Rosenthal's gift of $300,000 came to the university under unusual circumstances. Myron Segal, a heart surgeon with close ties to Nova (he was married to Marilyn 'Mickey' Segal, daughter of A.L. Mailman), had performed surgery on Ed Rosenthal. Rosenthal asked Segal what he would like in compensation for his medical skills. Segal asked for and received $350,000 from Rosenthal to set up a nursing facility at Memorial Hospital and requested that Rosenthal make a contribution to Nova University. Although Rosenthal had no connection to the university, he honored Segal's request and donated $300,000 to the school.[69]

In the early years of fund solicitation, many of the large donors were not from Fort Lauderdale as would be expected, but hailed from nearby Hollywood. Interested citizens formed the Hollywood Founders of Nova University as a voluntary group to raise the funds to construct a science education center. They were very successful in obtaining contributions, and since they were from Hollywood, the new building would be named the Hollywood Building. Because A.L. Mailman came forward with a generous sum to complete the construction, the final designation was the Mailman-Hollywood Building. It is not often that residents have their city's name inscribed on a building as principal donors.

Citizens of Davie, Florida, not to be outdone, formed a committee to conduct a fund-raising campaign to help pay for the construction of an apartment complex for married students. The Nova University Association, a group of "honorary alumni," was also formed to help raise money for the university.[70] Now that ground had been broken for the first building, area residents began to believe that this improbable idea might come to fruition after all and were eager to contribute. The Rosenthal building was completed and dedicated on May 21, 1967. Edwin M. Rosenthal, the octogenarian donor, described the ceremony as "the proudest day of my life" and urged the five hundred people in the audience "to take an interest in helping Nova become one of the outstanding universities in the United States."[71]

In February 1966, Winstead initiated the school's first recruitment of students by sending brochures to colleges and universities throughout the nation announcing Nova's PhD programs. Nova was prepared to accept students in science education, physical oceanography, and

Figure 1.4 A U.S. mailbox, one of the earliest structures to be erected on-site during the building construction phase in the 1960s. (By permission of Nova Southeastern University Archives, Fort Lauderdale, Florida.)

Figure 1.5 The first three buildings constructed at what was then called Nova University of Advanced Technology. From left to right: Rosenthal Student Center, Louis W. Parker Physical Sciences Center, and Mailman-Hollywood Building. (By permission of Nova Southeastern University Archives, Fort Lauderdale, Florida.)

physical sciences. With the first building completed and student applications coming in, there was an air of optimism among the administration and trustees that the venture might actually become a reality.

To persuade the public that the university was on sound footing and would survive, the twenty-five members of the board of trustees showed their faith in the institution's future by making monetary commitments worth some $4.4 million.[72] The original board of trustees for what was now an independent Nova University of Advanced Technology included the original members of the Oatmeal Club and the SFEC trustees. In essence, the leadership had not changed, and the same group of businessmen continued to guide Nova University during its first years of existence. Board members were James "Jim" Farquhar (chairman), W. Howard Allen, Warren J. Winstead, Stuart Synnestvedt; Robert O. Barber, Robert C. Ellyson, Henry E. Kinney, Henry D. Perry, Charles Forman, John J. Hines, William C. Mather, L.C. Judd, Robert E. Ferris, W. Tinsley Ellis, and Myron Ashmore.

On May 18, 1966, work began on the $2.65 million Louis W. Parker Physical Sciences Center. The university had $1 million from Parker, but lacked the funds to compete the building. Under these circumstances the university decided to build just the shell and wait until they could raise funds to finish the structure. James Hartley explained the reasoning behind the decision. He said that if Nova were to complete its vision of a viable university of technology, then the Parker Building—the physical sciences center—would have to be the primary academic building. So, rather than build one story, which is all they could afford, and add on to it later, they built the building's shell and completed the interior portion of the first floor. Later, when the university had accumulated enough money, Nova went ahead and built out the third floor so that the Germ-Free Life Research Center could move its headquarters to the building. The second floor remained unfinished until the early 1970s.

Surprisingly, Nova did not initially build a central power plant for heating and air conditioning—again, due to lack of funds. The power plant was part of the original design, but Louis Parker wanted his donation put into the Parker Building. As Hartley recalled, the man who gave the money made the final decision, so the power plant was not built in 1966. Nova finally constructed a state-of-the-art central power plant in 2011.[73]

One of Nova's most important early developments was the creation of the Physical Oceanographic Laboratory. To begin with, Fort Lauderdale and Port Everglades offered a perfect location for oceanographic studies. The idea for an oceanographic center at Nova evolved from Charles Forman, who had been instrumental in starting the oceanographic program at Florida Atlantic University (FAU). FAU, however, specialized in engineering, and Charles Forman and his brother Hamilton wanted oceanographic research on tides and coral reefs.

In July 1966, Nova hired William Richardson, who had been at the Woods Hole Oceanographic Institution and worked for the University of Miami, to be professor of physical oceanography. In August 1965, Richardson, writing to express his interest in Nova, noted that if he were employed to establish a center there, he would require technicians and electronics people as well as another scientist in physical oceanography. Richardson also requested a large two-story houseboat for a lab on the water and a forty- to fifty-foot diesel boat for use in the Florida Straits.[74]

After Richardson agreed to come to Nova, the university supplied him with almost everything he had requested. Richardson turned out to be a superlative hire. He was very well known in the profession, and because he brought with him several federal and scientific contracts, he could open for business immediately. Richardson had a $168,000 contract with the National Science Foundation to study tides and a grant from the Office of Naval Research to survey the Gulf Stream.

By September 1966, research was underway at the Oceanographic Center with a group of three professors, five students, and more than a dozen assorted assistants, associates, secretaries, and specialists. These new employees worked in a cluster of house trailers and in temporary quarters aboard a sixty-foot, two-story houseboat specially designed as a laboratory. The houseboat contained the instruments, library, machine shop, and radio room that were necessary for the center's research. From 1966 to 1970, the Oceanographic Center was located on the waterfront alongside Southeast 15th Street in Fort Lauderdale. In December 1970, the houseboat, staff, and equipment moved to its permanent location on the Intercoastal Waterway opposite Port Everglades.

Richardson had two major research vessels at his disposal, *The Gulf Stream* and *The Bellows*. He used the former to drop small torpedo-like tubes overboard at intervals to measure the Gulf Stream's flow, temperature, and salinity. Richardson indicated that the nature of this information was vital: "Regardless of what you want to do in the ocean—farm it, mine it, live under it, navigate over it—you first must know what the currents are doing."

The research could not proceed as efficiently as Richardson desired with the main lab on a houseboat, so he requested a permanent building on the ocean. Hamilton Forman, using his contacts and influence, "made the rounds of the county commission and was able to get them . . . to give us ten acres" of prime land at Port Everglades. The Forman brothers then built a $125,000 basin on the new property and moved the houseboat to its permanent location on December 10, 1970. The location, just south of the Port Everglades Inlet, placed it within minutes of the Gulf Stream. Leading oceanographers pronounced the location as outstanding. Work soon began on a 17,000-square-foot multipurpose structure that would house laboratories and administrative offices and a 6,000-square-foot warehouse. Richardson believed the facility would be a model for future centers in oceanography and thought it would be to international oceanography what the Nova complex was: "a showplace of advanced ideas."[75]

In April 1969, movie star Steve McQueen came to the Oceanographic Center for advice on making a major film on oceanography. Winstead reported that he met with McQueen and the writer of the script for the immensely popular film *Bullitt* to discuss using the Port Everglades property as the site for the proposed motion picture. The film would be produced by McQueen's film company, Solar Productions, which had produced *Bullitt*. Winstead later remarked that Nova was "led to believe that, should our site and university be selected for a film on oceanography, the film company might construct some buildings, [build] a submarine which would become the property of the university, and make a substantial cash gift." McQueen apparently lost interest and nothing came of the idea.[76]

The official opening of Nova University was targeted for September 25, 1967. The university planned for the event to be a "family affair," with trustees, faculty, students, and their families participating in an on-campus program. Prior to the opening of the university, on September 20, 1967, Nova put out several news releases explaining what the institution was about and what it planned to accomplish. The initial news releases were replete with hyperbole and exaggerated claims, but this promotion was designed to capture the attention of scientists and educators around the country. One began with the statement that Nova University had been called one of the great ideas in twentieth-century education. Abram Sachar, president of Brandeis University and a member of Nova's board of advisors, said about the school, "A university cannot be created in these times without a great idea—and you have here a great idea." The press release went on to claim that Nova University (although it had not yet opened its doors) "ranks unquestionably as one of America's most exciting responses to the swiftly advancing technological needs of the nation and the times."

Nova University, touted another news release, had been designed for the advanced, the gifted, and the creative student. The student would work in an enclave where he and his fellows would study together in an atmosphere dedicated to education and scientific discovery. Most students would be in graduate school, as the baccalaureate would not be offered as a terminal degree. The student-faculty ratio would be very low—one to five at most.

The university, continued the news story, believed that the "role of the humanist and scientist in our world are inextricably intertwined." Nova intended to equip its students with "the flexibility of mind and imaginative power necessary for creative work in our world of rapidly advancing scientific knowledge" and give them "the skills and appreciation necessary for a full and rewarding life."[77]

All of this rhetoric sounded exciting and challenging, but these ideas were theoretical and had not yet been proven. A closer examination of the Nova concept revealed that the idea of a graduate-level-only institution had no chance of success. The theory was impractical, unrealistic, and simply would not work. How could the university survive if there were only seventeen students, all of whom were on full scholarship? There would be no tuition money to pay the faculty and run the university. The university would have to depend on grants and donations to survive, but these essential funds would not be forthcoming, and the school would be on the verge of bankruptcy in less than two years. The founders and President Winstead were so caught up in and excited by the boldness of their idea that they missed the impracticality of the concept.

In pursuing its unique plan for higher education, Nova announced that it would not be organized into colleges and schools in the traditional manner. Instead, each group of closely related subject areas would constitute a center where the research professors and their colleagues would have mutual interests and an intimate working relationship. Each center would be autonomous, but there would be constant cooperation among them in developing research programs.

Abraham Fischler, head of the Education Center, held his first meeting in September 1967, with the faculty members of his new center. Fischler explained that the main focus of the Education Center would be to develop new methods of teaching and learning, and to train professional teachers to be more effective and productive. The center would have no formal courses or units, no semesters or quarters. Each student would be assigned to a committee of five faculty members who would assess the student's current level of knowledge, determine the student's goals, and provide the academic guidance for him or her to complete the work necessary to reach their goals. The Education Center would work closely with the public elementary schools and the high school in the Nova complex.[78]

To attract students and to provide detailed information about the new university to parents and other members of the community, Nova put out a brochure titled "Your Questions Answered." Some examples: (Q) Is the university tax supported? "The university receives no support from local or state tax funds, nor does it seek any. It is proud of being a private institution." (Q) Is the university accredited? "It has been accepted by the Southern Association of Schools and Colleges as a 'candidate' for accreditation, which means that it is progressing satisfactorily toward formal accreditation. Accreditation cannot be made official until the university awards its first degree." (Q) How are the students selected? "They are selected on the basis of their academic experience and academic goals, their experience and proficiency in research, recommendations from their professors, and their adjudged ability to perform successfully in the unique academic environment of Nova University."

Other questions answered in the brochure included: (Q) What is the relationship of the university to Nova Elementary School, Nova High School, and Broward Junior College? "There is no *direct* relationship, since these schools are public and the university is private. However, the design for the Nova Complex provides that there shall be an interchange of activities and ideas between the public and private sector . . . that the public schools shall profit from the research and studies developed at the university . . . and that to some degree the public schools shall serve as laboratories for the university's educational research programs." The university announced a capital campaign to raise $15,000,000 and encouraged donors to provide gifts in the form of cash, securities, and property, and noted that the gifts were tax deductible.[79]

The university also announced the first members of the faculty. In an unusual academic ratio, there would be seventeen faculty members to tutor the seventeen graduate students enrolled for the fall semester, thus a one-to-one ratio between faculty and students. The list of new faculty (only fifteen of the seventeen faculty were eventually hired) is presented below in alphabetical order by surname, with their position at Nova and the institution where they received their terminal degree:

Kuldip Chopra, professor of applied physics, PhD, Delhi University, India.

Abraham S. Fischler, dean of graduate studies and James Donn Professor of Education, EdD, Teachers College, Columbia University.

Charles E. Gauss, provost, PhD, The Johns Hopkins University.

Roy C. Herndon, associate professor of physics, PhD, Florida State University.

Robert J. Jones, assistant professor of psychology, PhD, University of Texas.

Aijaz Khan, postdoctoral fellow in solid-state physics, PhD, Osmania University, Hyderabad, India.

Joseph I. Lipson, professor of science education, PhD, University of California, Berkeley.

William A. Love Jr., assistant professor of psychology, PhD, University of Texas.

Peter P. Niiler, assistant professor of theoretical oceanography, PhD, Brown University.

Raymond Pepinsky, Robert O. Law Professor of Physics, PhD, University of Chicago.

William S. Richardson, dean of graduate faculty and professor of oceanography, PhD, Harvard University.

James Smith, research associate, science education, EdD, Stanford University.

Judith Rubenstein Steward, assistant professor of psychology, PhD, University of Connecticut.

Warren J. Winstead, president and professor of education, EdD, Harvard University.

Charles S. Yentsch, associate professor of marine biology, MS (biology), Florida State University.[80]

A careful study of the faculty members hired for the opening of Nova University reveals some interesting and surprising information. There was only one female out of the fifteen new professors. The entire faculty, with one exception, had EdDs or PhDs. The one exception was in oceanography, and he had the terminal degree in his field. Not only did they all have terminal degrees, but the degrees were also from the best universities in the country. These included Harvard University, Teachers College Columbia University, University of Chicago,

University of Texas, Brown University, Stanford University, the University of California at Berkeley, and the Johns Hopkins University. Several of the faculty had already published and were experts in their fields. All were working on research projects that coincided with the academic programs at Nova.

How in the world did Warren Winstead manage to attract such a well-qualified faculty to a barren campus with only one building, a significant lack of funds, only seventeen graduate students, and a flawed concept for maintaining a viable university? As with his recruitment of the board of advisors, part of Winstead's success was due to his charisma, his ability to sell the program, and his optimism that the Nova concept would work. He offered salaries much higher than the going rate and promised the faculty freedom to do their own research. The faculty was certainly attracted by the balmy weather in South Florida and the possible future benefits from living in a prosperous and rapidly growing area. They were also intrigued by the innovative ideas and creative possibilities of the new university. In Abe Fischler's case, he saw a great opportunity for his research as he could use the Nova schools as a living laboratory for his educational design to improve science teaching in the public schools, and he liked the innovative and flexible design of the new university.[81]

The initial list of university employees included thirty-eight staff members. The university claimed $9,500,000 in assets and $1,228,000 in promised research grants. Using the research report done by the firm of Hunter Moss, Nova predicted that when the university achieved its full growth by 1980, there would be 255 professors, 200 associate professors, and 250 support staff. The university estimated that by 1980, industries that Nova had attracted would employ 60,000 engineers, technicians, and service workers. The university estimated that its annual payroll by 1980 would be in excess of $600 million.[82] Nova University used these statistics to create a positive first impression and hoped the favorable predictions would garner increased support from the local community. Nonetheless, as indicated earlier, these estimations were a misrepresentation of the first order.

At this juncture, Nova University had accomplished its initial goals: it had hired a staff and faculty and recruited students, and was now ready to open its doors.

2

The Opening of the University

After all the planning, conflicts, crises, and obstacles, the SFEC and the board of trustees finally achieved its long-sought goal when Nova University welcomed its first class on September 25, 1967. Although twenty-one students were accepted for the fall 1967 term, only seventeen enrolled. The first students had been selected from approximately 250 applicants and all were on full scholarship. Of the original students accepted, seventeen already held master's degrees and would be working toward doctorates in science education, physical sciences, and oceanography.

Since the university was unknown, even in Broward County, press releases provided helpful information about the new campus, which was located in Davie, Florida, nine miles southwest of Fort Lauderdale. Temporary administrative offices and laboratories were housed in three buildings on East Las Olas Boulevard in Fort Lauderdale. One building had been completed on the Davie campus, the Rosenthal Student Center, which was being used temporarily for executive offices. Plans were for construction to begin in 1967 on the Hollywood Education Center and on a complex of ninety apartments for graduate students.[1]

When the first class of seventeen graduate students arrived at Nova University on September 25, 1967, the campus looked nothing like that of a university that aspired to be "the MIT of the South." It more closely resembled the abandoned airfield that it once was. Only one building had been erected, although the Parker Building was under construction. The campus, with the exception of a few trees, consisted of barren acres of weeds and sand.

Opening day turned out to be unseasonably hot. Despite the undeveloped campus and the warm weather, the occasion was joyous. The *Miami Herald* noted that "the arrival of the first students seemed auspicious to anyone who had a hand in shaping the brand new university. Finally, finally—after years of planning, talking, hoping, cajoling, arm-twisting, fund-raising, promoting, and recruiting, Nova University had opened its door. Even though the day was hectic, faculty and staff smiled, breathed a sigh of relief, forgot about how much more had to be done, and celebrated the fact that the dream of creating a major university in Broward County seemed one major step closer to becoming a reality. The opening of the first privately endowed technological graduate university begins with a small note that will be heard around the world."[2] Certainly the members of the original Oatmeal Club and the early SFEC trustees had reason to be proud of what they had achieved. They had persevered when the outlook for success was bleak and when they despaired of success. The SFEC's innovative idea had come to fruition.

After registration, the new students listened to university officials praising the remarkable accomplishment of establishing a new university. Warren Winstead emphasized the seriousness of the occasion and the importance of the first students: "You will make or break the university with your performance this year." The new president could not have known at the time that the students' performance would not be critical and that in three years the school would be near bankruptcy and he would be out of a job.

September 25, however, was a time of celebration, and Winstead excitedly proclaimed the opening of the new institution of learning. Professor Fischler stressed the freedom from traditional restraints in Nova's new approach to graduate education. He promised that the educational experience would be stimulating and urged each student to be self-motivated and to pursue research with vigor: "You don't learn to do research by staying on the sidelines any more than you learn dancing that way." After registration and speeches, the university sponsored a cocktail party for students, staff, faculty, and several hundred well-wishers.

That first class of seventeen students included fifteen men and two women. One member of the class was Leroy Bolden, an African American student who had been an all-American football player at Michigan State University and who had come to Nova from California

Figure 2.1 The first class of seventeen graduate students, 1967. (By permission of Nova Southeastern University Archives, Fort Lauderdale, Florida.)

to study science education. Gloria Cashin, one of two women in the class, held an MA from the University of Miami and had also enrolled to study science education. One student came from India and another from Venezuela.

These new Nova students were more mature than the typical graduate student. Most were in their twenties, had already acquired one advanced degree, and several were married with families to support. They were not interested in beer parties or spending time at the campus hangouts. They were already embarking on their life's work. Physics student Paul Viebrock said, "You need to be more self-organized here than in any other graduate school. You work at your own pace, but you're expected to achieve [knowledge] faster. Lectures are not required, but it happens we are always there."[3]

As Nova University embarked on its unique educational concept, the idea appealed to the imagination of educators who gravitated to proposals that were new, special, and different. Nova University represented a hope for higher education in South Florida, an institution that would keep the best and brightest students at home and would attract superior faculty and students to a rapidly developing region of the United States. By stressing the importance of science and technology, Nova could provide the leadership necessary to make the country more competitive in the new frontiers of the 1960s. Nova would be in a position to provide new and innovative approaches to teaching, research, and learning. As the premier institution in the South Florida educational park, the university would serve as a catalyst for implementing new educational models that would be copied nationwide. Nova would serve as a magnet for technologically oriented business and industry to locate in Broward County.[4] With such high expectations, now Nova had to live up to its promise.

Many national newspapers and periodicals, including *Time* and *U.S. News and World Report*, wrote lengthy articles on the opening of Nova University. A national audience of university presidents, administrators, and faculty—the most important group to whom Nova wished to appeal—read the *Chronicle of Higher Education*, the most influential U.S. educational publication. If Nova could secure publicity and approval from the *Chronicle*, that endorsement would help in establishing the university's credentials. The *Chronicle* presented a positive discussion of Nova University, its goals, and its innovative curriculum. It reported that Nova aspired to be "ranked quickly with MIT and Caltech." President Winstead, in a massive overstatement, noted: "We are doing what MIT and Caltech would do if they could start over today." The greatest fear expressed by Winstead and others was that, despite their heralded opening, they would have difficulty remaining innovative and flexible because of certain forces and bureaucratic requirements (accreditation) that would eventually inhibit change.[5]

Now that Nova University had opened its doors, it had to make the system work. Despite its auspicious opening and all the high-flown rhetoric about being the new MIT, Nova had neither the tradition nor the resources to operate successfully. Local support, commitment, and generosity of spirit would no longer sustain its radical plan for a graduate university.

In September 1968, one year after welcoming Nova's first class of graduate students, President Winstead greeted a second-year class of twenty students and twenty-three faculty. Fourteen of the twenty graduate students had enrolled in the Social and Behavioral Science Center. Winstead asserted that the first year had begun with anticipation; the second year would be one of "reassessment and consolidation." Despite retrenchment in some areas, Winstead announced new research initiatives in training courses for teachers and in oceanography. He revealed that progress had been made in student housing. Three student apartment buildings had been completed and were being occupied by graduate students, some faculty, and married students attending Broward Junior College.[6]

Winstead, looking to expand scientific research at Nova, asked the board of trustees for authorization to study the feasibility of acquiring the Germ-Free Life Research Center (GLRC), a cancer research center located in Tampa, Florida. The president indicated that the third floor of the Parker Building could be prepared to accommodate this activity at a cost of approximately $250,000.[7] By January 1969, after much discussion, the university had tentatively decided to try to establish the GLRC as an integral part of Nova University. The GLRC would form the nucleus of the life sciences program.

Support for the GLRC, a not-for-profit, tax-exempt laboratory, had come from contracts with the National Cancer Institute and from numerous other private sources. Joel Warren, the center's director, once served on the polio research team of Albert Sabin and was a highly regarded cancer researcher. In a presentation to the board of trustees, Warren explained that the research emphasis for the GLRC would be on the role of tobacco, chemicals, and viruses in causing tumors. The center hoped to develop a means of preventing cancer through the use of drugs and vaccines. To evaluate and test the potential of possible cures, the GLRC bred experimental germ-free mice in a germ-free environment.

While the board of trustees pondered the possibility of bringing the GLRC to campus, Winstead insisted this was "an opportunity that cannot be passed over. It will make this area nationally significant immediately in cancer research." Board member William Horvitz agreed that "this is one of the better opportunities the university has had, and we should not let it slip through our hands." Winstead announced that Theresa Castro would organize the women's group, the Royal Dames, to raise $250,000 for cancer research over a period of five years.[8]

The Germ-Free Life Research Center officially became a part of Nova University on June 1, 1969. In 1972, cancer research at Nova University entered a new phase, as the GLRC became the Leo Goodwin Institute for Cancer Research, named for Leo Goodwin Sr., founder of the Government Employees Insurance Company (GEICO) and a Fort Lauderdale resident. The Goodwin Institute would later evolve into the Life Sciences Center. Joel Warren would be the director of the Goodwin Institute and the Life Sciences Center, which was teaching and doing research in scientific fields other than oncology.[9]

As early as 1972, financial problems developed in the Goodwin Institute partly due to a decline in federal funding. Leo Goodwin Jr. apparently came up with the money to pay off some of the institute's obligations and provided it with a $50,000 electron microscope—the first one in Broward County. By 1975 the Life Sciences Center was again in debt. The failure to achieve a balanced budget prompted a letter from Abe Fischler stating that the university could no longer afford a center that did not balance its books and that the administration could no longer continue to subsidize life sciences. If the center had not balanced its books in one year, Fischler warned, then "drastic changes will have to be made, including asking some faculty members to leave."[10]

In the summer of 1973, the Goodwin Institute welcomed a distinguished visitor when Albert Sabin, a friend of Joel Warren's and the discoverer of an oral vaccine for polio, came to campus for a month-long visit. Sabin praised the development of the cancer research center and predicted it would become one of the leading research institutions in South Florida.[11]

In 1968, the main focus of the university was accreditation, for Nova could not survive without that imprimatur. On December 13, 1968, the Southern Association of Colleges and Schools (SACS) wrote Winstead to inform him that his institution had been designated as a Recognized Candidate for Accreditation. Candidacy was not accreditation, but SACS indicated that "steady and proper progress" was being made and implied Nova could be expected to achieve full accreditation by the time of its first graduating class. At that time SACS would then have an evaluation committee visit the university to determine eligibility for accreditation.[12]

In November 1969, the board of trustees decided to hire an executive vice president to ease the administrative burdens on President Winstead. The board chose Abraham Fischler, who accepted the position on the condition that the appointment would be temporary. It was clear at this point that President Winstead needed help. He had neglected some of his important duties, and the financial situation of the university was becoming desperate. Two weeks after assuming his new job, Fischler learned via a phone call from SACS, that a status report had to be filed with SACS each year until the institution became accredited, but Winstead had not sent in the initial report. Not only that, but Winstead publicly indicated that while accreditation by SACS would be nice, it was not so important because Nova had such an outstanding advisory board. So not only had Winstead not complied with the requirements for accreditation, he had also insulted SACS.

Fischler immediately sent off the delayed report, but the failure to comply on time proved disastrous as SACS notified Nova that it had been removed from candidate status due to its failure to communicate. In January 1970, Fischler and Jim Farquhar visited Gordon Sweet, executive director of SACS, at SACS headquarters to repair the damage done by Winstead's remarks and the late status report. The two men contritely asked SACS to reconsider its decision and assured them that Nova would cooperate with all the agency's rules and regulations and would soon provide an updated status report. In January 1970, Nova got a reprieve when it received a letter from SACS advising that it had been placed on correspondent status for a probationary period of six months.

Fischler immediately launched a self-study, and in April 1971, SACS sent an evaluation team to spend three days on campus. The nine-member team was headed by oceanographers from Woods Hole Oceanographic Institution and educators from such schools as Vanderbilt University, Emory University, and Texas Christian University and roamed the campus from April 12 through 14, 1971. The team filed a complimentary report, recognizing a "very real spirit of dedication to the university on the part of all members of the university community." The report referred to Nova as an "intriguing experiment in higher education" with a "highly individualized" instructional program. The evaluators rated the relationship between faculty and administration and between faculty and students as "remarkably good." In the case of the quality of its students, however, Nova did not get high marks. The report noted that any new school found it difficult to attract high-quality students—"So it is with Nova." The libraries were found to be inadequate, but the team softened this criticism by reporting, "The libraries are as unique as the institution itself."

On December 1, 1971, SACS announced that Nova was fully accredited for master's and doctoral programs. Nova would have to go through reaffirmation in four years, however, instead of the normal ten, at which time another self-study and site visit would take place. If reaffirmed in 1975, that accreditation would last for ten years. This decision enabled Nova to proceed with some major projects, including a law school and an off-campus doctorate of education program.

Accreditation also improved the university's chances of receiving grants and financing from private and government agencies.[13]

Someone at SACS, most likely Gordon Sweet, was looking out for Nova's interests. The school had failed to comply with the basic requirements of SACS and had been put on probation. In 1969–1970, Nova was essentially bankrupt; it had only a barebones campus and no library to speak of. By any standard, Nova probably should have been denied accreditation. SACS's decision to grant accreditation was yet another example of a favorable development for Nova at a critical juncture, for without accreditation, Nova would have been finished before it started.

In a time of economic distress, there were some positive developments. On February 18, 1968, Nova broke ground for what was then known as the $1.6 million Hollywood Education Center. Hollywood residents had raised $1.1 million, and the U.S. Office of Education added a $552,000 grant to complete the work. The building, which would house the social and behavioral sciences, opened to students on June 1, 1970. According to press accounts, the 49,000-square-foot, three-story edifice provided the graduate school with one of the state's most advanced facilities for research in education and behavioral sciences. The structure included a television studio (the university planned to telecast its own programs), a library, a 200-person lecture hall with a film projection booth, seminar rooms, and a computer center.

An entire wing of the Hollywood Education Center was devoted to the Institute for Human Development, directed by psychologist Marvin Rosenblatt. The institute dealt with serious social issues such as child rearing, marital disharmony, juvenile delinquency, crime, emotional disturbances, and educational problems. The new center received much-needed help when Birdie Einstein (no relation to the famous scientist) gave $100,000 to the library at the Hollywood Education Center.[14] The gift enabled Nova to make a significant improvement in one of its weakest areas.

A troubling internal schism over the university's vision and its future developed between Professor Ray Pepinsky, the Robert O. Law Professor of Physics, and Dean Abe Fischler. The initial conflict occurred when Fischler failed to endorse Pepinsky's recommendations for how the Physical Sciences Center should be organized. On May 20, 1968, the board of trustees offered new contracts to all faculty members except Pepinsky. The decision to terminate his contract, as explained by the board, was the culmination of a long series of annoyances, failures, and disappointments attributable to Pepinsky. He had neglected to adequately fund his department and was cited for "intolerant and unprofessional behavior."

Pepinsky appeared before the board on May 27, 1968, to answer the charges. He warned the trustees that his separation from Nova would have a negative impact on the physics program and would not be in the best interests of the university. The trustees were unmoved and decided that due to a lack of leadership on Pepinsky's part, Nova did not have a viable physics program. The board voted unanimously not to renew his contract. Fischler noted with some satisfaction that the university sided with his position and got rid of Pepinsky.[15]

Pepinsky's departure had a significant impact on Nova. Approximately seven of the physics students transferred, leaving Nova, in effect, without much of a physics department. With all of its financial troubles, Nova did not need to spend time on such divisive internecine warfare.

Professor Ed Simco, who had come to Nova as a member of the second class in 1968, recalled his decision to attend graduate school at Nova. His mentor had notified him of a new school, Nova University, which would provide an assistantship of $5,000 per year and would waive tuition. Simco had never heard of Nova, but with four children, he thought it was too good an economic and educational opportunity to pass up. He already had a master's degree in physics and planned to complete his physics PhD at Nova, but when he arrived, he discovered that the physics department was being phased out. With Abe Fischler's advice, he agreed to change his PhD to science education.

Simco not only lost out on his opportunity to complete his PhD in physics, but also, when he and his family arrived at Nova in 1968, his wife was appalled at the derelict campus. Simco said, "This is Nova University." His wife asked, "Where?" Simco, however, saw the university's potential and decided to stay. He had no tuition to pay, he had a $5,000 stipend, and the rent at the student apartments, then known as buildings A, B, and C, was fairly cheap. Simco completed his PhD in 1971, and then stayed as a postdoctoral student. He has been at Nova ever since.[16]

By the summer of 1968, the board of trustees, the governing board at Nova University, consisted of eighteen members and four honorary members. The board operated with five committees: executive, personnel, ways and means, building and grounds, and finance. At this juncture, finance was the most important and relevant committee as the board of trustees had finally recognized that they needed a dramatic and immediate solution to the deteriorating economic situation at the university. The trustees needed to begin a major fund-raising campaign as soon as possible, but one member cautioned his peers that "public airing of our dire need for operating funds would be harmful," as it would discourage giving to an institution that appeared unable to survive. The board even talked about selling the university property on Las Olas or going to the banks for a large loan to pay off its debts.[17] Nova's economic problems had worsened because of increased costs in faculty salaries and operating costs. Student tuition was virtually nonexistent and did little to allay the red ink. The new buildings needed books, furniture, and lab equipment; faculty expected to be paid; and vendors and suppliers were clamoring for the money owed to them.

Nova's original economic model had committed its financial future to an ongoing need for outside funding from research grants and private donations. Unfortunately, the initial projections by the New York firm of Tamblyn and Brown for fund-raising in South Florida had fallen far short of expectations. Nova had been given land and buildings, but needed unrestricted operating funds to pay the bills and keep the university open.

To some degree, Nova was a victim of its own excessive and optimistic public relations campaign. Nova had not yet created the massive economic impact on real estate, new jobs, and new industry as predicted by Hunter Moss and Company. It became abundantly clear that not only was Nova not going to solve all the problems of Broward County, but also might not be able to support itself. In the early planning stages, everyone was a dreamer and somehow thought the sheer force of their idea would be enough for success. Nobody planned for exactly how much money would be needed or where it would come from—the founders assumed that someone would come to their rescue. As their dreams met reality, some donors and supporters became disillusioned and began to question the inflated rhetoric touting Nova as the wave of the future.[18]

At the end of 1968 and the beginning of 1969, the financial situation reached an acute crisis point. Vendors were demanding payment for services, and some businesses would work with Nova only on a cash-on-demand basis. Faculty occasionally had to delay cashing their checks until the university could come up with funds. The power company threatened to cut off electricity. The federal government had served final notice on payment of withholding taxes and Federal Insurance Contributions Act (FICA), and pension commitments were not being met.

On April 22, 1969, President Winstead made a special report to the board of trustees about the financial crisis. He said that Nova needed to obtain more money from federal grants, ask some of their generous donors, such as Edwin Rosenthal and Louis Parker, for additional funds, and revive the $5 million fund-raising campaign in Fort Lauderdale. Unfortunately, only $150,000 had been raised in that campaign, and Winstead's only option was to cut expenses, what he called "belt-tightening." The business offices in the Las Olas property were moved to the recently completed first floor of the Parker Building, saving in clerical and secretarial personnel; the Las Olas property was then rented out. Several personnel changes were necessary. Winstead reported that the vice president for business affairs resigned and his position would remain vacant. Several secretarial positions were eliminated. Winstead warned that faculty and student morale was the lowest since the university's inception and that even with further belt tightening, the situation was so grave that the crisis could culminate in "the dissolution of the university."[19]

Most insiders realized that Nova was at a critical crossroads. Several members of the board of trustees remember discussing the rapidly deteriorating situation; for all intents and purposes, the university was bankrupt. One frequently asked question: "Does anyone know a good bankruptcy lawyer?" Robert Ellyson described the drastic change in attitude on the board in 1969. The board realized that they had to be realistic in terms of what they thought was going to work. They understood that they could not compete with the Caltechs and the MITs, and finally recognized that Nova was not going to get the money it needed from the federal government or local donors. Nova had to look for new opportunities. As Abe Fischler remembered, everybody realized that the original model "wasn't going to happen, that physicists weren't going to come down here, that engineers were not going to come down here. We had nothing to offer them. We didn't even have the resources to build them the laboratory they needed."[20]

Under these circumstances, the trustees began searching for an affiliation with another university. Inexplicably and unrealistically, they made overtures to MIT, Caltech, and Rensselaer. They should not have been surprised when none expressed interest in a merger. In 1969, the board of trustees contacted the University of Miami (UM), a private school. William Horvitz announced that he, Jim Farquhar, and A.L. Mailman had visited UM and had spoken with its president, Henry King Stanford, and the vice president for finance. The three emissaries revealed that President Stanford showed a strong interest in an affiliation and did not seem concerned about Nova's debt. The trustees then authorized Winstead to call President Stanford and tell him that the Nova board would be happy to meet with him once he cleared the matter with his executive committee.

As it turned out, the University of Miami lost interest in the merger. One major sticking point in the negotiations was that Nova was unwilling to give up the oceanographic center and Miami already had a flourishing maritime center. Stanford indicated that Nova lacked sufficient local support and that UM already had significant economic problems of its own, meaning it did not want to take on Nova University's debt. Tinsley Ellis thought Nova could have had a good working relationship with UM, "but they were not the least bit interested." By August 1969, UM had officially terminated any talks about a merger.[21]

Although it is difficult to ascertain whether Nova or Florida State University (FSU) initiated the first overtures about an affiliation, on May 15, 1969, FSU president J. Stanley Marshall wrote a letter to the Nova Board of Trustees making just such a proposal. Marshall intended to develop the Nova campus into a major graduate center for FSU and was willing to relocate a substantial number of faculty and graduate students to the Nova campus, possibly by September 1969. As a condition of a possible alliance, Marshall insisted that the graduate school numbers would have to be expanded significantly to make the new FSU campus economically viable, but he promised to maintain Nova's academic standards. He also agreed to honor all personnel contracts in the event of a merger. He understood that Nova had some unpaid financial commitments, and FSU would work carefully with the Nova board to resolve these issues. He proposed that the name Nova University be changed to Nova Graduate Center of Florida State University. Marshall admitted that he was only speaking for himself and that no discussions had been held with the state board of regents or with the chancellor of the university system.

The same day, the board of trustees met with FSU dean Phillip Fordyce to hear Marshall's proposal discussed in detail. Fordyce explained that if the merger took place, Nova would become a part of the state system and all property would be deeded over to the state. FSU would be willing to provide approximately $1 million to pay off Nova's debts and would continue Nova's graduate programs in oceanography and education while adding courses in fine arts and social welfare.

Winstead pointed out the advantages and disadvantages of FSU's offer. On a positive note, the merger would end Nova's financial problems, enable it to fully utilize all of its facilities, and expand its science programs with state support. However, Nova would lose the flexibility of a private institution and would be controlled by a politically influenced state bureaucracy. Nova's founders would have very little input in running the institution. Robert Ellyson argued that Nova would end up being a university far different from the one the SFEC hoped to create. The board, facing an uncertain future, ignored the negative aspects of a merger and voted unanimously to go on record as favoring the possibility of a partnership with FSU.[22]

By May 24, 1969, local papers had gotten wind of the possible merger and asked Winstead to discuss what negotiations had taken place. Winstead replied that any talk about a merger was "just a preliminary discussion," although he had recently met in Tallahassee with Stanley Marshall and Robert Mautz, chancellor of the State Board of Regents. Chancellor Mautz indicated that a merger with FSU was highly unlikely since the state would have to take over ownership of Nova. He said there might be the possibility of some sort of affiliation between Nova and FSU, but that possibility never materialized, and FSU broke off discussions with Nova.

Similar talks were held with Florida Atlantic University (FAU) president Kenneth Williams, who declared that FAU would be pleased to work with Nova in any appropriate way. The Nova board passed yet another resolution stating that Nova would be happy to have formal discussions with FAU about an alliance, but as with FSU, nothing came of this attempted union.

Jim Farquhar added to the list of possible affiliations when he remarked that Alexander Schure of New York Institute of Technology (NYIT) had called Winstead to express his interest in a merger. For the fourth time, the board approved a resolution of interest in an association with another institution and invited NYIT to make a presentation if it were still interested.[23] Nova University, desperately seeking salvation, had cast as wide a net as possible.

Although the board of trustees had approved a search for possible mergers with four different universities, Winstead insisted that while there were discussions going on, Nova had not initiated any of the talks and was not "seeking affiliations with any institutions at this point." The *Fort Lauderdale News* speculated that Nova was trying to get the state to take over the school for financial reasons, but Winstead said that idea would be "misleading."[24] How could the paper's view be misleading since it was an accurate depiction of Nova's objectives? Winstead's statement that Nova was not seeking any affiliations was an outright fabrication. In his defense, he tried to cover up the possible mergers because he knew the news that Nova was willing to give up its unique identity would negatively affect any possible financial contributions to the university.

Jim Farquhar had earlier observed that there had been a split on the board of trustees over whether Nova should remain independent or form some sort of partnership. Some board members feared that the driving motivation for an affiliation with another university was simply a strong desire by some members to get out of debt without understanding the importance of preserving Nova's uniqueness.

The desire in some circles to remain independent was borne out by the remarks of Cy Young, president of Gold Key at Nova. Young admitted that Nova "needed help" and had launched a new fund-raising drive "to unlock the great bulk of the community's resources" because "it seems to us imperative that Nova University be assured of sufficient financial strength to permit it to remain an independent institution." Furthermore, Young thought it possible that Nova could merge with another private institution "tuned to the Nova philosophy," but he ruled out any affiliation with tax-supported state universities such as Florida State.[25]

On June 7, 1969, the Florida State Board of Regents, the governing board of the state university system, set up a task force to explore the possibility of a state university merging with Nova University, but Chancellor Mautz made it clear from the beginning that there was no chance of establishing Nova as a separate state university. By early July 1969, the Board of Regents task force concluded that there would be no more exploratory talks about an affiliation with Nova because the state system already had too many other commitments, including two new universities, and did not have enough money to finance a takeover of Nova. In essence, the state was no longer interested in taking on a private school with debt. This decision, in effect, eliminated FAU and any another state university as a possible partner. Meanwhile, President Winstead had focused his attention on NYIT; on July 2, he went to New York for more discussions about a possible merger.[26]

Prior to Winstead's visit to NYIT, Nova officials, disheartened by their inability to find a partner, in a hasty and imprudent move, tried to form some sort of relationship with Fort Lauderdale University (FLU), formerly Drake Business College. Secret negotiations had been going on for some time, and the newspapers reported that Nova had approached FLU "in order to loosen the financial death grip that had threatened to undermine the five-year-old institution." It was not certain if FLU was an accredited institution, but apparently that did not dissuade Nova as the university proposed that FLU students use some of its classroom space and empty buildings and have the benefit of being taught by some of Nova's top science people. In exchange, FLU would give Nova $250,000 to pay off its debts. Not surprisingly, the FLU board turned Nova down. Stanley Drake, president of Fort Lauderdale University, revealed that they opted out because "they [Nova] wanted us to become tenants only and we are interested in becoming one big university." Drake went so far as to allege that because of its financial situation, "Nova needs us much more than we need them." The rejection by a business school was the ultimate dismissal. The situation at Nova had become so hopeless that it would approach a former business college for a bailout, but even an unaccredited business college was unwilling to form an affiliation.[27]

President Winstead, visibly embarrassed by the inability to arrange any sort of union with another institution, denied that he had sought an affiliation with FLU or the University of Miami. Winstead observed that FLU was a two-year business school trying to become a four-year university, and the two schools had totally different concepts about education. Nova was a small, high-quality, research-oriented institution. "We want to stay that way," said Winstead. Nor had Nova, he continued, approached any other university for affiliation. Winstead said he wanted to counteract the rumors that "we were trying to market the university" and called attention to the fact that he had collected "letters refuting statements that we were bidding for affiliation with other institutions."

One cannot imagine from whence those letters would come, certainly not from the Nova Board of Trustees, who were on record for unanimously encouraging just such mergers. Winstead alleged that all contacts "originated outside the board of trustees, undertaken by various individuals who felt they saw ways in which Nova" could eliminate its debt. Once again, the overriding reason for Winstead's remarks appeared to be that all the talk about mergers had hurt the school's ability to raise funds. An unrepentant Winstead proclaimed that Nova, faced with some financial problems, had "firmly rejected all proposals that would have turned this university into an institution of lower stature and lesser quality."[28]

Winstead's comments defied credulity. The meetings with Stanley Marshall of FSU and the board of regents, as well as the talks with FAU and the University of Miami, had been widely reported in the

press. Certainly the university administrators and the board of trustees knew better. The question is did Winstead make these remarks
on his own, or was he instructed to do so by the board? There is no
indication in the board of trustee minutes that they had requested he
deny attempts at affiliation, so he must have done so on his own. If so,
it undermined his credibility with the board.

On November 3, 1969, the Nova community was shocked to learn
of the sudden resignation of Warren Winstead, the university's first
president. The board granted him a nine-month sabbatical and full
pay, but he cleaned out his desk and departed before the nine months
were up. Abe Fischler, the executive vice president, now had to assume
greater responsibility for running the university.

Why did Winstead resign? Certainly some members of the board
of trustees were unhappy with Nova's progress under his tenure. He
had not been able to raise sufficient money, and the financial situation had gone from bad to worse. His greatest failure probably was
his inexplicable decision not to submit a status report to SACS, and
then he downgraded the importance of accreditation by SACS, the
only accrediting agency. His shortcomings in dealing with SACS came
close to undermining the viability of the university and were inexcus-
able. The president had also failed to arrange a merger with another
university and denied that Nova sought such mergers and tried to
blame individuals outside the board of trustees for the unsuccessful
approaches.

There was some talk that Winstead had personal problems and
had been too involved in social activities. Critics pointed out that he
did not always attend to the details of his presidential responsibilities.
Abe Fischler remembered that when he took over Winstead's office,
he found bills that had not even been posted. Fischler thought Winstead failed not only because he did not tend to essential university
operations, but also because he just did not realize that the original
concept would not work. Fischler commented that Winstead was unable to see the real picture: "He kept his eye on the hole and not on
the doughnut." Winstead was a good guy, continued Fischler, but "he
lost sight of why he came down here."[29] Despite the initial hoopla and
big promises at the beginning, with the departure of Winstead, Nova
had no president and was one step from closing its doors. One never
knows for certain, but a combination of these failures likely led to the
board asking for Winstead's resignation.

Winstead was a better salesman than an administrator. He traveled all over the country successfully selling Nova and attracting

top-notch people like Bill Richardson and Abe Fischler to the campus. His ability to persuade some of the best scientists in the world to sign on as advisors was nothing short of phenomenal. He generated a lot of enthusiasm for the university, getting national exposure with his appearance on the *Today* show and an article in *Time* magazine. He managed to raise some money with innovative methods. Many who worked with him described him as a visionary and a delightful colleague. But the challenge of building a new university from the ground up, especially one with only a graduate school, would have tested anyone's capabilities. Certainly there was no personal animosity against the man; board members praised him for his significant contributions in getting Nova established.

Once again, Nova University faced adversity. The school was now leaderless and had been unable to find an institution with which to merge, and its financial stability became more precarious each day. Board members and some outsiders thought this noble experiment would end in 1969; there were just too many obstacles to overcome. But Nova, like the mythical phoenix, rose again from the ashes. As before, Jim Farquhar and other stalwart friends came to the rescue. The university finally managed to conclude a merger with the New York Institute of Technology and found a president, Abe Fischler, who, over the next twenty-two years, would lead the school out of the educational wilderness to become a successful institution of higher learning.

3

The Abraham Fischler Presidency
Change and Growth During 1970–1985

As Nova struggled to survive, a few key individuals and some pragmatic decisions helped to right the ship. Perhaps the most important event in 1969 was Jim Farquhar's timely intervention. Farquhar, who had come to the rescue on several occasions, once again bailed out the university.

Farquhar later reflected on the tense situation that prevailed in 1969: "We owed a lot of money, and we would have to just go out and scratch for it and pay the bills and get going again." Robert Ellyson said that on many Fridays it appeared that Nova would not make the payroll. Ellyson would include notes with the paychecks asking the recipient to hold it for a few days if they did not need the funds immediately. Ellyson praised Farquhar for coming forward time and again to help meet the payroll, often with statements like, "Well, if you need another $20,000, I'll see what I can do."

Farquhar remembered a finance committee meeting where they had decided, "This is it, boys, we have to do something or close the doors." He had already pledged 100 acres of farmland to Nova, and with Abe Fischler's encouragement, Farquhar agreed to sell eighty acres of the donated property. In fact, he sold it that very day for $7,500 per acre. Within two weeks of the sale date, August 6, 1969, the school had $600,000 to use for expenses. The university used the money to satisfy the IRS and to pay off some bank loans. The board of trustees wanted to keep the land because it was contiguous to the campus, but at that time they did not envision a use for the land in the near future. The board was desperate for money, the university was in

Figure 3.1 Abraham Fischler, EdD, president, 1970–1992. (By permission of Nova Southeastern University Archives, Fort Lauderdale, Florida.)

survival mode, and the land sale seemed the most prudent thing to do. The board of trustees understood that the one-time land sale was not a solution, only a reprieve.[1]

A more hopeful development occurred on May 17, 1970, when Nova University held its first commencement exercises. Five students, including two women, were the first to earn PhDs at this inaugural event. The five graduates were Michael Yost Jr. (science education), Earl Hughes (science education), Robert Kendall (oceanography), Clarice Moreth (oceanography), and Marilyn "Mickey" Segal (behavioral science). Abe Fischler presided over the joyous occasion, and honorary degrees were awarded to Louis Parker and Jim Farquhar. The accomplishments of the five new graduates encouraged the faculty and administration that there would be many more successful students in the future.[2]

Merger with New York Institute of Technology (NYIT)

Behind the scenes, however, the board of trustees was searching for a way to save the university from collapse. The most hopeful and perhaps final possibility was a merger with the New York Institute of Technology (NYIT). Pursuit of a possible affiliation began in 1967, when Abe Fischler heard a speech by Alexander (Alex) Schure, the president of NYIT, outlining his educational goals. Impressed with Schure and his innovative approach to education, Fischler encouraged Warren Winstead to meet with Schure.

The first official contact between NYIT and Nova University took place in June 1968, when Winstead reported to the board that he had received a proposal from Schure to establish an undergraduate college at Nova. Winstead went to New York to meet with Schure and apparently made great progress in planning a union. Immediately following the visit, Winstead sent Schure a draft of the articles of incorporation between Nova and NYIT, to be known as the University Federation, Inc. Schure responded that the articles looked fine and hoped to proceed with the arrangement. In May 1969, the Nova Board of Trustees invited representatives of NYIT to make a presentation to Nova about a possible affiliation. In July 1969, NYIT vice president David Salten journeyed to Nova to discuss the financial aspects of an agreement.[3]

At the time, NYIT had locations in Old Westbury, Long Island, and Manhattan. Alex Schure and his family founded the school in 1955;

it was chartered by the State of New York in 1957. The original charter, for a two-year technical school, was amended in 1962 to include
the granting of four-year degrees and approval to operate suburban
campuses. As of 1970, NYIT had approximately 4,200 students and
awarded bachelor's degrees in computers, fine arts, business, and
communication arts, as well as a master's degree in business.

Alex Schure earned two doctoral degrees, one in education and one
in communications. His family made a fortune in electronics, and he
decided to use his specialty—applying technology to teaching—in the
development of an educational center. He pioneered the use of au-
tomated teaching machines and computers. Schure believed that the
key to education was not so much the content as the delivery system,
and he saw a day when education "via satellite and communication
systems" would be available in learning centers, corporations, and
homes. Schure was an early champion of computer animation, and
NYIT gave research funding and a home to a computer brain trust
that would later evolve into Pixar Animation Studios.[4]

After some preliminary discussions about finances, on June 25,
1969, David Salten arrived in Fort Lauderdale to meet with the Nova
Board of Trustees. Salten stated that since both institutions were private and innovative, NYIT would be interested in joint programs.
Most of NYIT's courses were at the undergraduate level, so it was
willing to establish a master's degree in business and some undergraduate courses on the Nova campus. Nova would continue as a separate
graduate school, and there would be a combined board of trustees
representing both universities. NYIT would agree to extricate Nova
from its immediate financial difficulties, and as security, the New York
institution would accept fifty acres of campus land as collateral. NYIT
wanted Nova to adhere to its experimental concept and did not plan
to make any additional changes in its faculty or programs.[5]

After some deliberation, in 1969 NYIT reneged on its original proposal and resolved not to make an agreement with Nova University at
that time, although Schure had written to tell Winstead that the initial
articles of agreement looked fine. Abe Fischler recalled that the NYIT
representatives "did not trust Winstead." Alex Schure was reluctant
to fund Nova partly because of Nova's ongoing debt and because
Winstead kept insisting that Nova wanted to be the MIT of the South.
Schure told Winstead, "If you want to be MIT-oriented, you need financing on a scope which is beyond what we have to offer, and if the
community [Broward County] can't provide it, you have to come to
one of two choices—either change the objectives of the institution

and go on from there, or reexamine how you do your financing and find some other way to do it."

Schure indicated that while they were interested in Nova, they could not satisfy the large financial requirements to fund a major research university. NYIT was also troubled about a lack of local students. Until the issue of financial security was rectified, Nova would not garner much local support and would have to look outside of Broward County for financial contributions.[6]

It appeared that the initial effort to lure NYIT into an agreement had failed, but Abe Fischler was not willing to give up. He had known Schure for some time, liked him personally, and was excited about what was going on academically at NYIT. Fischler, interested in the concept of self-learning through technology, approved of NYIT's implementation of some of these concepts, especially in science education.

Therefore, in May 1970, when Fischler was still executive vice president of Nova University, he decided to go to New York and visit Schure. Fischler knew that Schure was interested in the entrepreneurial spirit at Nova and that a merger would afford Schure the opportunity to pursue some of his creative educational concepts. Schure and Fischler shared a philosophy of learning, and their respect for each other made it easier for them to discuss a new arrangement. Within thirty minutes, according to Fischler's recollection of the meeting, Schure came up with a scenario for a NYIT-Nova federation. Fischler said that when he told the Nova Board of Trustees that he had obtained a verbal agreement on a merger from Schure, they did not believe him. The next day, the board called Schure to confirm the offer. When Schure indicated that he did want an official merger, negotiations began in earnest. Fischler visited NYIT again in June 1970; the gist of their conversation would form the core of the final agreement. Once Winstead resigned, Fischler, as the executive vice president, was the chief executive officer of the university and had the permission of the Nova board to pursue a merger with NYIT.

The main difference between NYIT's refusal of a merger in 1969 and the agreement in 1970 was primarily due to Fischler and Schure's friendship. They liked and trusted each other and now that Winstead had departed, they were free to pursue an affiliation. Schure said he felt positive about a merger since Nova had a dedicated board of trustees, a top staff and great professionalism. He thought Nova's graduate students would fit in well with NYIT's undergraduates.

Schure expected the joint venture to go well since both were independent universities with great flexibility.[7]

On July 1, 1970, NYIT and Nova signed the official document setting up a federation between the two schools. This agreement saved
Nova from having to close its doors and affected its future more
than any other event up to that time. Schure and Fischler had already
agreed to the general terms of the contract, and Fischler reported the
essence of these terms to the Nova University of Advanced Technology Board of Trustees (BOT) on June 17, 1970. The BOT accepted the
basic overview of the federation and agreed to work out the details
at a later date.

The July 1 agreement indicated that each university would maintain its not-for-profit legal entity and name. Six of the present board of
trustees at Nova University (Charles Forman, Ellis, Farquhar, Young,
Ellyson, and Horvitz) would be members of the new joint board. The
remaining Nova trustees would have to resign. NYIT would then appoint nine members of the new unified board of trustees, giving Schure a controlling vote on any proposal. Thus the new board would
consist of fifteen members plus the chief executive officer of each college: Schure and Fischler. NYIT in turn agreed to elect two members
of the Nova board (Fischler and Farquhar) to the NYIT Board of
Trustees. Alex Schure took the title of chancellor of Nova University.
Fischler would serve as president of Nova University and would report to the chancellor. By the terms of the agreement, Schure was the
presiding officer of both schools and would be paid a generous salary
by both institutions. Since the chancellor needed to be on the Nova
campus on a regular basis, Nova supplied Schure with an apartment
on the beach in Fort Lauderdale.

The official agreement specified that Nova University would continue its PhD programs and assist in developing similar programs at
NYIT. The academic programs at Nova were to be enlarged to include
a number of master's and undergraduate programs sponsored by both
NYIT and Nova. The boards of trustees at both universities could
allocate faculty of either campus to the other's campus when it was
deemed that their experience could be best utilized.

To insure Nova's financial integrity, NYIT agreed to contribute
$60,000 a month for twelve months to Nova for operating expenses.
The final sum to be paid by NYIT to get Nova out of debt would
be $720,000, paid by June 30, 1971. In addition, NYIT promised
to pay by December 13, 1973, the sum of $224,000, which would

cover Nova's current pension debt, FICA, Internal Revenue Service withholding debt, money owed to creditors, and restricted fund indebtedness. Finally, NYIT accepted the responsibility for repaying Nova's long-term obligations. NYIT would pay $147,000 the first year and $147,000 the second year for debt reduction. These fiscal terms would be invalid if Nova had any hidden debts or if the figures given to NYIT were incorrect.[8]

NYIT thus provided approximately $1.2 million to Nova ($720,000 at $60,000 per month and a payment of $147,000, another payment of $129,000, and $224,000 for FICA and IRS debt) in the form of prepaid rent for NYIT to function on the Nova campus. The NYIT Board of Trustees would not have approved merely giving $1.2 million to Nova. If the money were used for prepaid rent on a lease arrangement, then the $1.2 million would not show up as a debt in NYIT's accounting ledger. In essence, Nova leased some 30,000 feet of space to house NYIT activities and courses and the personnel who would develop these programs.

While the infusion of funds from NYIT saved Nova from insolvency, its financial woes had not been resolved. There were still deficits, and the administration struggled every month to make the payroll. Charles Forman, pleased with the final agreement with NYIT, made the motion for the board of trustees at Nova University to accept the merger. Forman reasoned that Schure knew education and had run a profitable institution. "We need his programs and his ideas," said Forman, and his money would give Nova the funds to operate and a chance to grow the university. Forman, recognizing that the financial situation at Nova was uncertain, thought that Nova had "sold" Nova University as a good investment for Schure, otherwise he would not have agreed to the contract. Forman said to the Nova board that if they agreed to the federation, "we are all going to be heroes or goats, and I hope we are heroes."[9]

Persuading the Nova University Board of Trustees to finalize the merger proved more difficult than anticipated. Several local citizens voiced their disapproval of a takeover by some "damn New Yorkers." About half the board did not like the deal and thought it was a mistake to sell out to a not very prestigious New York university that no one had ever heard of. Some trustees feared they would lose local control since NYIT had a voting majority on the board. A few members resented those "New York carpetbaggers" coming down to tell Nova how to run its university. Some of Nova's founders were concerned that the agreement would end up betraying the university's origins and purpose and would not be in Nova's long-term interests. Others resented Schure's high salary as CEO of both universities.

There were also some hard feelings from the nine Nova University board members who were forced to resign. The nine trustees had agreed to resign for the good of the institution because they thought the NYIT merger was the only option, otherwise Nova would have had to close down. Tinsley Ellis said, "We did it to survive, pure and simple, because it wasn't a good fit to begin with, but it did serve its purpose over a period of years. I'm glad we did it. Otherwise we wouldn't be here today."[10]

The *Fort Lauderdale News and Sun-Sentinel* praised the new federation: "The expansion of Nova University is good for the community. Its trustees and administrators should be congratulated." One of the advantages of the new alliance, declared the paper, was that Nova would be better able to fulfill its original intent of being a school that citizens of Broward County could attend. With the implementation of undergraduate courses, a local student could start in first grade at Nova Elementary and continue through high school, college, and graduate school—all at the Nova campus.

Nova, with only twenty-four graduate students, hoped to expand enrollment to 300 with undergraduate courses beginning in the fall of 1971. Fischler explained that Nova's immediate debts would be paid by December 31, 1970, and the university would begin paying down its long-term debt. He predicted that by gaining control of its finances, Nova would be able to recruit outstanding faculty and increase the number of students and course offerings.[11]

The transition to the federation was initially difficult for Nova since the university lost some control over its curriculum and administrative decisions. Now, with a new partner, Nova faced a crisis of confidence and identity. The school had abandoned its original concept, had almost gone bankrupt, had been essentially invisible to the community, and had merged with a New York institution that very few ever heard of. Nova had to redirect its energies and make the most of its new affiliation.

In the beginning, Nova leaders worried that NYIT would exercise total control over the university's decision making. Most of the individuals involved in the merger, however, claimed that NYIT chose not to interfere with Nova administrators' decisions. Tinsley Ellis said that for the first three years the New York board members did not overrule any decision the combined board made. Schure had ultimate authority but did not use it. In the early years of the union, Schure

and Fischler were friends and operated in a congenial and cooperative manner. Ellis contended that Schure "left a great deal of the authority with Abe Fischler because he had a great deal of confidence
in him." Hamilton Forman insisted that Nova had not sold out with
the merger and continued to do pretty much what it always wanted
to do.[12]

Initially, Nova ran the NYIT classes on campus, and NYIT cov-
ered program expenses and took any profits earned from the programs. Nova complained that its overhead expenses were greater than
NYIT's allocation to cover those costs, so from 1973 to 1977, NYIT
allowed Nova to share in the small net surplus the federation earned
and to take 10 percent of the income from the joint programs to assist with overhead costs.[13] That 10 percent was helpful, but it did not
alter the bottom line.

From the time of his arrival on campus in 1966 to the end of his
presidency in 1992, Abraham Fischler had an indelible impact on
Nova's survival and subsequent success. Born in Brooklyn, New York,
Fischler was a product of public schools. He matriculated at City College of New York (CCNY), but after one year went into the U.S. Navy
as a medic, serving in 1946 and 1947. He received his BS degree from
City College in 1951 and his master's in science education from New
York University. When he completed his doctorate at Teachers College, Columbia University, Fischler accepted a position as assistant
professor of science education at Harvard University for three years
and later became a full professor of education at the University of
California, Berkeley. Fischler's main focus in his academic career was
improving the way students learned. Rather than having students restricted by arbitrary time periods, Fischler proposed that the curriculum be tailored to each student's needs, with content delivered in a
manner and at a pace consistent with each student's learning style.

Fischler, described by a local newspaper as a "pipe smoker with a
keen, flashing wit and smile," made a momentous decision in 1966,
both for himself and for Nova, when he left a tenured position at one
of the most prestigious institutions in the country to come to Fort
Lauderdale to a new university that had not even opened its doors.
He was attracted by the innovative possibilities of founding a new
university and intrigued by the possibility of expanded research on
how students learned, and he never regretted his choice.[14]

During Winstead's presidency, Fischler was the dean of graduate
studies and director of the Behavioral Science Center. On November 4, 1969, the day after Warren Winstead abruptly resigned, the

board of trustees of Nova University made Fischler the executive vice president. Although Winstead, who was on sabbatical, remained on campus for a while, from November 1969, Fischler was the acting president, in authority if not in title.

While acting president, Fischler negotiated the merger with NYIT and began making draconian cuts in expenses to keep the university operating. He acted as executive vice president until the board chose him as the second president of Nova University in August 1970. There is some dispute as to whether the board of trustees had begun a national search to find a replacement for Winstead. If so, they did not have to look far. Fischler did not think there was a formal search, and his recollection was that he got the job because Alex Schure said the merger would not go through unless Fischler became president. Also, Fischler could not imagine why anyone else would want the job, what with the university's deplorable situation at the time. Joel Warren, director of the Germ-Free Life Research Center; William Richardson, head of the Oceanographic Center; and Fischler were the only three experienced administrators left, and neither Warren nor Richardson wanted to give up his current position. Fischler told Jim Farquhar that he would accept the presidency for just one year until the university had stabilized and made some strides toward profitability.

The board's August 24, 1970, decision to select Fischler as president had enormous ramifications for Nova's future. This move probably did more than anything to ensure its survival, as Fischler would demonstrate strong leadership for the next twenty-two years. As would often be the case for Nova, he would turn out to be the right leader at the right time. Trustee Cy Young, upon Fischler's appointment as president, described him as "a remarkable man. He's a scholar, he's a scientist, he's an expert in education. And now it turns out that he's a damned fine administrator. And that's very unusual to find those qualities combined in one man."[15]

In September 1970, Fischler presided over the opening session of the fourth year for Nova University. Twenty-six graduate students, thirteen of whom were new, registered for classes. Fischler announced that the third floor of Parker Physical Sciences Center had new chemistry and immunology laboratories and the permanent facilities at the Oceanography Center were nearing completion. The new leader declared that the affiliation with NYIT would give Nova the necessary resources, faculty, and knowledge to move into a new growth period.[16]

Nova University formally installed Abe Fischler as president on October 4, 1970. He received the symbols of his new office from board

Figure 3.2 Alexander Schure, PhD, chancellor of Nova University, 1970–1985. (By permission of Nova Southeastern University Archives, Fort Lauderdale, Florida.)

of trustees chairman Jim Farquhar at the newly completed Mailman-Hollywood Education Center. The occasion served to introduce Nova University supporters to NYIT officials and executives. Nova awarded Alex Schure, president of NYIT and chancellor of Nova University, with an honorary doctor of engineering science degree. The degree recognized Schure as the founder of NYIT and cited his expertise in educational technology and for blending technology and education.

In his inaugural address, Fischler promised that new programs would be developed jointly with the business and industrial community of Broward County. He hailed the federation with NYIT, saying that the merger brought together two complementary institutions and was a "truly symbiotic relationship." Fischler praised the business leaders who founded Nova University and expressed great pride in its early period of growth and development, which he characterized as its "infancy." While the early period required "much nurturing, tender loving care and dependence; it did allow us to unify and solidify."[17]

On November 15, 1970, Nova University dedicated the Mailman-Hollywood Education Center and invested Schure as chancellor of the university. In his address, he proposed that the university should continuously search for indestructible virtues and the betterment of the community. Schure hoped that in time Nova would broaden its curriculum, and he encouraged the development of additional academic specialties in medicine, law, environmental studies, and informational science.[18]

When Fischler characterized the relationship between Nova and NYIT as "symbiotic," he overstated the case. Immediately after his inauguration, Fischler faced significant difficulties in establishing successful undergraduate programs on the Nova campus and continued to be plagued by ever-increasing financial problems. Many of Nova's debts had been paid, but the cost of running a university with twenty-six graduate students and a comparatively large faculty, no tuition, and a lackadaisical response from the local community to the merger made life difficult for the new president. Fischler needed an additional $800,000 for expenses during the 1971–1972 school year just to maintain current programs and pay outstanding bills.

In the beginning, Schure kept all of the money NYIT earned from its programs at Nova; that decision restricted Nova's ability to expand. By 1973, as noted earlier, Schure opted to give Nova 10 percent of the earned income from NYIT courses. The extra income helped but was not enough; from 1970 to 1985, Nova lived on the brink of financial failure. Fischler must have frequently recalled the significance of

Schure's comments in his investiture speech: "There are many details of the relationship still to be worked out. There will undoubtedly be many problems and will require much mutual patience, cooperation, and . . . forbearance in order to solve them."

Fischler knew about the problems inherent in organizing a merger and the forbearance necessary to keep all parties happy better than anyone else since it was his responsibility to work out the details. He obviously did good work during his first three years as president, because in 1973 the board of trustees offered Fischler a four-year contract at $45,000 per year. The board commended him for his outstanding job "under tremendous pressure in a difficult and thankless position." While they were in session, the board changed the institution's name from Nova University of Advanced Technology, Inc., to Nova University, Inc.[19] Nova was no longer a technical and scientific graduate school, and the new name more accurately reflected the undergraduate programs and the university's revised mission.

In 1973, the most stalwart and faithful friend of the university, Jim Farquhar, citing health reasons, resigned after ten years as chairman of the Nova Board of Trustees. Abe Fischler publicly praised Farquhar for his many contributions to the university: "He didn't have a bad bone in his body. I never saw him angry. I never saw him overly upset. He would do it rather than ask you. An absolutely unusual guy." Fischler recounted the number of times that Farquhar had come to Nova's aid. He had given land worth millions of dollars, loaned the school money to meet payrolls, and worked tirelessly as chairman of the board during the institution's ten most difficult years. In 1979, Nova honored Jim Farquhar at a testimonial dinner given in recognition of his many years of devotion and service to the university. At the dinner, Fischler lauded the honoree for his generous contributions to the advancement of education and the arts and for his part in the development of the South Florida Education Center. Fischler noted that most people kept the money they earned, but Farquhar contributed to the lives of others and made a difference in those lives. Fischler designated Farquhar as "Mr. Nova."[20] Nova would not have survived without this gentleman's advice, commitment, and generosity.

In an attempt to attract more students and to ramp up interest in the new federation, Nova placed a prominent ad in the *New York Times*, which garnered approximately 9,000 responses.[21] The ad gained some notoriety for the school but did not result in a large number of new applications. Despite ongoing economic issues, Nova pushed ahead on four fronts: persuading prospective students to attend Nova, improving student housing, creating a law school, and expanding off-campus educational programs.

With formal accreditation achieved in 1971, Nova decided to launch a law school in 1973 and planned to offer an off-campus doctorate of education program in nine major U.S. metropolitan areas. The other area of concern had been partially addressed when the three buildings in the Davie Founders residence halls were opened. The dormitories were named for large contributors to the university: Jim Farquhar, Earl and Adella Vettel, and A.D. Griffin. Once completed, the buildings were immediately occupied, but these apartments still did not solve the housing problem. Nova continued to investigate new ways to increase the number of student quarters.[22] Although at the top of Nova's agenda, the law school and additional dormitories would be costly to develop, and Nova lacked funding for these projects. Fischler hoped the off-campus programs in educational leadership would offer a panacea for Nova's economic shortages.

Educational Leadership Program

To increase Nova's revenue, Fischler devised the blueprint for the first distance education program in the nation in which students could earn an EdD degree. The concept was ahead of its time and in many ways was the forerunner of today's online education programs. The idea was to find alternatives to campus-bound degree programs, redefine the traditional notion of a college, and take the campus to the student to foster external, field-based courses—in short, long-distance education. Fischler's degree program, called the Educational Leadership Program, was aimed at principals and superintendents in public schools around the country who wanted to earn an EdD degree but were working full-time. Fischler set up "clusters" of students in metropolitan areas around the country, hired top-flight professors to teach the courses, and then flew the faculty into the city for a weekend of classes and seminars. These field-based courses enabled school administrators to progress in their career by acquiring an advanced degree without interrupting their current employment. To be admitted into the EdD program, participants had to have a MA degree and be employed in an administrative position.

The initial curriculum offered courses in leadership, curriculum, supervision, school finance, and evaluation. Ed Simco, one of Nova's early instructors, recalled that when teaching an off-campus cluster class, he would meet with the students on Friday night and get them oriented toward their class on Saturday. The class usually met once a month, and students were given assignments to complete prior to class. The professor would teach the cluster for eight hours on Saturday, lecturing, discussing issues, breaking out into small groups, and having students submit projects for evaluation by the entire class. The class ended late Saturday afternoon, and the faculty member would return home on Sunday.

For Fischler, it was a cost-effective model that led to increased income for the university. He paid the professor's salary, plane fare, and hotel, but he did not have to pay health benefits or retirement. Fischler sometimes had to pay rent for a facility to hold the classes, but frequently was able to take advantage of academic institutions that had unused classrooms on the weekend. The same professor taught the same course wherever and whenever it was held. Fischler and others had a network of contacts in the educational field and thus hired some of the best professors in the country who taught the same courses they taught at their own universities. Most traditional universities would try to use their own faculty to teach off-campus courses, but no school would command the experts that Fischler could call on to teach his clusters. Nova officials expected criticism of this novel idea of distance education, but they believed that the high-quality faculty would mitigate such criticism.

Each cluster included a local coordinator who held an advanced degree and lived in the area. The coordinator was available to handle problems and provide guidance for students who needed help. The coordinator would ensure that classrooms were available and that the students had their books. The students would then travel to Nova University or another location for a one-week intensive session in the summer. Written and oral exams ensured that the candidates had mastered the material. Each student had to complete a major applied research project to be approved by the Nova faculty. Since all students held full-time jobs, the course work required a significant amount of self-discipline to succeed.

Fischler liked the cluster idea because of the camaraderie and dialogue it generated between the twenty-five to thirty people in each cluster. The students read each other's papers and shared professional experiences, and could immediately apply what they learned to their daily activities as school administrators. In essence, they had their own research laboratory—they could try out new methods as administrators in their own schools and report the results to their classmates. The students learned from a knowledgeable mentor who gave them feedback and guidance as they pursued their degree.

Fischler had discovered and filled an important niche in higher education, providing an opportunity for individuals to get degrees without vacating their job or leaving their geographic area. Nova would come to them. The program began in 1971 with four clusters. Fortunately for Nova, the external degree program quickly won approval from Gordon Sweet and SACS in 1971, with the provision that the program be evaluated every year. John Scigliano, then director of admissions, designed the programs, and Fischler hired Donald (Don) Mitchell as the director of the Educational Leadership Program. In 1972, the program received a big boost when the Ford Foundation awarded Nova a grant of $70,480 to be used in the planning and the implementation of the clusters. Mitchell said the "Ford grant will be used for the improvement of study materials, for an evaluation of the program, and for the coordination of the national lecturers input."

John Scigliano observed what Don Mitchell had done with principals in elementary and secondary schools and decided that the same could be done for community college administrators. Fischler liked the idea of a field-based program for community college administrators. If the program proved successful with primary and secondary school principals, why not community college administrators? Scigliano wrote a concept paper, SACS approved that program, and it became very successful. Ultimately the university would develop similar programs for city and state executives and courses for employees in the criminal justice system.

When Fischler first proposed the idea of external programs, some members of the board of trustees were concerned whether Nova would be able to maintain the quality of the programs and worried that Nova might be characterized as a diploma mill. Once SACS approved the idea and the programs were accredited, however, those board members changed their opinions. If SACS approved the Educational Leadership Program, it must be sound, they concluded. The board also understood that Nova could earn some sorely needed money from the program, and that new income was enough of a positive factor to mitigate any criticism that was bound to come. Tinsley Ellis saw it as an institution-saving decision because Nova needed the money to keep functioning. As for the expected attacks on course quality, Ellis said Nova had to show that the program was of high quality and had to respond to any and all attacks.

By 1973, the Educational Leadership Program had 817 students from 23 states and the community college degree program included 707 students. Nova then added a doctorate in public administration for county and city managers. According to Fischler, by 1973 the income from the various programs amounted to about half of Nova's budget. The welcome influx of funds from the distance education courses kept Nova at least close to stability.[23]

Despite a large student enrollment in the off-campus programs and steadily increasing income, the Nova field-based courses faced serious challenges from various states and universities who looked on Nova's incursion into their territory as unwanted competition. The more successful Nova became in the 1970s, the greater the resistance. Each state had its own method of determining the educational opportunities that would be allowed within its boundaries, and Nova had to be licensed in most states just to be able to conduct its classes. As Nova's numbers and influence grew, several states worked hard to keep Nova out of their jurisdiction. The political bureaucracy did not want outside universities coming in and offering courses that their state universities already taught. Tenured professors did not like the idea. They viewed Nova as an unworthy interloper trying to rob them of students. Nova had to fight several costly legal battles to protect its concept and to continue to offer classes.

One typical legal challenge was when North Carolina refused permission for Nova to teach its classes in the state. Nova went to court arguing that state universities were competitive institutions and had no right to exclusive jurisdiction over an educational concept. The North Carolina Supreme Court agreed, ruling that state law did not give the North Carolina Board of Governors authority over Nova's courses since the school granted its degrees in Florida, not North Carolina. Refusing Nova permission to teach classes in North Carolina would be a restriction of free speech.

Nova won the North Carolina lawsuit but faced many other challenges throughout the country. Nova had to file lawsuits everywhere it was opposed or had to get injunctions to allow the university to operate in that state. Arkansas challenged the Nova courses because they did not teach Arkansas history; Massachusetts objected because Nova did not have a library at its classroom sites.

Texas allowed Nova to have two clusters in Dallas, but when it opened another cluster in Galveston, the Coordinating Council for Higher Education in Texas said Nova had to cease and desist in Galveston—it could operate only in Dallas. So for three years, Nova had to fly students from Galveston to Dallas for their instruction. When Fischler planned to challenge the Texas ruling in court, Gordon Sweet asked Nova not to oppose the decision. SACS had received letters from North Carolina and Texas threatening to withdraw from SACS if SACS continued to support Nova. SACS could not afford to lose two prominent states from its association. Fischler, deeply indebted to Gordon Sweet, agreed to withdraw his challenge to the Texas ruling. The commissioner of the Texas college and university system said that Nova agreed "they won't operate any more clusters in Texas and I won't raise any more hell about the ones that are already here."

On an earlier occasion, Sweet had replied to an attack on SACS for being "misguided" in giving accreditation to Nova's program. Richard Morland of Stetson University had described Nova as "a diploma mill," and Sweet assured Morland that Nova had been "the subject of a number of evaluations by respectable and reputable persons from recognized colleges and universities." Sweet concluded that Morland was guilty of sensationalism, uninformed judgments, and irresponsible charges. Sweet's defense of Nova helped establish the university's bona fides and helped, at least briefly, to stem the tide of the angry attacks.

Other states used various ingenious means to thwart Nova, and Nova often responded in kind. New Jersey ruled that students who took Nova's courses in the state could not use them for credit in getting a superintendent's license or certificate in New Jersey. Although the courses continued to be taught in New Jersey, Nova had the students certified in Pennsylvania. Because of reciprocity, the students would then be certified in New Jersey. In Puerto Rico, Nova attorney Tom Panza reported that when Puerto Rico tried to close down the cluster there, he flew down for a hearing on the issue. The entire hearing was conducted in Spanish, and when Panza protested that he did not speak Spanish, the local officials said, "Too bad." Once again Nova got creative and chartered a boat to take the students out to sea to attend classes beyond Puerto Rico's legal jurisdiction.

Resistance came not only from other states, but also from the State of Florida, which tried to restrict the program by preventing Nova from using adjunct faculty to teach the clusters. Florida wanted to require prior state review and approval of "branch classes" established more than thirty miles from a school's main campus. Hamilton Forman and Tom Panza traveled to Tallahassee to change the minds of the cabinet members. Fischler knew how important this vote would be—if the restrictions held, Nova would not be able to carry out its field-based programs. Fischler said, "Seven hundred and fifty people would be unemployed, 6,000 students would no longer be going to school, and Nova University would have to close its doors." Within a few days, Forman had persuaded five of the seven state cabinet members to rescind the restrictions.[24]

Until 1978, the off-campus programs expanded and prospered, but the many objections to the program began to create problems for Nova. The *Cincinnati Enquirer* wrote an editorial referring to Nova "as a mail-order diploma school reported in 1976 to be operating out of Florida." The newspaper's editor was upset because administrators in Ohio had received pay raises and promotions based on "spurious" EdD diplomas from Nova: "The doctoral degree traditionally has been too highly valued to be had without the most rigorous academic investment. The Nova program, in all honesty, was a conspicuous shortcut."[25]

President Fischler fired off a letter defending the degrees and pointing out that SACS had accredited Nova's programs. The board of trustees gave Fischler permission to pursue redress in the courts. Nova sued the newspaper, the editorial writer, and the publisher. The legal brief defended Nova's programs and explained that SACS had given Nova University full accreditation in 1975 and that the nineteen-member inspection team included faculty from Harvard University, the University of Wisconsin, UCLA, and the University of Washington. Nova was neither a "mail-order diploma mill" nor an illegitimate university. The suit argued that the *Cincinnati Enquirer* published these erroneous facts maliciously, knowing they were false. As a result, Nova University "had been defamed, held up to contempt, ridicule, and disparagement before the public," and its reputation had been harmed. The suit asked for $5 million in compensatory damages and $5 million in punitive damages. Nova won the defamation suit, and the *Cincinnati Enquirer* printed a retraction.[26]

In 1979, the Educational Leadership Program suffered another setback as the National Council for Accreditation of Teacher Education (NCATE) denied accreditation of Nova's doctorate program. The group concluded that the program had only one strength—the use of recognized authorities as instructors—and had several weaknesses. The students did not meet with the lecturers for enough hours, Nova's library facilities were inadequate, and the fiscal stability of the program and the university was questionable. Although Fischler did not address the negative aspects listed by NCATE, he dismissed the ruling because the NCATE was unwilling to recognize the value of a nontraditional program.[27]

Throughout its existence, Nova University constantly had to defend its off-campus programs. At one point the university hired a marketing company to help frame an effective response to the attacks. The Barton-Gillet Company stated that Nova had the toughest marketing task of any educational institution it had studied. The firm urged Nova to emphasize the many and varied programs it offered and to point out the favorable reports from school principals and superintendents around the country.[28] As a result, Nova launched a positive series of ads about its offerings.

In 1980, the *Chronicle of Higher Education* published a balanced article about Nova's distance education program. The *Chronicle* quoted Fischler as saying, "If our programs had come out of Harvard, they would have been the greatest thing coming down the pike in higher education." Other Nova University officials constantly complained about the critics who had been unwilling "to consider the facts and judge the program on its merits." The *Chronicle* also included negative comments from educators who maligned external programs because they did not have a critical mass of students and faculty necessary for the collegiality and interchange that existed in a good graduate program. Any good graduate program required quality labs and libraries, which Nova did not have, and also required an intensely researched dissertation, not a work project. Some educators who objected to off-campus programs simply resented the amount of money Nova made and did not believe external programs provided the same quality education as internal programs. The article concluded with a comment from a Nova official, who pointed out that the University of Massachusetts and Pepperdine University were offering off-campus courses much like Nova's: "They know this is the future. They are taking our model and running with it."[29]

Tom Panza, an attorney for Nova, always believed that the university would survive these difficult times, partly because Abe Fischler would not let it fail. Panza thought the distance-learning idea was good and that it was the wave of the future. Because Nova was an independent institution, it could act decisively and effectively because the school did not have to go through all the bureaucracy required of a state university. Nova could develop a curriculum that met a particular need and could do so in a reasonable period of time.[30] Today, when almost all major universities use distance learning, the concept has become widely accepted. At the time, however, Nova had to put up with the sniping and criticism to get the revenue it needed.

University School

Marilyn Segal, who earned her doctorate in behavioral science, was one of the first five graduates of Nova University. After receiving her degree, Mickey, as she was known, presided over a small experimental preschool and kindergarten at Temple Beth-El in Hollywood, Florida. The school, known as the Pre-School Private School, was initially the brainchild of Myron Ashmore and a pilot program in which disadvantaged preschool children and tuition-paying students shared an educational experience. Segal, the daughter of A.L. Mailman and mother of five children, earned her degree in English from Wellesley College in Massachusetts and her master's from the McGill University School of Social Work in Montreal. At the preschool, Segal administered a very innovative type of open classroom environment with individualized instruction.

Abe Fischler knew about Segal's preschool and was impressed with its initial success. He needed a student population to continue his research into how children learned educational science concepts. Fischler wanted a school with easy access, and he persuaded Mickey Segal to move her academy onto the Nova campus. The new school would be known as the University School, and the Mailman Family Foundation gave Segal $60,000 a year to run the operation.

At the beginning, in 1970, the University School was affiliated with and located on the Nova University campus. Fischler assured the board of trustees that Nova had not taken over financial control of the school. Nova University assumed responsibility for the school's academic affairs and management, but the University School had its own separate board of trustees.

In 1971, President Fischler requested that the board consider incorporating the University School into the Institute of Early Childhood Education. He argued that bringing the University School aboard would complete the promise made to the SFEC—to provide an educational continuum from the time a child is born through to the PhD. The board balked. They were willing to give the land and supervise the school, but were adamantly opposed to assuming the University School's $85,000 debt and would commit to a building only if the money were raised through a fund drive.

Eventually, A.L. Mailman agreed to assume the outstanding $85,000 debt and to assist in getting a bank loan for the cost of the new building. In November 1972, after being located on the campus for two years as an independent school, the University School and its assets officially merged with Nova. It would continue to serve as a laboratory school for research in the Behavioral Science Center and for Fischler's graduate students in education.[31] It should be noted that the University School at Nova University was a private lab school and was distinct from Nova High School, which was tax supported and part of the Broward County public school system. The two schools were often confused because both were new, innovative schools and the campuses were very close to each other.

Fischler was perhaps a bit disingenuous in his request for the University School to be affiliated with Nova. He tried to persuade some of the Oatmeal Club members who were also on the board of trustees with his pitch about the cradle-to-the-grave concept, but he also wanted the school on campus for his own research. As the University School grew, Nova had problems housing the students, first in the Rosenthal Center and later in the Parker Building. The acquisition of the University School proved to be a drain on university resources at a time when the school was constantly in debt.

In November 1970, the University School did a self-study explaining its educational strategy and how the school was organized. In 1970, there were 290 students from age two and a half to fifteen. The University School made a concerted effort to recruit African Americans and Native Americans, and enrolled children of all racial and religious backgrounds. The school hoped to maintain a delicate balance between an open classroom setting, a school without walls, and a disciplined freedom while promising to be flexible, innovative, and self-critical.

The University School stressed individual accomplishment relative to one's ability and expectations rather than performance in comparison with a group. There would be no letter grades. The institution tried to maintain an unthreatening climate; fear of failure was absent. The full development of the child, academically and socially, was the top priority.

In its early years, the University School continued to be a financial liability for Nova, but the school slowly grew and with an increase in student enrollment gradually paid down its debt. By 1975 the University School had a $2 million school complex located on seventeen acres of university land. There was a 42,000-square-foot main building with a library, classrooms, offices, media resources center, auditorium, and cafeteria. In 1979, there were 950 students supervised by 63 faculty and administrators. Some 60 percent of the faculty held graduate-level degrees. The school had been accredited by SACS and the Florida Council of Independent Schools. It had become the official Head Start Center for Broward County and served as a model training center for other Head Start personnel in the county.[32] The University School would eventually become one of the better laboratory schools in the nation.

Promoting Diversity

From the outset, Nova University placed a strong emphasis on recruiting a diverse student body and faculty. Abe Fischler worked diligently to persuade an African American student, Leroy Bolden, to become a member of the first class at Nova. Fischler wanted the community to know that Nova was going to be an integrated institution and that it welcomed minorities on campus. Fischler believed setting the right tone and being sensitive to racial issues should be a major responsibility of any university. Furthermore, he argued that a university campus should create an environment where people would be more accepting of racial and cultural differences. At Nova, the school considered only the capabilities of the individual, not the color of their skin.

Fischler recalled that during the late 1960s and early 1970s in Davie and Broward County, he could not take an African American friend to lunch at the Rolling Hills Country Club. In 1967, in conservative Davie, Florida, there was much local opposition to the transition into an integrated school system. The Ku Klux Klan had a very active presence in Davie, and even in the 1970s, hundreds of people turned out for Klan parades on Davie Road.

In 1972, Fischler risked a firestorm of protest when he invited congresswoman Shirley Chisholm to give an address to the first summer institute of the Educational Leadership Program. In 1968, Chisholm became the first black female elected to Congress, and in 1972, she was the first woman to seek the nomination of the Democratic Party for president of the United States. In her 1972 quest for the Democratic nomination, although her life had been threatened on several occasions, she campaigned in twelve states and won twenty-eight delegates.

Chisholm was heavily involved in her campaign for president when she arrived in Fort Lauderdale in August 1972. Her appearance galvanized the Klan and led to many complaints about Nova inviting a person of color to speak at a university-sponsored event. Fischler refused to retract the invitation, and Chisholm addressed some 250 educational doctoral students. She began by encouraging the local schools to hire more black and minority teachers. If integration of the schools were to succeed, she cautioned, it must be seen not only in terms of race, but also in terms of culture and should be considered pluralism, rather than assimilation. As expected, there was an outcry of protest and a few local citizens urged the board of trustees to fire Fischler because he was "rubbing their nose in" racial integration. The board refused their entreaties.[33]

Davie was also a hotbed of anti-Semitism, as Jews had long faced discrimination in South Florida. In the 1950s the Anti-Defamation League of B'nai B'rith singled out Fort Lauderdale as "intractable in their discriminatory attitudes"; more than 80 percent of Fort Lauderdale resorts and hotels displayed "restricted clientele" signs. In 1960, Fort Lauderdale remained one of the "sore spots of Florida" since 60 percent of its hotels retained odious discriminatory policies. Abe Fischler described the high level of anti-Semitism when he arrived on campus in 1966. A few members of the board of trustees had reservations about choosing a person of the Jewish faith as president of Nova. Fischler, as president of the university, could lunch at the Rolling Hills Country Club and the Fort Lauderdale Yacht Club, but could never become a member since neither club accepted Jews.[34] However, over a period of years, anti-Semitism waned as members of the Jewish community rose to prominence as leaders and contributors to progress in Broward County.

Law School

In 1973, Alex Schure and Hamilton Forman, looking for a way that Nova University could garner local support from the people of Broward County, declared that it was time for Nova to establish a school of law. A law school was the only realistic option as a professional school since a medical school was out of the question due to cost. Schure and others thought the university, with most of its students off campus in distance-learning classes, needed a strong tie to the community. The law school would be the foundation that would bind Nova to the community.

Broward County citizens did not usually interact with students and faculty at the Davie campus and generally did not know what was going on at Nova since few courses were available except for graduate study. NYIT's attempt to start undergraduate classes had not met expectations, and Schure thought that if Nova could develop a good law school, it would be popular with the community and local citizens would send their children to study at Nova. There was a large base of potential students in South Florida since there was no law school of any consequence in the region other than at the University of Miami. Backers argued that the law school would fill a need for more attorneys in the area and would have a favorable economic impact on the county. A key advantage to setting up a law school would be the infusion of tuition money into the leaking university budget and the long-term prestige of having a law school on campus.

Abe Fischler was reluctant to open a school of law since it would be very expensive and he did not want to take on any new debt—Nova could barely meet its expenses as it was. He knew it would be very difficult to build a law school from the ground up. Fischler also knew that Schure wanted the law school and controlled nine votes on the board of trustees, so Schure could get the proposal passed if he so desired. Fischler agreed to charter a law school if the trustees raised $1 million. If they did so, Nova could open its doors in September 1974, but Fischler reminded everyone that Nova did not have the cash to start a law school. He pointed out that the university had to hire a dean, at least four faculty members, and needed a large law library to gain accreditation. All of that cost money. An active fundraising drive for the law school, led by August Paoli, ran into difficulty with local donors and managed to raise only $250,000.

Due to the lack of funding, Fischler was unsure how to proceed. The board of trustees phoned Schure and asked what they should do. Schure replied that they should go ahead and open the law school and he would find some way of providing the funding. The NYIT Board of Trustees approved Schure's decision, and he then pledged NYIT's resources and its endowment to the American Bar Association (ABA) as a guarantee that the law school would meet the required ABA's standards.

Schure believed the law school would be essential if Nova were to endure. He likened the situation to a military campaign: even if you did not have the resources, if the time is right, you have to gamble and move ahead rapidly. The commitment to build a law school in desperate economic times was yet another example of Nova's entrepreneurial bent and the school's belief in taking measured risks. Without Schure's willingness to pursue his goal in an uncertain economic situation, Nova would not have opened its law school in 1974. Nova succeeded in part because of its flexibility—its ability to modify and change the original concept when necessary and to be always alert to new opportunities.

When first informed of the possibility of a law school, most members of the Nova Board of Trustees were indifferent, while others opposed taking on more debt in such precarious economic circumstances. Some of the local lawyers opposed the idea, contending that there were enough lawyers in the area already. Robert Ellyson favored the law school. He said that nobody ever built a church with money on hand; rather, he said, "You kind of built it with the faith that you are going to get it. You've got to believe somehow that it's going to happen." As in the past, an unwavering belief in the future of the university helped carry the day.

Abe Fischler used the $250,000 that the Paoli committee raised to pay the professors and dean. He borrowed about $500,000 to stock the law library, and local law firms helped by donating books. Fischler borrowed other funds to renovate the first and second floors of the Parker Building for the library and classrooms. By the second year, enough tuition money was coming in that Fischler did not have to take out any new loans.[35]

Fischler began organizing the law school by hiring its first dean, Peter Thornton. Thornton earned his JD and LLM degrees from the Brooklyn Law School and was a professor of law at the University of Notre Dame. Thornton was mainly concerned with the basic problems of putting together the foundation of a good law library, a sound curriculum, and an expert faculty. He hired four faculty members and a librarian. He persuaded some local attorneys to fill in as adjunct professors until a full faculty could be recruited. Thornton had a difficult time getting senior faculty to come to a university that barely had its head above water and to begin work in a new law school without a library and cramped facilities. Nonetheless, he managed to attract some highly qualified junior faculty.

Dean Thornton announced that the law school would operate as a full-time day division and would accept only full-time students. No night classes. The applicants had to be eighteen years old and must complete undergraduate requirements prior to entering law school.

Some of the first-year courses would include contracts, property, procedure, criminal law, constitutional law, and legal research. Thornton projected the first-year enrollment at 150 students, with an ultimate enrollment of 500. In 1973, approximately 840 students applied for admission to Nova, 327 were accepted, and 175 ultimately enrolled. The first class averaged a score of 555 on the Law School Admission Test (LSAT) and had a grade point average of 3.09. Acceptance to Nova's law school was based on the student's performance on the LSAT, academic achievements, personal character, and aptitude for the study of law. Nova's applicant pool included several local residents, some of whom were looking for a second career, and many of whom were older than the average law student.

For a student, choosing to attend a new law school was a tricky business. The law school was not accredited in 1973, and without accreditation, a graduate could not take the bar exam. The faculty was new, and the facilities were less than stellar, so anyone who came to Nova was taking a risk. In 1974, the campus was still sparse, with only three completed buildings. One person said it looked like a moonscape. Ronald (Ron) Brown, NSU professor of law, remembered when a law student from Montana, who had not previously visited the campus, came on-site for the first time. After viewing the desolate, underdeveloped landscape, she just sat down and cried.

Nova's Center for the Study of Law, the fifth law school in the state of Florida, opened its doors on September 5, 1974, to 175 students. The chief justice of the state of Florida attended the opening ceremony, along with a group of distinguished jurists and attorneys. About 56 percent of the new class was under 25 years of age, 14 percent were women, and 45 percent were married. There were five Hispanic students and one African American student in the class.

The Nova law school faced an unusual obstacle in attaining accreditation from the American Bar Association (ABA). The ABA required that all law school faculty have tenure, but Nova University, a nontraditional school, did not offer tenure to any of its faculty. They were all on one- to three-year contracts. Fischler opposed giving tenure to any faculty member since a more traditional law school would be bound and constrained by structure and organization and less willing to be innovative and buy into Nova's vision of the entrepreneurial spirit. However, the ABA refused to even come to the campus for an inspection visit until Nova established tenure for the law faculty. Nova and Fischler had no choice but to comply, and in 1975 the board of trustees set the standard for law faculty to obtain tenure. A law faculty member had to demonstrate scholarly work and outstanding teaching ability during a probationary period not to last longer than seven years.[36] In practice, Nova was now a hybrid university—part traditional, the law school, and the rest nontraditional.

Although the law school would eventually pay its own way with tuition money (tuition was increased to $2,600 per year in September 1975), the first few years were difficult. The university tried a fund-raising campaign for the law school, but despite persistent activity, only $15,000 had been accumulated by March 1975. Fischler complained of an extremely tight cash-flow problem in the law school and asked NYIT for assistance to sustain it through this period.

Peter Thornton, who had no previous administrative experience as a dean, had difficulty adjusting to both Abe Fischler and the nontraditional, creative academic environment. Citing the "undue pressure of administrating," Thornton resigned effective June 30, 1975.[37] The first dean had lasted barely two years.

Fischler moved quickly to select a new dean, choosing Laurance M. Hyde, a faculty member at Nova who had arrived in 1974. Hyde earned his BA and JD degrees from the University of Missouri and came to Nova from the University of Nevada. Shortly after Hyde assumed his duties, on August 12, 1975, the law school received provisional accreditation from the ABA. Provisional accreditation meant there would be an obligatory three-year waiting period, until the first class graduated, before the law school could apply for full accreditation. During that time, the ABA would monitor the law school. Fischler reminded everyone how important ABA approval was. It meant that every current and future student could sit for the state bar exam to be licensed.[38]

The Nova law school began its second year in 1975 with fourteen full-time faculty members and a student body of 330. In 1976, with the completion of the second floor in Parker, the law school had access to four classrooms, three seminar rooms, and a new library. Louis Parker, the original donor for the Parker Science Building, would occasionally walk into the building and say, "What is this law school doing in my science building?"[39]

Law professor Ron Brown, who took up his post as an assistant professor in the fall of 1976, said that he had accepted the position at Nova partly because of the climate and partly because of the challenge and excitement of starting a new law school—"a speculative adventure." Mark Dobson, also a new professor, admitted that the campus was not very pretty, but he did not mind. He was willing to commit to Nova for the experience of building something from the ground up.

In Brown's view, the facilities in the fall of 1976 were less than adequate. There was a very small library on the second floor of the Parker Building and a limited number of classrooms. The classrooms were not well insulated. Instructors had to tell the students to speak up so they could be heard over the class next door.

Brown shared an office with a colleague. Unfortunately, the space was divided by a partition that did not go all the way to the ceiling, so they could hear each other counseling students. If a faculty member needed an office repainted, the professor did the work himself. Brown claimed that one big advantage was the smallness of the law school. It was an intimate group, and they were all in it together. He said, "[In] the early days it was much more like a commune" than a conventional law school. Some of the more mature students were older than Brown, but the age difference did not matter.

In exchange for his salary, the law school expected Brown to perform scholarly research, participate in the annual ABA accreditation evaluation, and teach two classes each semester. His first students were a mixed bag. Some were trapped in the area and chose Nova because of geography, others because they could not gain entrance to the other state law schools. The married students and those seeking a second career, according to Brown, were "absolutely terrific." Brown taught a number of weak students who required more attention, but that was typical of a new law school. In later years, Brown noted that the academic quality of the students improved dramatically.[40]

Dean Hyde, knowing that the size and quality of the faculty had to be improved or the center would not get approval from the ABA, hired eight new faculty members in 1976. He also hoped to develop a more scholarly student body as the second class, in 1975, had a composite LSAT average of 539 and a GPA of 2.93, slightly lower than the original class. From that point on, the number of applications and the LSAT scores of entering students increased. Hyde notified Fischler that a student bar association had been organized and that the *Nova Law Journal* had been established. The Florida Bar Association reviewed the first issue of the law journal and deemed it "an outstanding publication" with a good balance of subjects and with topics of interest to judges, lawyers, educators, and law students.[41]

The ultimate and overriding goal for Fischler and the Nova law school remained full accreditation. Provisional accreditation came quickly, but Nova could never aspire to be a superior law school without full and official approval from the ABA. Early problems that the ABA provisional inspection team cited included concerns about the university's financial state, inadequate facilities, and an inferior library. The ABA expected Nova to improve the student-faculty ratio and to hasten curriculum development. In 1978, the ABA refused to extend the law school's provisional accreditation because it lacked an adequate building for classes, offices, and the library, and because of Nova University's financial instability. Nova's failure to get the money from the Goodwin Unitrust (see Chapter 4 for a full discussion of the Unitrust controversy) hurt its chances, as that money that had been legally donated to Nova by Leo Goodwin Sr., but distribution of the funds had been held up by lengthy and intense litigation.[42]

During the ABA's annual inspection of Nova University law school, team members found some areas of improvement, but also some lingering and troublesome problems. The team noted that the law school administration appeared to be strong and competent, that there was an active board of governors, and that student and faculty morale was high. The publication record of the faculty was reasonable, considering that most were relatively inexperienced, and the library's core collection was solid, but there was an immediate need for a library addition. A promised sum of $5 million from the Goodwin Unitrust would be essential for the effective functioning of the law school as the school had counted too much on revenue from tuition.

The ABA feared that if a school were dependent on tuition, there would be a temptation to process students simply to get their money, rather than set high standards for admission. The evaluation team again expressed grave concern about Nova University's financial stability and thought that the law school paid more money than the other centers to the central administration to the detriment of the law students. The team worried about Nova's relationship with NYIT and that the New York school might in some way extract funds from Nova for its own use. The inspection team cited several areas of needed improvement: faculty compensation was low in relation to comparative schools; there was only a minimum amount of student scholarship aid; the faculty-student ratio of twenty-eight to one was too high; the bar pass rate was lower than other Florida schools; and the school needed to make efforts to recruit more highly qualified students.[43]

The law school faculty constantly objected to the university's use of money derived from law school tuition. They thought of themselves as the "cash cow" of the school and believed that they were subsidizing the rest of the university—and to a large extent they were. In

1978, the law school contributed $590,000 to the university's overhead. The law school had increased its tuition in 1981 from $4,050 to $4,250 and expected that money to be used for faculty salaries and improvements to the library.

Dean Hyde wrote President Fischler a stinging letter in September 1978 expressing the law school's anger: "The law school protests and refuses to acquiesce in the budget process . . . which has attempted to unilaterally increase the amount taken from the Law School's revenue to support the university and other university programs. . . ." This action deprived law students of the benefits of legal education and deprived "the law school of its autonomy in making educational decisions." Hyde said the law school felt isolated from the rest of the university, and much of the ill will and alienation resulted from quarreling over allocation of funds.[44] Fischler, fearful of a burgeoning movement to make the law school autonomous, faced a growing rift between his office and the law faculty. The money issue would eventually be solved when Nova received the funds from the Goodwin Unitrust.

Dean Hyde resigned in September 1978. This exposed an early difficulty for the law school: instability in the administration with the rapid turnover of deans. Thornton lasted only a little over two years, and Hyde resigned after three years. The subsequent choices of a triumvirate and dual interim deans to lead the center proved to be unsatisfactory solutions to the problem. Fischler ended the temporary reign of the co-deans when he hired Ovid C. Lewis as the third dean of the Center for the Study of Law on June 10, 1979. Lewis took office on July 1, 1979, and began a period of stability at the law institute.

Dean Lewis matriculated at Rutgers School of Law and obtained a JSD at Columbia University in New York. He came to Nova after a stint as professor and acting dean at Northern Kentucky University Chase School of Law. Ovid Lewis chose Nova because he viewed the law school as a strong, solid, traditional program in an experimental academic environment. Like many other early faculty, he saw "incredible potential" for Nova to become a respected, quality law school. He came partly because of his faith in Abe Fischler as a visionary leader. The law faculty was relieved to get someone who was a worthy leader from an intellectual viewpoint and who gave high promise of being a permanent fixture. Ron Brown found Lewis to be stimulating with many interesting ideas: "He was exciting, fun, and good-hearted." Mark Dobson noted that the students loved him, although they did not always understand what he was saying: "He exuded erudition to a fault."[45]

When Dean Lewis began his term as dean, he was aware of the money problems and the limitations of the library and facilities, but his initial focus was on hiring the best faculty he could find. He encouraged the faculty to become more scholarly and urged them to get more involved with the other centers on campus because interdisciplinary academics would be beneficial to everyone. Lewis declared that essentially he had the autonomy to run the law school as he saw fit.

Dean Lewis knew that Nova was a backup school for many students and that the typical applicant did not earn high scores on the LSAT, nor did the early classes do well in passing the bar exam. Upgrading the academic quality of future students became a priority. Foreseeing the importance of technology, Lewis had eight computers installed for students to use in their research and writing. He called them his "computer confessionals—little cubicles where students could go and confess their ignorance to the computer."

A major part of Lewis's agenda was a visiting professors program; he achieved a major coup when he persuaded Arthur Goldberg to become the first Leo Goodwin Sr. Distinguished Visiting Professor at the law school. Goldberg, a U.S. Supreme Court justice from 1962 to 1965 and a former U.S. ambassador to the United Nations, would teach one course on constitutional litigation.[46] Goldberg's presence on campus gave the law center much favorable publicity and endeared the dean to students and faculty alike.

While Lewis was working to improve the faculty, students, and library, two issues demanded much of his and Fischler's time and energy. First was the ongoing pursuit of adequate facilities for the law school, without which they could not earn accreditation. In the search for appropriate quarters, the university's attention was directed to the International Union of Operating Engineers Local #675 Building at 3100 Southwest Ninth Avenue, in south Fort Lauderdale, about nine miles from the Davie campus. The local union had built an office building on speculation with money from its pension fund and was preparing to move from its Ninth Avenue building into a new facility.

The union never completed the second through the fifth floor since it did not plan to use the building for very long. When representatives from the law school visited the site, they saw that the auditorium would be perfect for the law library and surmised that they could build out floors two through five to suit the needs of the law school.

Olympia and York Florida Equities Corporation had expressed an interest in either acquiring a building or constructing a new facility on or off campus to lease back to the university for the law school's use. Olympia and York chose the union building at Southwest Ninth Avenue. After the appropriate renovations were completed, the university leased the building on a lease-purchase from Olympia and York for twenty-three years at an annual rental of $346,500, payable in monthly installments of $28,875. Nova eventually purchased the building for the law school.[47]

The leasing arrangement with Olympia and York was a great deal for Nova since the school did not have the money to either purchase or refurbish it. Olympia and York, and eventually the university, got a good deal on the building since the union needed to sell. The law school persuaded the ABA that although the law school leased the building, it was and would be university property. The ABA accepted the law school's argument, thus removing a major obstacle to accreditation. In August 1979, the Nova law school moved into its new 64,000-square-foot building. The $2.35 million facility had been renovated at a cost of $750,000.

The new building was perfect for the law center: there was plenty of parking, and it was on the east side of town, closer to downtown and the courts. The old union hall became the library, and the school used the first floor for administrative offices. The third floor contained classrooms, and the fourth floor held faculty offices. By 1979 the faculty had increased to twenty-three, with a ratio of students to faculty of twenty-two to one, and the incoming law class numbered 210, up from 180 the previous year.[48]

In 1981, the American Bar Association wrote Fischler and Lewis that it had made a close study of the on-site team's 1980 inspection report and had reassessed the financial status of NYIT and Nova. With the money from the Goodwin Unitrust now available and a new law school completed, the ABA awarded Nova full accreditation.[49] The ABA approval proved to be a huge achievement for Nova. The university now had a fully accredited professional school, which increased Nova's prestige and tied the university closer to the community. Local attorneys would teach courses at Nova and could use the law library, and now parents in Broward County could send their sons and daughters to the local law school. Best of all, the law school would generate a significant amount of money through tuition.

Behind the law school were five acres of land and buildings that were owned by the Fort Lauderdale Oral School, a school for the hearing impaired. By 1979–1980, the Fort Lauderdale Oral School was in financial difficulty and was obviously not operating at full capacity. Mickey Segal took Abe Fischler to visit the Oral School, where they found only six children, from ages three to sixteen, enrolled. Segal thought it was a shame that the school had all those facilities and were not using them. She proposed bringing the school onto the Nova campus. Segal thought it would benefit the hearing-impaired children if they were mainstreamed into a school serving children with normal hearing and given the individual care they need.

Jack LaBonte, a member of the Nova Board of Trustees and chairman of the Oral School, met with Fischler, and they agreed that if Nova would erect a $1 million building on campus, the Oral School would raise the money to pay for it. LaBonte made the agreement because otherwise the Oral School would have failed, and he thought the school would be a valuable addition to the university.

In January 1983, the board of trustees approved the acquisition of the Oral School. The Ralph J. Baudhuin Oral School, as it came to be known, was integrated into the University School, and eventually a new building was constructed to house it. The Oral School became the Baudhuin School because Ralph Baudhuin was president of the advisory board of the Oral School and later gave it an $800,000 bequest.[50] Again, an unexpected gift coupled with an effective business strategy led to the expansion of the campus while satisfying the needs of the hearing impaired in the community.

Nova University had made significant progress in the preceding few years. The merger with NYIT saved the institution and, to some degree, stabilized its finances. The Educational Leaders Program provided a new source of income, and the law school gave Nova academic respectability. The University School and the Oral School expanded Nova's community outreach and helped realize the founders' vision and commitment to a cradle-to-the-grave educational system. In 1970, Nova had a viable partner and in Fischler a new leader who would guide the university through turbulent times.

4

The Goodwin Trust and the Disappearance of the Research Vessel *Gulf Stream*

A controversial event that had a significant long-term impact on Nova's future occurred on May 3, 1976. On that date the trustees of the Leo Goodwin Sr. Foundation of Fort Lauderdale notified Nova University that it would receive "all of the net corpus of the Leo Goodwin Sr. Unitrust after certain distributions to Holy Cross Hospital and the Fort Lauderdale Oral School." By the terms of the trust, executed by Leo Goodwin Sr. on May 21, 1971 (one week before his death), the Fort Lauderdale Oral School would receive $10,000 and Holy Cross Hospital would receive the sum of $45,000 plus the greater of either $1,000,000 or 12 percent of the net unitrust corpus. The remainder of the unitrust, 87.5 percent, would go to Nova. The funds were to be distributed in 1976 after a five-year waiting period. During this five-year period the income from the trust would be used to pay off personal tax liabilities and other estate debts. The document specified that "none of the undersigned Unitrust Trustees (Leo Goodwin Jr., Helen Furia, and Alphonse Della-Donna) have now, have had in the past, or will by agreement or understanding have in the future control over University expenditures." The Goodwin Unitrust Board of Trustees further certified that they had made "no commitments whatsoever with respect to the expenditure for educational purposes of any funds that may be distributed to Nova University."

The unitrust was a gift in the memory of Leo Goodwin Sr. "for the use of the University exclusively to further its educational functions, to be expended or added to an endowment—as determined by the [Nova] University Board." The legal document expressed the hope that Goodwin "would be suitably memorialized" and indicated that the current net value of the unitrust exceeded $8 million. The trustees pointed out that the unitrust was in negotiation with the Internal Revenue Service about paying estate taxes and the money would not be released until that controversy had been resolved.[1] The Goodwin gift was manna from heaven for Nova and apparently totally unexpected, although Leo Goodwin Jr. had been a member of the Nova Board of Trustees.

Abe Fischler hoped that this important donation would solve most of his financial problems—the law school would get $5 million, enough to build a new law school and have enough money outside of tuition to get accreditation, and Nova could pay off some of its debts.

Leo Goodwin Sr., the founder of the Government Employees Insurance Company (GEICO), was, at the time of his death, one of the wealthiest men in America. When Goodwin Sr. executed the unitrust in 1971, the charitable gift consisted of 800,000 shares of GEICO and $4 million in cash. At that time, 800,000 shares of GEICO stock was worth some $48 million. However, by 1976, due to huge underwriting losses by the company, the stock value had plummeted and was then estimated to be worth between $8 million and $12 million.[2]

Although the terms of the Goodwin Unitrust could not have been more precise, Alphonse Della-Donna, a local attorney and a trustee for the unitrust, decided that he would try to hold up the disbursement of the funds. Della-Donna, who emigrated from Italy in 1948, was a certified public accountant who earned his law degree from the University of Miami in 1964. He had persuaded Helen Furia, who had been Leo Goodwin Sr.'s secretary, to vote with him. Della-Donna thus controlled two votes and could force the trustees to accept any position he desired. When Leo Goodwin Jr. died, his wife, Fran Goodwin, replaced Leo Jr. as one of the three trustees. Della-Donna was the only trustee with a legal background, so he called the shots.

In anticipation of receiving the Goodwin money, Abe Fischler went about fixing up the Union Hall building on the east campus for the law school and committed the university to additional campus expenditures. Fischler soon faced a dilemma: Della-Donna did not want to release the funds, because as long as he controlled the money, he continued to earn legal fees. He had already received $1 million for his work with the unitrust foundation, and he wanted more. Initially Della-Donna proposed setting up a new foundation separate from the unitrust foundation, and he would be in charge of disbursing the funds to Nova University. Fischler refused to agree to Della-Donna's proposal for a separate foundation because the Goodwin Unitrust was an unrestricted gift to Nova University and, Fischler said, "unrestricted means unrestricted."

Tinsley Ellis, who often negotiated with Della-Donna on behalf of the university, said that every time he thought he had an agreement with Della-Donna, the attorney would come up with a new request or add a different concept or change part of the legal agreement. In April 1978, Della-Donna announced that he would go to court to stop what was by then a $14.5 million bequest to Nova University from the Goodwin Unitrust because the 1970 agreement between NYIT and Nova University essentially gave control of Nova to a New York institution. According to Della-Donna, because of the NYIT merger, Nova was not an independent institution, nor was it a local Broward County institution. Della-Donna said he was certain that Goodwin had reserved his funds for local Broward County charities and would not want to leave money to a New York university.

The Nova University Board of Trustees, trying to appease Della-Donna, went so far as to pass two resolutions declaring that Nova was not controlled by NYIT and that all of the Goodwin monies "would be used exclusively for institutional facilities in Broward County" and nowhere else. Della-Donna insisted that although the resolutions had been passed, they did not mean anything because the trustee resolutions had not been ratified. "If these resolutions had been ratified," testified Della-Donna, "I would have given up the money." Fischler replied that the resolutions "had been passed, ratified, and hand-delivered to Della-Donna's office" to prove to the attorney that the resolutions had been fully approved by the board.

Della-Donna then accused the Nova Board of Trustees of fraud for lying to him about certain facts and providing him with false information. Fischler vigorously denied the charges. He pointed out that Della-Donna had been on the Nova University Board of Trustees and had served on the finance committee, so he knew what was going on at the university and could not say he was uninformed.

Judge George Richardson of the Seventeenth Judicial Circuit Court in Broward County, in a law suit filed by Della-Donna to prevent issuance of the proceeds from the fund, had already ruled that the Goodwin Unitrust was an unrestricted grant and the trustees had no right to rescind the original commitment to Nova. The money, ruled the judge, should be paid forthwith. Della-Donna, unrepentant, refused to give up the fight and continued to play out this legal charade—all the while getting paid for his time. He said he was determined to prevent the Goodwin money from leaving Broward County and going to New York. Della-Donna's argument was a clever ploy to appeal to local citizens since some Broward County residents already resented the influence NYIT had on Nova. The Nova administration asserted yet again that the university was not a satellite of NYIT.

Della-Donna, ever crafty, decided on a new tactical move: a bit of coercion. He had learned that the ABA had given accreditation to the Nova Center for the Study of Law but could remove it if a law school building was not erected in the immediate future. He knew Nova University did not have the funds for the new building, so he proposed giving $5 million of the $14.5 million unitrust bequest directly to the law school for the purpose of putting up the new law center. Della-Donna stipulated that the $5 million would not be available to the law school unless control of the law school was removed from the Nova University Board of Trustees and, by inference, control by NYIT. Here the attorney tried appealing to the law professors who wanted the money and resented being the university's "cash cow." He also asked that the law school be moved away from the Nova campus. Several trustees and Nova administrators wanted the law school at all costs and were willing to settle for the $5 million just to keep the law school viable and on the Nova campus.

As Della-Donna expected, the new proposal to give $5 million directly to the law school ended up splitting the Nova Board of Trustees into warring camps. One group of trustees did not want to continue the legal fight. They wanted the law school to become a reality and feared that if they did not take the $5 million, they would never get any of the Goodwin Trust and the law school would lose its accreditation. Better to take the $5 million in hand, end the cost of litigation, and get on with the progress of the university. Of course, if the board of trustees agreed to accept the $5 million for the law school, the remaining $9.5 million would revert to the unitrust, controlled by Della-Donna.

Abe Fischler finally decided that he had compromised enough with Della-Donna. He concluded that Nova would never get its money unless the university went to court and sued Della-Donna for control of the corpus of the Goodwin Unitrust. Fischler believed that Della-Donna would draw out litigation until Nova finally gave in and settled for a lesser amount. Fischler, in addition to dealing with the huge cost in time and money contesting Della-Donna's legal actions, was trying to run an institution and the failure to obtain the Goodwin money had put the university's existence in danger.

Fischler accused Della-Donna of continuing to come up with various legal challenges and pointed out that he had brought suit against Nova in three different legal jurisdictions. According to pleadings in Broward County Circuit Court files, Della-Donna had initiated twenty-seven lawsuits and appeals and unsuccessful libel and slander actions against President Fischler, Nova attorney Terry Russell, and the *Fort Lauderdale News and Sun-Sentinel*. Mary McCahill, chairman of the Nova Board of Trustees, argued that if Nova gave in to Della-Donna's demands and accepted the $5 million, it would be admitting the truth of his charge that Nova was not locally controlled. The cost of litigation was eating away at the value of the unitrust, and the only way to stop Della-Donna was a multimillion-dollar lawsuit.[3]

With the future of the university at stake, the board of trustees met on April 17 and 25, 1978, to determine the best course of action to take in regard to a legal challenge against Della-Donna. The heated discussion centered on whether to settle for the $5 million or to begin what would certainly be a lengthy and expensive lawsuit. Chancellor Alex Schure argued that to accept Della-Donna's offer would be to violate Judge Richardson's order that specifically directed the funds to be paid to Nova without restriction. He pronounced Della-Donna's charges of fraud and lies as "specious and after the fact." Schure reminded the group that Leo Goodwin Jr. had been on the Nova Board of Trustees and Della-Donna had also been on the board since December 15, 1976. The two men could not plead ignorance about Nova's activities.

The trustees of the unitrust, continued Schure, could not arbitrarily withdraw Nova as the beneficiary and could not impose unreasonable conditions on the payment of those funds. Della-Donna originally proposed that Nova agree to restrict the funds' use to Broward County. The Nova Board of Trustees did so, only to have Della-Donna reject the very stipulation he requested. Schure repeated that Nova was not dominated by NYIT, but what was really at stake was "whether or not we're going to appease someone that is unappeasable and whether this institution is going to retain its independence; whether it is going to protect its academic freedom and whether these trustees [Nova] would exercise their discretion as they are charged to under the law and the bylaws" Schure proclaimed that Nova's only option was to enforce the university's rights "to the fullest extent permitted by the law."[4]

At the same meeting, trustee David Salten, vice president at NYIT, added some venomous comments about Della-Donna's behavior. The attorney's charges were not only malicious, Salten said, but also a public affront, and the conditions he sought were "as imperious in tone as they are defective in content." Salten accused Della-Donna of having been paid legal fees of some $900,000. Della-Donna replied that the accusation that he had received $900,000 in fees was "absolutely false," and that he had billed only $100,000 for his legal work with the unitrust. He said that he had received $950,000 in fees, but that money came from the Goodwin probate estate and not the unitrust. Della-Donna raised the stakes when, in a new filing, he included a clause that if Nova lost its court challenge against him, then it would get nothing, not even the $5 million to be set aside for the law school, and would forfeit all rights to the law building, the law school, and the law school's land. Della Donna added, with hubris of the highest order, that he regretted the Nova board did not "feel that we are dealing in good faith, because we always have."

After much discussion and argument during two meetings of the Nova University Board of Trustees, the twenty-member board (the number had been revised from the original agreement—in April 1978, Nova and NYIT each had ten voting members) came to a decision. The initial vote was nine to nine, with two members absent from the first meeting. Board member Cy Young said that he hoped the law center would become a reality and thought Nova could not wait the length of time it would take for the courts to decide the legal issues of the unitrust. "If they [Nova trustees] don't give in a little bit, they are going to destroy this university as sure as I'm sitting here," said Young.

A majority of the board chose to ignore Young's concerns and finally voted to pursue the lawsuit against Della-Donna. As a result of this decision, board members Lester Moody and Clinton Lagrosa resigned, as did Robert Ellyson, who did not approve of the way the dispute had been handled and felt that some resolution should have been worked out. Ellyson's resignation was accepted with "deep regret" as he had rendered yeoman service to Nova over the years. The resignations of Moody and Lagrosa were accepted without comment. Then the board of trustees, in a completely unanticipated move, decided to oust trustee Cy Young. The board accused Young of leaking detrimental details of the conflict to Della-Donna and the press, which led to some damaging stories about Nova's motives. Young, after being unanimously removed from the board for actions detrimental to the university, called his eviction "a surprise and disappointment."[5]

Nova did not have long to wait for a resolution to its lawsuit against Della-Donna. On August 3, 1978, in the Seventh Judicial

Circuit Court, Judge Richardson, in a summary judgment, upheld his previous 1976 ruling that the entire $14.5 million unitrust should go to Nova on an unrestricted basis. (It should be noted that the final disbursement value depended on the value of GEICO stock at the time.) The judge ordered Della-Donna to turn over $6.5 million of the fund within ninety days. The remainder would be turned over when the estate's tax liabilities had been settled. Nova agreed to pay his law firm $1.1 million to cover its fees and costs. In exchange, Della-Donna promised that he would end all appeals and other legal proceedings. Fischler said he was "delighted with the decision" and immediately planned to allocate $5 million from the unitrust to the law school.[6]

Fischler, Schure, and Nova had been vindicated, but it had been a long, hard, costly two-year battle that stymied university growth and drained $2 million from the unitrust corpus. Della-Donna, in a clear example of personal greed, had broken his promises, drawn out the court fight, and antagonized and frustrated everyone at the university. He did, however, eventually get his comeuppance.

In 1988, the Florida Bar Board of Governors prosecuted Della-Donna for violating his ethical and fiduciary responsibilities in several cases, including the Goodwin Unitrust. The bar association investigation spanned six years and cost $104,700, making it the most expensive disciplinary investigation in the history of the bar. The board of governors concluded that instead of properly representing his clients, Della-Donna "initiated, maintained, and encouraged the frivolous litigation for personal and financial gain." The Florida bar charged him with mishandling the Goodwin estate with "baseless and unjustified litigation" to prevent the disbursement of the unitrust funds, in the process nearly bankrupting Nova University and slowing accreditation for the law school. The $1.1 million settlement paid to Della-Donna to end all appeals and litigation "constituted a clearly excessive, illegal, and unwarranted fee" and "was tantamount to extortion." The bar wanted Nova to be totally reimbursed for the $1.1 million. That amount, with interest, would come to $1.9 million. After a thirty-five-day hearing, referee Hugh Macmillan agreed with the Florida bar and ruled that Della-Donna be disbarred for three years, pay the costs of the investigation ($104,700), and return $100,000 to Nova University.[7] On June 22, 1989, the Florida Supreme Court upheld most of the rulings by the Florida Bar Association and ruled that his misconduct warranted a five-year disbarment. The court did not ask for the return of Della-Donna's $1.1 million fee to Nova because the court had no authority to determine if the legal fees were excessive.[8]

During the time that Abe Fischler and the university attorney, Terry Russell, were exerting such energy and expense in fighting Della-Donna over the Goodwin Unitrust, Nova University had fallen on hard times. However, during the fiscal year 1980, Nova received an infusion of $920,000 in cash and 500,000 shares of GEICO stock, which then had a market value of $6 million. Another $9,841,828 in treasury bills, cash, corporate bonds, and other stocks was later awarded. By the time all of the money had been distributed on June 30, 1979, the amount was $15.9 million.[9]

In anticipation of the Goodwin Trust, the university expended money it did not have and the university went deeper into debt each year. Nova had given $5 million to the law school and paid Della-Donna his $1.1 million fee and some $700,000 in legal fees to its own attorneys. The corpus of the trust had by then been reduced by approximately $7 million. Nova quickly spent much of the unitrust money, paying off its loans and other debts, FICA and pension funds and investing part of the gift for future operating expenses. Nonetheless, the university still faced significant deficiencies in payments to FICA, pension funds, salaries, and withholding taxes.

Once again, Alex Schure and NYIT came to the rescue. Since the local banks refused to lend money to Nova, Schure let Nova use NYIT's line of credit with a California bank for a loan of $1.5 million. Even so, Nova still had to cut $900,000 in expenses to remain solvent. Survival was once again the primary goal. Most of the cuts were in personnel. Nearly fifty vacancies went unfilled and several major positions had already been eliminated.[10] These personnel and spending cuts reduced morale and caused some griping and grumbling among faculty and staff, who also expressed anxiety about if and when their next paycheck would arrive and if they would have the money in time to pay their mortgages and bills. Despite these tense times, there remained an air of optimism, and most who worked at Nova still believed the school would survive.

The conflict over the Goodwin Unitrust, the local displeasure with NYIT's alleged dominance over Nova, and Nova's continued financial dependence on NYIT led to a serious rift in the relationship between the two schools. These issues and other events would eventually lead to the final breakup in 1985. David G. Salten, a vice president at NYIT, complained in a "confidential" memo that was leaked to the

Fort Lauderdale News and Sun-Sentinel that Nova was constantly in need of financial help and its situation was becoming "increasingly unrealistic." Salten also accused Nova administrators of mismanagement and that the university's financial reports were so confusing that a person trained in accounting practices could not understand them. Furthermore, Salten alleged that communications between the two schools were inadequate. Nova had downplayed NYIT's contributions to the "point of extinction" and exaggerated Nova's contributions to the federation "to such an extent that one is reminded of Stalin's rewriting of Russian history after the purges." Fischler denied that Nova had downplayed NYIT's contributions, but had no comment on the mismanagement charges.[11] Salten's negative comments angered Fischler and other Nova supporters and was yet another issue in the deteriorating relations between the two schools.

While Nova leaders grappled with the controversy over the Goodwin Unitrust, from 1976 to 1980 Fischler struggled mightily to maintain the viability of the Life Sciences Center, which needed new faculty and more space for research. Director Joel Warren, lacking adequate funding, had been unable to hire the talented young research scientists he needed, and by 1978 it became clear that he would be unable to realize his goal of establishing a top-notch research institute at Nova. Since the Life Sciences Center had never been in the black and Nova had to make deep cuts in spending, Fischler sent letters to the Life Sciences Center faculty in September 1978 indicating that all faculty contracts would be terminated unless funds became available. When the necessary funds were not forthcoming, President Fischler, in 1979, announced the dissolution of the Life Sciences Center and the severing of relations with the Leo Goodwin Institute for Cancer Research.

Warren resigned as director effective June 30, 1980, and the Goodwin Institute left campus and moved to new laboratories in Plantation, Florida.[12] The failure and the departure of the Life Sciences Center, one of the first three centers on the Nova campus, was a blow to the prestige of the university. Fischler and others had high hopes for science research, especially in cancer, but the lack of funds and the failure to get significant grants had undermined the center's ability to stay afloat.

While Fischler coped with problems in the Life Sciences Center, the Educational Leadership Program was being battered by intense criticism from all over the country. Nova continued to defend the program with letters to editors and expensive lawsuits. Fischler also had to fight for law school accreditation. He went through two law deans until he found one who could stabilize the leadership of the law center. In short, from 1976 to 1980, Fischler's plate was full, and with all these problems, observers wondered how much longer Nova, teetering on the brink of insolvency, would survive.

Nonetheless, the Goodwin Unitrust payment helped to resolve some of Nova's difficulties. Of the initial $6.5 million payment, $1.5 million was used to pay off the $1.5 million loan to NYIT, and Fischler designated $5 million to the Nova Center for the Study of Law. Of that $5 million, $1 million was used to establish the Leo Goodwin Sr. professorship and the Leo Goodwin Sr. Scholarship Fund. Approximately $2 million would be invested and the accumulated interest used for the new law school building. Income from an endowment would be spent on normal maintenance in the law school building. Income from another endowment of $1.5 million would be set aside to fund interdisciplinary programs and to purchase law library materials. Fischler recognized that the funds from the Goodwin Unitrust and money from NYIT had once again enabled Nova to continue. Without it, Fischler said, "We would never have made it."[13]

The Disappearance of the Research Vessel *Gulf Stream*

In January 1975, Nova University suffered a great tragedy when the university's research vessel, the *Gulf Stream*, and its five-man crew vanished in the Atlantic. Nothing was recovered except for the body of James Riddle, as well as one drawer from the galley and a life preserver (the life preserver is currently housed in the NSU Archives). How could an experienced crew in a well-equipped ship disappear almost without a trace?

The *Gulf Stream* was a 48-foot, steel-hulled former oil-drilling support vessel powered by two 460-horsepower diesel engines. The ship had all the necessary safety equipment, a magnetic compass, an automatic pilot, two 110-volt generators, and two separate radio units. One of the generators had been recently overhauled, and the steering cable had been repaired. All of the equipment had been reported in excellent working condition, except for the radar equipment, which had been removed prior to September 1974.

The crew consisted of five men: William (Bill) Richardson, age 51, director of the Nova University Oceanography Center; William Ben Campbell, age 49, captain of the vessel; Jack Spornraft, age 25, a mate on the ship; James David Riddle, age 41, a research technician; and John Wayne Hill, age 28, the assistant development engineer.

Figure 4.1 Nova University research vessel *Gulf Stream*, 1974. (By permission of Nova Southeastern University Archives, Fort Lauderdale, Florida.)

Richardson, the popular director of the Oceanographic Center at Nova University, led the expedition. He was a Navy pilot in World War II and an experienced sailor. He held a BSc and a PhD in chemistry from Harvard University and was a well-known and highly regarded oceanographer. Richardson had taken over as director of the Nova Oceanographic Center in 1966 and had been slowly building the center to elite status. Much to President Fischler's delight, Richardson had received many grants and directed one of the profit-making centers at Nova.

Captain William Ben Campbell, who joined the Nova staff in 1968, spent much of his life working on and sailing boats. Spornraft, who was hired in 1974, and Riddle, who came on board in 1970, were experienced seamen. The final member of the crew, John Wayne Hill, was employed by the Scripps Institution of Oceanography and had been invited to accompany the expedition so that he could test some of Scripps's buoys.

The purpose of the trip, as had been the case on many similar voyages, was to perfect a heavy weather buoy testing system. The results would provide vital information to a number of large national and international programs in oceanography and meteorology. Richardson designed the buoys to drift with the ocean currents. The buoys would then transmit data via satellite on their positions, as well as air and water temperature, wind velocity, and the salinity of the seawater. The ultimate purpose was to obtain a better understanding of the oceans and their impact on climate change. Richardson explained that oceans can store enormous amounts of heat, and the absorption or radiation of just a small amount of that heat could cause atmospheric changes in the United States.

Richardson had chosen Maine as the launching point for testing the buoys for a variety of reasons: "We need a place to test those buoys where the seas and weather are nasty. Maine is it. You have quite deep water close to land and excellent facilities at Boothbay." The director had every confidence that the *Gulf Stream* would do fine in heavy weather: "Oh, she's a good old boat. We've been in some bad stuff. She can handle the Gulf of Maine if it does not gang up on her." Prior to departure in the cold month of January 1975, Richardson expressed concern about the possibility of ice: "I've been thinking about that. We don't have much high superstructure, but I don't think the ice will bother us."

Richardson estimated that the *Gulf Stream* had gone onto the chilly waters of Maine to attend to the buoys at least fifty times, so the crew had experienced January weather before. The crew's actions in gathering buoys and recording the scientific information was routine, something the crew had done many times. The crew was upbeat and optimistic about the trip and did not worry about danger, especially since the weather report indicated that the weather would be good from January 4 to 6.

The crew's plan was to leave Boothbay Harbor on Saturday, January 4, and recover eight buoys scattered thirty to forty miles south of the harbor. They would first pick up buoy number one, which was one of the larger and more difficult buoys to get on board. After securing the other buoys, they would put into Gloucester, Massachusetts, for the night; on the following day, Sunday, January 5, they would return to Boothbay Harbor.

At approximately 10:00 a.m. on January 4, 1975, the *Gulf Stream* left Boothbay Harbor with its five-man crew. What happened after that point is not precisely known. The ship simply disappeared. It has never been determined if its disappearance was due to bad luck, errant judgment, foul weather, or an accident. Many theories have been put forward about the cause of this disaster, and there is little agreement about the ship's fate, but there were some clues to the possible circumstances.

A few witnesses saw the ship before it sailed. Francis Pierce, owner of Pierce Marine Services in Boothbay, knew that Campbell had filled the forward fuel tank to 175 gallons—only half of its capacity because he did not want excess fuel to weigh down the bow. The aft tank had been filled with 500 gallons. At an average speed of sixteen knots and consumption of forty-two gallons per hour, the ship would have had enough fuel to operate for sixteen hours.

Bill Richardson and Charles Yentsch, a former Nova employee and now director of the Bigelow Laboratory for Ocean Sciences in Boothbay Harbor, had agreed that Richardson would contact Yentsch by radio or telephone when the ship made port in Gloucester and if the ship were not going to return to Boothbay on January 5. Yentsch needed this information so he could notify Jerry Erich, pilot of the Nova University plane, to bring the plane to Gloucester. In Gloucester the plane would pick up the *Gulf Stream*'s automatic direction finder, which would then be placed inside the aircraft to help in locating the buoys. Since the original plan had been for a quick one-day turnaround, the call would have been made on either Saturday, January 4, or the morning of Sunday, January 5. The call from Richardson never came. There had been a phone call to Yentsch's house, but the babysitter did not answer the phone. Could it have been Richardson? Possibly, but there was no way to know.

By the morning of Monday, January 6, with no word from Richardson, Yentsch notified the Coast Guard that the vessel was missing. The Coast Guard in Boothbay reported that it had received a transmission at 10 a.m. on January 4: "Coast Guard Boothbay, this is R/V *Gulf Stream*. Over." The Coast Guard responded, "This is Coast Guard Boothbay. Can we be of assistance?" The response: "Coast Guard, this is the *Gulf* . . . ," and the transmission abruptly ended. The Coast Guard's attempts to reestablish contact on January 4 failed. Nothing further was heard from the *Gulf Stream* until Yentsch notified the Coast Guard on January 6 that the ship was missing. The Coast Guard issued an alert on January 6 but did not manage to contact the ship, nor did the Coast Guard begin a search for the ship. However, on Tuesday, January 7, at 11:30 a.m., the Coast Guard received a message: "U.S. Coast Guard, this is the R/V *Gulf Stream*. Over." The

Coast Guard again tried to respond but was unable to establish contact with the ship.

Wilson Francis, a local lobster fisherman, reported that at around 10 a.m. on Monday, January 6, he spotted the *Gulf Stream* "coming around Squirrel Island, near Boothbay Harbor, not Gloucester, heading in a southerly direction at approximately fifteen knots."

John Hammond, another fisherman, was certain that he saw the ship heading south from Squirrel Island at about 10 a.m. He commented to his wife, who also saw the vessel, "There goes the *Gulf Stream*. It's the only research vessel around here that does any work."

Yet another witness testified that he recognized the voice of Captain Campbell on January 6 on a radio transmission. He said the call was not a distress call and was short and routine in nature. Since he could only hear the ship's side of the transmission, he had no idea as to the recipient of the call.[14]

It was unclear why, after forty-eight hours, the *Gulf Stream* was still cruising close to Boothbay Harbor and why the vessel had inexplicably been out of contact with Yentsch and the Coast Guard for that same length of time. The Coast Guard had received an abbreviated message from the ship at 11:30 a.m. on Tuesday, January 7, so if the dates were correct, the *Gulf Stream* was still afloat on that day.

If the ship were navigating the waters off the coast of Maine on January 7, it would have been in deep trouble as the weather had deteriorated rapidly. The crew would have faced low visibility, and the danger of ice in the freezing waters was a high probability. By January 7, the Coast Guard had launched a sea search for the *Gulf Stream*, but the cutter *Cape Horn* encountered twelve-foot seas and strong winds, so they called off the search and returned to base. Later, there were reports of twenty-foot seas with forty-knot winds.

As the wind increased and the seas rose, the crew must have realized that they might not survive the vicious storm. Anyone who has been at sea under those conditions (probably an eight or nine on the Beaufort scale—a strong gale) can attest to the paralyzing fear of being at the mercy of a rough sea. The ship would pitch and roll violently, blowing spray would reduce visibility, and the rain would hammer into the windshield so loudly that you could not hear yourself talk. Twenty-foot waves would roll over the ship; each time a large wave struck the vessel, it must have appeared that the vessel could not stay upright. At some point, the crew must have accepted the fact that the ship would sink and they would perish. The terror of those last moments must have been unendurable. Henry David Thoreau knew well the fury of the ocean off Cape Cod: "It will ruthlessly heave these vessels to and fro, break them in pieces in its sandy or stony jaws, and deliver their crews to sea monsters. . . ."[15]

The ship was probably strong enough to ride out the storm, and it had faced similar circumstances, but apparently it did not manage to ride out this particular storm. There were several possible explanations for the sinking of the ship. Since Campbell filled the forward gas tank only to half of its capacity, the ship might have run out of fuel, and the captain would have been unable to maneuver the ship perpendicular to the waves. The vessel would have tossed and rolled helplessly against the angry sea and may have succumbed to a series of large waves. Witnesses testified that the *Gulf Stream* crew had loaded the heavy buoys onto the back of the ship rather than towing them—a safety hazard in high seas. A rogue wave could have capsized the vessel. Prior to the trip, Richardson had pointed out that the ship did not have a high superstructure, and he had been somewhat worried about ice since it was January in the Gulf of Maine. The Coast Guard never reported a distress signal, but the ship could have had a problem with its radio as two earlier transmissions had ended abruptly and the Coast Guard could never reestablish contact with the *Gulf Stream*.

Charles Yentsch always believed that a larger vessel had run over the ship. The ship was small and not easily visible on radar, and they were operating at night and in bad weather near shipping lanes, so a supertanker could have hit the ship without knowing it unless there had been severe damage to the propeller or rudder.

Of course, there were the usual irrational explanations. Some Nova students thought the ship had become a victim of the Bermuda Triangle, even though the *Gulf Stream* was nowhere near that area. One wag thought the crew had merely escaped to Hawaii or Mexico or Brazil. Another story had the ship sunk by a Russian submarine. One knowledgeable person said he heard that the crew had plugged up the drains to put in some instrumentation, the ship took a wave, and the water could not drain out.

The parents of Jack Spornraft, seeking closure, hired a psychic or a "parapsychological consultant" named M.B. Dykshoorn, who claimed that a huge wave washed over the boat and sent it to the bottom. He also claimed he could pinpoint the exact place on the map where the ship had gone down. Interestingly enough, scientists at Woods Hole, after much calculating of wind, drifts, and weather, came up with almost the same location as Dykshoorn.

On April 14, 1975, the U.S. Coast Guard submitted its final report on the fate of the *Gulf Stream*: "There is no evidence that any act of misconduct, inattention to duty, negligence, incompetence, or willful violation of any law or regulation on the part of licensed or certified personnel contributed to the casualty. There is no evidence of any mayday or distress signal sent from the *R/V Gulf Stream* at any time. It is recommended that no further action be taken and that this case be closed."

Since there was no specific knowledge of what happened to the ship, the Coast Guard could not possibly have known that no misconduct or inattention to duty had occurred and had no evidence to make such a claim. The Coast Guard report, however flawed, proved to be beneficial to Nova. The insurance company had balked at paying for a ship registered in Fort Lauderdale that went missing in twenty-below-zero temperatures in Maine, but since it could not prove the crew had been at fault, the company had to pay.

The disappearance of Richardson and three members of his team saddened the university community. The campus was small, and everyone knew Richardson and the other crew members, so the loss was personal. Richardson's death was significant for the university because he had successfully organized a first-rate oceanographic center. Now, half of the ocean sciences department, as well as its research vessel, had been lost, and it would take years to restore the center to its previous level of excellence. On February 7, 1976, to honor Richardson, Nova University named the library at the Oceanographic Center after him and initiated a campaign to get $750,000 to endow the William S. Richardson Professorship of Physical Oceanography. The university reprinted an epitaph dedicated to the five men lost at sea: "The story we tell is not a pretty story, the ending certainly not a happy one. Although there are no memorial stones to mark your graves, there is a record of who you were. The scientists, the adventurers, the researchers, the engineers, the mariners—all of you lovers of the sea, respectful of its powers and mysteries. The who, the what, the why, and the when shall ever be unknown to us."[16]

Richard Dodge, later the dean of the Oceanographic Center, recalled the situation at the center when he first arrived in 1978 as a coral reef geologist and biologist. The center had gone into a tailspin in 1975 after Richardson's death. Not enough grants were coming in to keep the center in the black. In 1978, in hopes of reviving the center, Nova hired three new faculty members with grant-writing skills: Julian "Jay" McCreary, a physical oceanographer; Pat Black-welder, a geologist; and Dodge. A new director had also been hired. In 1979, however, the difficult fiscal position of Nova University required Fischler to notify the center's faculty that the university would no longer award academic contracts and faculty would be on soft money. Fischler informed the staff that if they had grants, they were encouraged to stay and use them, but if they did not have grants, he could not guarantee support. Despite some demands that Fischler shut down the center since it was a drain on the university, he refused to do so: "I wouldn't shut it down. I just fought that battle through" and saved the center.

As a result, some faculty and staff departed. The end of the 1970s saw the staff reduced to a few faculty and support personnel and only one academic program, a PhD in physical oceanography. Compounding the center's problems, both the houseboat and the Forman Building, named for Charles and Hamilton Forman, were in bad shape. In the early 1980s, to attract more students, the Oceanographic Center created a master's in coastal zone management and in marine biology. The center stayed afloat with grants from the State of Florida, the Environmental Protection Agency (EPA), the National Science Foundation (NSF), and the Nature Conservancy. By 1982, the Oceanographic Center was operating in the black once again.

Slowly but surely, the center began a period of growth and over time added additional faculty and staff. In 1990, it acquired the Schure Building, formerly owned by New York Institute of Technology. The center renovated the Schure Building in 1992 with an NSF award and constructed new geology and biology labs. In the late 1980s, Charles and Lucy Forman gave the center funding to create an endowment for research. By 1986, the center received approximately $800,000 in grants and contracts, employed seven researchers and faculty members, and enrolled approximately fifty students in its graduate programs.[17]

Nova College

In 1976, in an attempt to attract undergraduate students, Nova set up an experimental undergraduate school known as Nova College. The original idea for the college came from Gordon Sweet, the director of SACS. Sweet thought it would be important for Nova's development as a full-service institution if the school would come up with a strong academic program for underclassmen. Sweet said he would like the college to be accredited by SACS and encouraged Nova to move forward on his suggestion.

Abe Fischler, interested in the experimental and educational aspects of Nova College, came up with a plan for a three-year undergraduate school. He created several interdisciplinary, broad-based "circles" of learning: behavioral science, business and finance, and leadership. The circles met three hours a day, four days a week. Students studied each of the circles for nine weeks and then went on to another topic. In addition to their work with the circles, all students were required to take English and math. Within each circle of learning, students pursued several provocative themes: change and tradition; human nature and the individual; leadership and greatness; the individual and social organization; essence and existence; and wealth and poverty.

At the outset, approximately 100 students were enrolled, all on scholarship. The students were to read, gather facts, and then debate and write about the philosophical concepts. The purpose was to teach them to analyze and synthesize the material they read and studied. Fischler viewed the concept of general education at most traditional universities as flawed. Students took a few courses in English and math that were not interrelated or interdisciplinary and not designed conceptually. Fischler's circles/courses would help students think critically and give them the intellectual tools to excel in their chosen field of study.

In later years, the Florida state legislature, enamored of the innovative concepts created at Nova College, gave the university money to build a small science building; a voucher to make up the difference between tuition at Nova, a private school, and a state institution; and a grant of around $350,000 to implement and expand the program. Fischler was grateful to the state legislature for its largesse because the money helped out Nova's bottom line. The legislature's support gave the school some welcome publicity and indicated that Florida was willing to use public tax money to benefit private independent universities in the state.

SACS accredited Nova College in 1980, but the circles concept did not succeed for a variety of reasons. First of all, Nova University had difficulty marketing the program since it did not correspond to what most parents and students thought a college curriculum should be. Because the program was much more intensive (twelve months in length) and time consuming than the regular curriculum, several students, who wanted a summer vacation, dropped out. Nova College lived on as Fischler and others ended up compromising on the original concept. The final result was still innovative but vastly different from the original idea. Fischler noted that if Nova College had come from the faculty instead of the administration, it might have been more effective. He had implemented a program that was simply too esoteric and complicated to work, and in the final analysis Nova could not "implement it to the extent that one wanted."[18]

Athletics and Student Affairs

In 1980, to boost the limited undergraduate enrollment, Nova University and its board of trustees decided to sponsor and organize student activities, including athletics and social events. In 1981, Charles "Sonny" Hansley, the first director of athletics at the university, faced the monumental task of starting an athletic program at Nova. It had no established sports programs, no facilities, very little money, and only 200 to 350 undergraduates to participate on the teams. In 1982, Nova administrators decided they needed to choose a sport that would not require a large initial outlay. They decided that men's basketball would be the first sports team since the players needed only shorts, shirts, and sneakers, and they could use the local high school gyms for games. In 1982–1983, the men's basketball team, known as the Nova Knights, with Hansley as the coach, began its inaugural season as an independent program, unaffiliated with any conference.

As one might imagine, organizing a basketball team at a mostly graduate university was a formidable challenge. Very few potential recruits had even heard of Nova. As the season began, Hansley had only eight healthy players and no gym or locker room. The players changed into their uniforms in their dorm rooms and then drove over to the Lutheran High School gym, their home court, to begin play. This was no-frills basketball, where the team used a high school classroom as their locker room. Player Tim Moore, who played basketball at Pompano High School, said playing for Nova was worse than high school. At least in high school, griped Moore, the manager would wash the uniforms. "Here, we take them home. At least they give us a lot of clean socks."

Nova made a bold move in 1984 by adding men's soccer, women's volleyball, and men's and women's cross-country. These new sports did not require a large amount of funding and could be played on the athletic fields already available on campus or at the facilities of Broward Community College and local high schools. As Frank DePiano, the first coach of the men's cross-country team, recalled, basketball players needed a uniform, shoes, and a place to play, but in the warm Florida sunshine, cross-country runners needed only shoes and shorts and could roam all over the Nova campus.

In the fall of 1985, although the undergraduate enrollment had dipped to 222, Nova joined the National Association of Intercollegiate Athletics (NAIA) because it needed to be a member of the NAIA to add new sports. In 1987, with enrollment up to 1,000, the university augmented the athletic programs with baseball, women's tennis, and men's golf. Despite meager resources, some of the early teams found success. The women's volleyball team finished its second season with a record of nine wins and four losses. As might be expected, the other programs struggled to achieve a winning record, although basketball had a respectable 11-13 season during its third year.[19]

Nova University had made a concerted effort to increase athletics and other intramural activities to attract undergraduate students, but the campus lacked any sort of social planning or social activities for them. Zeida Rodriguez, an undergraduate student in 1983, liked the university and enjoyed her classes but was disgruntled with the lack of social amenities. There was no cafeteria on campus, so students had to leave campus for fast food. She had no place to relax and hang out with her peers except for a small room in the Parker Building. Rodriguez liked the small classes at Nova, however, and was impressed that the faculty was accessible to students on a personal level. A cursory glance at the student newspaper, *The Nova Knight*, from November 1983 until the end of 1986, indicates that students were constantly complaining about the dearth of social activities and demanding that the university build a proper student union.

The Student Government Association (SGA) sponsored several events in an attempt to get students to remain on campus and get to know their fellow students better. The SGA held a free picnic on the Wednesday prior to Thanksgiving 1983, coupled with a canned-food drive "for those in need who might not be able to celebrate the holiday without our help." The SGA held its annual holiday party on December 22, 1983, featuring the "hottest disco sounds." Unfortunately, the party had to be held in the cramped confines of the third floor of the Parker Building as no other venue was available. Of course, various organizations on campus held other typical student events, such as movie nights and "Get Blitzed Night."[20]

The SGA saw itself as a watchdog for student rights and besides parties, planned fund-raising events for more important purposes, such as providing scholarships for needy students. The *Nova Knight* urged students to vote in every election, both local and national. The paper had culinary reviews of local restaurants and provided information about concerts by U2 and Julian Lennon. Staff members wrote reviews of new albums by Van Morrison and Bob Dylan.[21]

The student newspaper took great pains to inform students about important university-sponsored events, like the forum on U.S. and Soviet affairs presided over by David Brinkley of *NBC News*. The *Knight* encouraged students to attend Nova's "Distinguished Speakers" series to learn about world affairs. The first event featured Sir Edward Heath, prime minister of the United Kingdom from 1970 to 1974.[22]

The main focus of the newspaper from 1983 to 1986 was a continual plea for a central student union and an on-campus bookstore. The students complained about the service and the high prices at the privately owned Corner Book Store and urged the university to set up its own not-for-profit bookstore. The *Knight* asked the administration for a career information center to help graduates find jobs and a computerized central catalog for the library. The paper pointed out errors and misinformation in the 1984–1985 university catalog and asked for more convenience in class scheduling.

The loudest and most frequent grievance remained the lack of a student center. The editor of the *Knight* found a "high degree of apathy" among Nova students. Student indifference was not surprising "considering the basic resources that have been made available to us till now, including a degrading, dirty student lounge and an almost complete absence of school-based activities on campus." The *Knight* repeatedly expressed the need for more campus-based events.[23] These complaints were made as late as 1986, but the university moved very slowly to accommodate student's needs. Abe Fischler believed he had more important things on which to spend money, and with the university constantly in debt, student athletics and social events were a very low priority. If Nova intended to increase its undergraduate numbers, that attitude would have to change.

International Programs: Panama

Desiring to take advantage of the physical proximity of South Florida to Latin American countries and expand its off-campus programs, Nova University decided to start an overseas program in Panama.

Nova initiated its program in 1977 just after the United States agreed to return the Panama Canal Zone to the people of the nation of Panama by the year 2000.

Aware that Panamanian officers would eventually man the Canal Zone, the U.S. Canal Zone Police knew they would have to turn to some other form of police work and requested that Nova set up a master's program in criminal justice. Nova organized a program essentially limited to the Canal Zone police force, but this initial venture led to other contacts with the Panamanian authorities and eventually to Nova's Panama Center. Nova recognized that the Republic of Panama served "as a bridge for understanding and cooperation among peoples of the Americas through the educational process." First conceived as a limited off-campus program, the venture quickly developed, and on March 15, 1982, the president of Panama signed a decree recognizing Nova University as an autonomous official university in Panama. At the time, it was the first and only institution of U.S. origin so honored.

By 1986, the center offered intensive English- and Spanish-language courses and had graduated American and Panamanian students with bachelor's of science degrees in the professional management program, master's degrees in business administration, master's of arts in teaching English as a second language, and doctoral degrees in public administration.

During the Cold War, the stressful period of diplomatic animosity between Russia and the United States, Camilio Fabrega, chairman of the Nova University Panama Center Board of Governors, expressed pride in having Nova University in Panama. With 4,000 Panamanian students being educated behind the Iron Curtain, Fabrega noted that Nova had played a significant role in providing education at a democratic institution instead of in totalitarian Soviet Union. In 1986, Dominador Kaiser Bazan, the Panamanian ambassador to the United States, said that Nova's presence and its influence on the 1,000 or so students enrolled on an annual basis had a major impact in curbing Soviet influence in the area. "The relations between Panama and the United States are very good now," he said, and education was the key to continued peace between the two countries.

Martin Taylor, the chief administrative officer, directed the daily operations in Panama. From 1977 to 1987, Nova created a professional-level university to provide educational and cultural services to personnel and dependents of the Panama Canal Commission, the Department of Defense, the U.S. Agency for International Development, the U.S. embassy, the government of the Republic of Panama, and the private sector. From 1979 until 1987, a total of 335 students had graduated in all the programs.

The Nova University Board of Trustees assessed the Panama program as very successful since it raised the university's prestige in international circles and made a profit. The board wanted the Panama program to have a more visible presence and insisted that a permanent classroom/office building was essential for future progress. With proper facilities and an expanded curriculum, the center became self-supporting.[24]

Nova University Administrative Structure: 1975–1985

By 1975, Nova University administration had become more stable and efficient. The hierarchy began with the board of trustees, then the chancellor of the university, Alex Schure, followed by the president of the university, Abe Fischler. The dean of graduate studies reported to the president, as did the directors of each of the five centers: the Nova Center for the Study of Law, Behavioral Science Center, the Life Sciences Center, the Center for Professional Development, and the Oceanographic Center. In 1975, university faculty participated in most academic matters, including curriculum and degree requirements, but had little influence on the actual running of the university.

Nova faculty used the university senate as the primary vehicle for administrative and academic recommendations to the president. Meetings were held four times a year and were open to all members of the university family. The chairman of the senate chose voting members, and there were student representatives from each of the five centers.

More important to the decision-making process was the administrative council. Composed of the president, the chairman and chairman-elect of the university senate, and the directors of each of the five centers, this group met monthly and advised the president on important matters. The latter group was smaller than the university senate and could discuss and act more efficiently than the larger body. Over time, depending on the president, the administration could— and in Fischler's opinion, should—ignore the university senate and provide them with the necessary information about the university's direction.[25] Due to the critical economic circumstances and the university's uncertain future, it was perhaps inevitable that the president would end up making most of the key decisions.

During this early period, Fischler ran the university without a provost or all the layers of bureaucracy that characterize most universities. Fischler preferred it that way because he favored a system that he described as "each tub on its own bottom." He chose the leader of each center, calling them directors instead of deans, and they served at his pleasure. When they began their time as director, Fischler told them that they had to do two things: maintain the academic quality and economic viability of their center. If they were successful, Fischler would leave them alone. If not, they would be replaced. If they came up with new ideas and demonstrated that the concepts would work, the president would give them the tools and funding necessary to implement these new programs. Fischler's operating system was another example of the university's entrepreneurial focus.

Fischler wanted the centers to keep most of the money that they earned as an incentive for them to earn more. To pay for operating expenses for the entire university, Fischler asked each center to contribute 25 to 30 percent of their earnings. The administration—that is, Fischler—operated as the service arm for the university: secretarial, administrative, and accounting.[26]

In 1977, on the tenth anniversary of its opening, Nova University held its first convocation to honor the founding trustees and other civic leaders who aided in establishing the institution. Among those honored were Jim Farquhar, Robert Ellyson, Tinsley Ellis, Myron Ashmore, Robert Ferris, and some of the major donors to the school—William C. Mather, Leo Goodwin Sr. (posthumously), Louis W. Parker, and William Horvitz. In his address, President Fischler traced the development of the institution's growth, commenting that the school started with only seventeen graduate students and now had approximately 8,000 students in twenty-three states and three foreign countries. The annual budget had increased from $500,000 in 1967 to $19.2 million in 1977. Fischler observed that Nova's struggle was not over: "Our infancy is over, but we need nourishment as we enter adolescence. We need the two-way dialogue. We need both your intellectual stimulation and your monetary support."

Fischler pointed out to his audience that independent universities like Nova were competing with tax-supported institutions that were also receiving private philanthropic support, so Nova would "require even greater support in the future." The president stated that private universities educated around one-fourth of the more than 11 million students currently in universities and thus saved taxpayers around $6 billion per year to educate those students in state schools. The country, said Fischler, needs independent universities because they provide diversity and choice in the educational marketplace, are more flexible and enterprising than public universities, and are relatively free from political pressure by the state legislatures. The public sector and the state legislature needed to recognize that a dual system (public and private) of university education is in the public interest.[27]

If one were to take a snapshot of the university's activities from 1978 to 1985, one would focus first on the economic situation. Nova's economic status remained precarious and unstable, and the school had to be bailed out yet again by Alex Schure and NYIT. On the surface, however, Nova officials discussed the future as if everything were proceeding in a positive direction. In 1979, when Fischler published "The Report of the President on the 15th Anniversary of the Founding of Nova University," no public mention was made of the acute financial distress. The major purpose of this document, as well as the 1977 report, was to bring the public's attention to the university's significant achievements in its fifteen years of existence. Also, despite a reluctance to face fiscal reality, Fischler used the bully pulpit to allay fears of the school's imminent demise. Fischler stressed that Nova's programs were mission oriented and designed to improve the performance of professionals. The university announced several new initiatives, including a master's program in criminal justice that targeted employed professionals in the criminal justice system—law and the courts, the police, and corrections. The National Graduate Teacher Education Program offered graduate courses for K–12 teachers.

A new and very successful off-campus program was the Center for Public Affairs and Administration, aimed at midcareer officials in government, universities, and public service areas. The program awarded a doctorate in public administration (DPA); from 1973 to 1979, 198 men and women had been awarded a DPA from Nova.

The university, continuing its idea of cradle-to-grave education, set up the Institute for Retired Professionals (IRP). Nova understood that professionals often felt lost at retirement and faced physical, emotional, and intellectual strains. The university decided to involve retirees in activities that would establish a sense of self-worth and provide a place where "highly trained retired professionals can expand their intellectual life and learn from teaching each other." Max Salzman, the associate director of IRP, said, "What we have is wisdom . . . a lifetime of accumulated knowledge and experience. It's all just a matter of bringing these people together and convincing them that they are a valuable resource." The course offerings included poetry, literature, contemporary affairs, music, art, theater, estate planning, and conversational French. IRP members served as both teachers and students in their twice-daily classes. Libby Klinghoffer, a recent retiree, declared that the IRP offered "a very broadening and stimulating experience." Participant Charles Weiss talked about the challenge of a new lifestyle and emphasized the need to stay mentally active.[28]

One on-campus center that expanded quickly was the Behavioral Science Center (BSC), which focused on the study of man and his behavior and offered an EdD in early childhood education. Also offered were master's of education degrees in mental retardation, reading, the gifted child, elementary education, and health education. The center included the Foster Parents Training Program, which trained welfare workers, and a biofeedback laboratory. The Department of Psychology offered a PhD program in clinical psychology, child psychology, and research and evaluation. Students could earn a master's of science degree in counseling, gerontology, applied psychology, and school psychology. The center opened several mental health clinics around the county, with one clinic specifically designed for children. Nova was beginning to expand its services for the local community and increase its interaction with local residents, and was thus becoming better known in Broward County.

In 1981, the Florida School of Professional Psychology merged into the Behavioral Science Center. The School of Professional Psychology, which lacked regional accreditation, had 120 students paying $4,700 per year in tuition; this new income provided a financial boost to the center. The merger enabled the center to begin offering a PsyD, the professional degree, in addition to the PhD, the academic degree. In 1983, the American Psychological Association gave full accreditation to the PsyD program.[29]

All of these new initiatives and expanded programs raised Nova University's profile and added money to its coffers. The new injection of funds, however, was still not enough to keep Nova in the black. Nonetheless, the programs in psychology and early education, the public administration program, the master's in criminology, the courses for national teachers' education, and others would form the basis for a successful and viable Nova when the university eventually separated from NYIT.

Due to insufficient funds, certain academic areas suffered more than others. As is often the case, the library was shortchanged financially as the administration tried to get by with as little funding as possible. Robert (Bob) Bogorff, the director of libraries at the time, bemoaned the administration's lack of interest in library holdings. There was no central library in the early years, so the books were crammed into a small library in the Mailman-Hollywood Building. The Parker Building also had a small library with limited space, and the Oceanographic Center had its own library, but the holdings for the university were limited. The library got help in the late 1970s when the School of Psychology ordered many volumes when the SACS representative came to evaluate the university. The SACS investigator recognized the library's plight and, after getting a laundry list of the most-needed materials from the director, made certain that those needs were met so it wouldn't imperil Nova's accreditation. Eventually, by the mid-1980s, the university began to fund the library to build up collections that had been ignored. For the first fifteen years, Bob Bogorff recalled, library staffing was inadequate, and "it was not a satisfactory university library."[30]

Early Technology at Nova

Another area of concern for the growing university was technology development, computers in particular. Abe Fischler had long been a proponent of new technology, and all of the original graduate students at Nova had to learn Fortran, a general-purpose computer programming language. Fischler predicted that ultimately technology would be used for his distance-learning programs. Nova later developed a comprehensive program in computer education, including a master's in computer science and computer applications. Soon computer science became Nova's most popular major at a time when few campuses in America were offering such courses. Nova broadened its offerings with an EdD in computer education. Fischler knew that this new technology was the trend of the future and made certain that computers were "in the very fabric" of all doctoral programs. He also began to devise a plan to use this new technology for the university's off-campus programs.

Technological innovation came quickly in the 1980s. In 1984, Nova established the Center for Computer-Based Learning, which included master's and doctoral programs in information science, computer education, and computer science. In 1985, the university revolutionized distance education with the development and implementation of the electronic classroom for delivering synchronized online courses. By 1992, with the advent of audio teleconferencing, Nova could service all courses via online computers from the Nova campus. In 1987, the Center for Computer Science was set up to contain both the graduate and undergraduate computer science degree programs previously housed in the Center for Computer-Based Learning.[31] Nova University, along with a few other institutions, had changed the focus of higher education in America. First, with the idea of off-campus programs and later with the technology that enabled Nova to teach these programs online from campus.

Nova University had suffered a tragedy with the loss of the *Gulf Stream* and its crew, but it finally received the long-overdue funds from the Goodwin Unitrust. Nova slowly recovered on several fronts: rebuilding the Oceanographic Center; offering academic, social, and athletic opportunities for students; and upgrading its technology. Nova was now ready to free itself from its alliance with NYIT and embark on its own as an independent university.

5

End to the NYIT Merger

Nova Finances: 1975–1985, Prelude to the Dissolution of the NYIT Merger

From 1964 to 1985, when Nova first earned a surplus, the university faced critical funding shortages and was always looking for new sources of income. Part of the difficulty in juggling budgets came when, to pay the bills, Abe Fischler had to siphon money from the law school or the Educational Leadership Program, the only successful earners in the early years. There was resentment and tension on the part of the centers, which expected to keep most of the money they earned. Throughout the 1970s and early 1980s, Nova's cash-flow problems moved from severe to critical. Many bills were not paid on time, and on one occasion the school was within one week of having its electricity turned off because of past-due bills.

One example of Nova's tardiness in paying bills was a letter from B.K. Dorsey of Boone Industries in North Carolina to President Fischler requesting payment for a $123.62 invoice that was six months overdue. Dorsey wrote that she had been informed that a Mr. Rosenburg (she meant Rosenblatt), vice president for financial affairs, had already mailed a check, but "[e]ither the Pony Express is extremely slow or Mr. Rosenburg has not attended to this matter. . . . In all our years of business I have never had such a problem in collecting unpaid invoices. I am sure that this is not the image you wish Nova University to project."[1] This was one of many such missives. If Nova had trouble paying a bill for just $123.62, one can imagine the headaches when Nova was faced with paying off substantially greater amounts.

At the board of trustees meeting on September 12, 1975, President Fischler reported that the extremely tight cash flow was partly due to capital expenditures for the law school. The university had been unable to reimburse its off-campus lecturers for out-of-pocket expenses and owed them a total of $65,000. This failure to pay the lecturers caused unrest and many problems among the affiliated faculty, who were reluctant to continue teaching without being paid. The off-campus programs were a main source of Nova's income, and if the school could not pay the instructors, then the program would collapse and that income would be lost. The university also had accounts payable of $910,000. Where would it get the funds to pay those past due bills?[2]

Nova officials, of course, continued to look for ways to reduce expenses, but the costs of renovating campus buildings like the Parker Building and the Rosenthal Center and a reduction in expected income from the off-campus programs overwhelmed their good intentions. The university continued its capital fund drives and urged local citizens to contribute, but without great success.

A fairly typical budget was for the 1976–1977 fiscal year. The percentage allocated to each center was divided up as follows: law school, 7.8 percent; University School, 8.6 percent; debt service, 8.2 percent, behavioral sciences, 7.5 percent; EdD community college program, 7.6 percent; Human Performance Research Institute, 9.5 percent; physical plant, 5.9 percent; university administration, 6.2 percent; Nova College, 4.9 percent; public administration center, 4.9 percent; oceanography, 4.7 percent; life sciences, 4.5 percent; criminal justice, 3.6 percent; library, 1.6 percent. Other percentages were scattered among the printing office, the computing center, and development.[3] A quick reading of the list indicates that the university administration and the physical plant took very little of the university's expenses, demonstrating that the personnel in these two areas worked frugally and efficiently. Most of the other centers received similar percentages, although the amount spent to expand the University School seems high since the school provided very little revenue and was usually in the red. The university constantly reduced expenses by decreasing the size of the development office, curtailing an alumni program, and making significant cuts in life sciences.[4]

In 1983–1984, the deficit ballooned to $3 million and Nova had to borrow $4 million just to cover its expenses. To counteract these losses, Nova increased tuition 8 to 12 percent depending on the program. The university eliminated all pay raises while refusing to reduce salaries. Nova consolidated programs, reorganized staff, and cut back on travel. Secretaries and faculty members were reminded to turn off lights and adjust thermostats.

Despite the continuing financial difficulties, Fischler realized that he needed to invest in additional administrative support. He strengthened his top-level administration team with the appointment of James Guerdon as vice president for administration and finance; Ovid Lewis, the former law dean, as vice president for academic affairs; and Helen Graham, the first woman chosen for an upper-level administrative position, as director of human resources. The board of trustees recognized the need for the university to have knowledgeable and effective representation in legislative matters in Tallahassee, as it coveted increased financial support from the state. Realizing the dire need for creating an endowment, the university, after cutting back personnel in the development office, reversed field and appointed Stephen Goldstein as the university's first vice president for corporate and foundation development. Nova had to ramp up its capital funds drive as it had acquired only $100,000 in donations the previous year. Nova asked its trustees to increase their own level of giving and to find one other person to do the same. Fischler understood that publicity about the university's deficit hurt contributions, but the president wanted to show Broward County residents that Nova could "function in a more businesslike manner."

Community support often depended on visibility, but most of Nova's students did not live in Broward and Nova had not been around long enough to build up a core of loyal alumni. The *Miami Herald* summed up Nova's dilemma: "Without a large undergraduate presence and the collegiate atmosphere that comes with it, Nova can't muster the kind of alma-mater sentiment that can move a community to open its heart—and its pocketbook."[5]

Throughout the period from 1970 to 1985, NYIT frequently loaned money to Nova. The university paid off some of its loans but continued to pile up new loans with interest payments to NYIT. Acutely aware of Nova's financial problems, Chancellor Schure offered to make a $2 million loan to Nova, but as several board members pointed out, that would just prolong and extend Nova's debt to NYIT. By 1985, they realized that there was no way for Nova to sustain itself and grow to financial stability without extricating itself from an ever-growing financial obligation to NYIT.

The End to the NYIT/Nova Federation: 1985

Nova University's desire to part with NYIT had emerged as early as July 1978, when trustee Cy Young urged Nova to sever its ties with NYIT immediately. Young contended that NYIT continually siphoned off cash from the financially hard-pressed institution. The cash that Nova paid to NYIT included interest on loans, revenue sharing on any of Nova's profitable programs, and the $65,000 annual salary plus benefits for Chancellor Alex Schure. Young asked, "If the New York crowd shares in the profits, why can't they share in the losses?" Young said that Nova already owed NYIT more than $2.6 million and that sum would surely grow, putting Nova under the total control of NYIT. On the other hand, David Salten and others at NYIT expressed displeasure with the Nova's inefficient administration and its constant demand for money. The school "has always been in need of money—usually desperately, occasionally urgently."[6]

The *Fort Lauderdale News* editorialized that the agreement with NYIT was bad for Nova because NYIT dominated the federation and did not have Nova's interests at heart. The paper fervently hoped that Nova could be saved from the federation so that it could serve the interests of Broward County and not NYIT.[7] It became obvious by 1978 that there was increased tension between the two schools, and by the end of 1985, both NYIT and Nova wanted to end the association.

Earlier, during the period from 1976 to 1978, both parties had tried to salvage the agreement. At that time Chancellor Schure wanted the relationship between the two universities strengthened and expanded, and he made several suggestions to the board of trustees in that regard. Schure advocated the expansion of Nova College, the development of a school of architecture, an MA and PhD equivalent in criminal justice, courses in social work and engineering management, and cable television for publicity.[8] Nova University's response to these ideas was muted at best, showing no great desire to take on Schure's suggestions.

Abe Fischler, who admired Schure and was deeply indebted to him for saving Nova on several occasions, tried to put the best face on the deteriorating relations with NYIT. In a statement to the board of trustees on April 25, 1978, Fischler noted that the relationship with NYIT had been "a great asset to Nova University." He pointed out the importance of the original $1.2 million that NYIT made available

and the other instances when the New York school had lent money
to Nova. NYIT had put up its resources and guaranteed the viability
of the law school to the ABA. In addition to financial help, NYIT
had made available "human resources" and expertise to guide Nova
through some difficult times. Fischler said the arrangement must be
beneficial for both institutions and that he planned to do his best to
make it work.[9]

Schure regularly cautioned the Nova administrators that they had
to curtail some of the building program and eliminate those courses
that did not make money. Nonetheless, in the spirit of cooperation,
NYIT listened to Nova's complaints that they were paying the overhead for the programs (faculty salaries, secretaries) while NYIT
reaped the benefits. Over a period of years, NYIT agreed to give Nova
10 percent, then 20 percent, and finally 50 percent of the net gain
from the successful programs. This gesture helped out, but to Nova,
NYIT was still taking out more money than they were putting in. By
1985, President Fischler estimated that, as the on-campus programs
increased enrollment and earned more money, NYIT's take had increased from $200,000 a year to $500,000 a year. Nova could not
build and innovate if NYIT continued to absorb such a large amount
of money.

On September 10, 1985, the administrations of both schools tried
to resolve their governing and financial differences during a series of
meetings intended to create a revised relationship between NYIT and
Nova. A combined task force of Nova and NYIT faculty met on several occasions in an attempt to resolve the issues, but finally decided
there was not much they could do together. Frank DePiano recalled
one of the meetings where little common ground was found and both
parties left the unpleasant gathering with negative emotions.[10]

On September 24, 1985, in an effort to preserve the 1970 agreement, Alex Schure sent a proposal to the Nova University Board of
Trustees. In his letter, Schure indicated that the 1970 agreement had
worked well and had built an exceptional educational institution at
Nova. He declared that NYIT had advanced significant amounts of
money to Nova during the past fifteen years and had devoted "substantial, time, energy, and guidance in the development of Nova from
a PhD degree–granting institution of 127 students and twenty-four
faculty in 1970 to a broad university granting bachelor's, master's,
and doctoral degrees" and a student body of 6,000. NYIT and its officers had provided their academic experience to Nova and had guaranteed the establishment of the law school. In calling attention to the

significant benefits afforded to Nova in its arrangement with NYIT, Schure appeared to claim credit for all of Nova's advances in the previous fifteen years, much to the displeasure of the Nova adherents on the board of trustees.

Schure's September 24 proposal reaffirmed the 1970 agreement and declared that NYIT retained the right to appoint one-half of the members of the board of trustees at Nova University and one-third of the executive committee. Further, it would take a three-fourths vote of the Nova Board of Trustees to adopt the annual Nova budget, sell real estate, or change the terms of the contracts between Nova and NYIT. Net revenues of the shared programs would be divided equally by NYIT and Nova. Schure hoped that the university federation between Nova and NYIT would be strengthened through new academic programs and new technology. Finally, once Nova agreed to the new proposal, the document prevented Nova University from ever challenging the original July 1, 1970, agreement with NYIT.[11]

A casual observer could see how Schure's excessive demands would offend Nova supporters. First, he once again seemed to be claiming all the credit for Nova's success, especially the founding of the law school. Second, and perhaps most troubling, NYIT could exercise complete control over Nova by virtue of its right to choose half of the members of the board of trustees. Since a vote of three-quarters of the board would be necessary to adopt a budget, sell real estate, or change any contracts, NYIT could block any decision it did not like. The three-fourths majority requirement was a direct insult to Nova. Schure made it appear that the Nova trustees were incapable of making wise decisions on any matter and that this new requirement would lead to even greater control by NYIT. Schure's desire to keep half of the income from shared programs upset Fischler and others since they had already objected to NYIT taking too much money out of Nova. Perhaps most important, by signing this agreement, Nova could never get out of the July 1, 1970, association, which it wanted to do, and could not later legally challenge Schure's 1985 addendum.

Shure's September 24 proposal followed a contentious meeting of the Nova Board of Trustees in Davie on September 12, 1985. The main topic for discussion was a $1.5 million loan from NYIT to Nova. A sum of $750,000 would be immediately available for Nova's use to catch up on accounts payable. NYIT, however, had not released that money. A previous document showed that there had apparently been a proposal that Nova could end the federation with a payment of $10 million. Now the Nova trustees accused Schure of forceful coercion. They thought he was holding up the delivery of the $750,000 in order to get Nova to come up with $10 million to dissolve the federation.

Schure replied that the earlier document requesting $10 million had not been intended to influence the $1.5 million loan and that the earlier amount was merely a starting point for discussion. Chancellor Schure, angry and offended by what he considered unfair charges from the Nova Board of Trustees, expressed his displeasure at being summoned from New York to attend a board meeting in Florida. He reminded the group that he had saved the university at least four times and fought for Nova with the NYIT board, which had frequently expressed impatience and displeasure over the association with Nova. The NYIT board had long demanded that the chancellor have more control over activities at Nova University since NYIT was spending large sums of money to keep it solvent. There had been resistance to the federation from the NYIT board from the beginning, but Schure always defended the association. Schure proclaimed that over the federation's fifteen-year period, he had never made a demand of Nova— a dubious statement at best, since Schure had forced Nova to establish a law school (a good decision, but a demand nonetheless) and exerted influence in other areas.

Schure apologized if the first draft of his September 24 proposal, requesting $10 million to end the 1970 agreement, ruffled some feathers. He admitted that some of the language had been intemperate and he did not intend to force the document on Nova. He reminded the trustees that he was one of Nova's most faithful supporters and did not appreciate being put in a position of having to defend his leadership of NYIT and Nova.

Some Nova board members, angered by Schure's comments, decided that one way to end the federation was to question the legality of the original 1970 agreement. The Nova supporters on the board tried to come up with any legal loopholes whereby they could extricate the university from its association with NYIT. Robert Steele, a Nova board member, could not see why Nova University would send $1.5 million to NYIT as payment for a loan since NYIT had taken more than that sum from money earned entirely by Nova. Steele characterized the $10 million offer to end the association as "ludicrous." Nova did not have nor could it raise $10 million. Nova could not even pay back the $1.5 million loan from NYIT. This large amount of money that Schure demanded from an insolvent school struck some observers as being the height of arrogance and greed.

Schure responded testily to Steele's comments and to the implied threats of legal action against NYIT. He insisted that NYIT should retain 50 percent of the shared programs since, in his judgment, "Nova had neither the talent nor the capability to sustain the field-based programs," and because of this ineptitude, the revenue from those off-campus programs would diminish. Schure did not think it was in Nova University's best interest to publicize its squabbles, but "if the trustees wanted to go to war, so be it."

August Paoli, another board member, demanded that Schure apologize for threatening the trustees and the university. Schure replied that while he felt he was being treated shabbily, he was not threatening anyone.

In a last-minute attempt to broker some sort of settlement, Abe Fischler revealed that the Nova University Board of Trustees proposed that NYIT's take from shared programs be capped at $500,000, no matter how much money had been earned. Schure, by now vexed and displeased with the Nova board, refused to agree to a cap on NYIT's revenues. Fischler believed that if Schure had accepted this solution, even at that late date, the issues that confronted the two institutions might have been resolved and the association saved.[12]

At this point, however, relations between the two universities had been irreversibly broken. The confrontation between Schure and Nova devotees at the board of trustees meeting hastened the end of the federation, but there were other reasons for Nova to curtail the relationship with NYIT. The major issues were money and control. As Tinsley Ellis recalled, many supporters in Broward County wanted Nova to be a local university, not dominated by a New York institution. The founders of the university had spent years building up Nova and did not want it to be a satellite of NYIT. Nova backers favored a split from NYIT partly because many potential local contributors saw Nova as an out-of-state-managed institution and refused to contribute to Nova's fund-raising efforts.

The cost to Nova of the NYIT association had accelerated to the point where it was restricting Nova's growth. To survive and prosper, Nova had to proceed as a completely independent institution. The Nova administration had for some time resented the fact that NYIT was taking out more money than it was putting in. The money exchange was excessive and becoming increasingly unfair. Nova was not flourishing but just getting by, and Nova saw NYIT as an exploitive partner.

Abe Fischler gave credit to Alex Schure for saving Nova numerous times from bankruptcy and for creating the law school. He remarked several times that Nova would not be having these conversations without that help and support from Schure. Despite his friendship with Schure, by 1985 Fischler knew that the relationship had to end and Nova had to develop on its own. Fischler also realized that the agreement was not working from an intellectual point of view. The two faculties did not mix well, and NYIT operated under different conditions than Nova. NYIT was unionized, whereas Nova was not. Schure, as chancellor, had authority over Fischler, the president, and Schure began to view himself more as the employer and Fischler as the employee. With Schure's intent to expand NYIT's influence over Nova, it became more difficult for Fischler to run the university as he saw fit, so Fischler reluctantly accelerated his efforts to bring the association with NYIT to an end.[13]

Changed circumstances at NYIT exacerbated relations between the two schools. NYIT, under pressure to increase its income, did not want to give up the funds it was receiving from Nova. The NYIT board looked on Nova as a drain on NYIT resources and thought Nova was ungrateful for the many long-term benefits from its association with NYIT. NYIT was exercising its financial muscle because it had superior economic strength at the time and NYIT wanted to push Nova in a direction favorable to NYIT. Nova board members did not like that kind of pressure and worked harder to end the agreement with NYIT.

To complicate matters, Alex Schure was no longer president of NYIT. After a series of conflicts with his faculty and the NYIT board, he turned control over to his son Matthew, leaving Alex Schure with little day-to-day authority. Schure realized, however, that he still "owned" a university since he was still chancellor of Nova. He thought he could turn his full attention to Nova University and implement some of the programs he had always envisioned.[14] Fischler and others sensed that Schure wanted to increase his influence at Nova and moved quickly to thwart that possibility.

Another issue that caused some hard feelings was Schure's attempt to persuade Nova to purchase some computer equipment, a VAX 11/750 computer system, from Computer Graphics Lab in New York. Computer Graphics was a for-profit company and a wholly owned subsidiary of NYIT. Schure sent Nova some computer software packages and informed Nova that the university had "to use these systems." Ed Simco, director of the computer center, wanted to cancel the order because delivery of the VAX computer system had been delayed by fourteen months, the hardware was too expensive ($131,000), and Simco could get better equipment for a much lower price.

On August 15, 1985, Simco received a telephone call from Chancellor Schure demanding immediate payment of the $131,000 for the VAX 750 because the bill was fourteen months overdue. Simco replied that all of the equipment on the invoice had not been received. Schure responded that other equipment had been substituted, Nova had everything it was supposed to have received, and the price of the VAX system was fair.

Schure also said that he was getting heat from NYIT auditors and the NYIT board over nonpayment of the bill. Schure reminded Simco that he and NYIT had helped Nova many times over the years and "had helped Nova by giving them educational programs which were money makers and which Nova kept the largest portion of the income, and how thankless Nova was for all this, and this is what he gets for everything he has done for Nova." Schure added that he was tired of being "punished and beaten" by Nova, as they continued to make statements that were half-truths. Schure disliked the attitude of the people at Nova, and felt that this computer incident had "done more to sour him on Nova than any other incident in fifteen years."[15]

Although Schure expressed anger and displeasure with Nova over the purchase of computers, there was no assurance that he would willingly give up his salary and perks as chancellor. Nonetheless, the acrimony over the computer purchase had embittered Schure on any future interaction with Nova University.

Fischler and others, unable to work out a compromise with NYIT, decided to fight NYIT in the courts. Nova thought a legal confrontation with NYIT would be the best way to pressure the school to end the agreement. In a legal draft that was never filed, Nova asked for declaratory and injunctive relief from Alex Schure and NYIT. Nova's attorney, Terry Russell, argued that in the 1975 shared programs oral agreement, NYIT agreed to transfer control of certain bachelor and master's programs to Nova and to divide the net income fifty-fifty. Russell asserted that since 1975 Nova had distributed some $1.7 million to NYIT via the fifty-fifty split. Florida statutes declared that a not-for-profit corporation may not distribute its profits to contributors, whether they be members, shareholders, officers, or directors. Any profits must be devoted to the corporation, and since NYIT contributed to the administration of the shared programs to Nova, NYIT could not seek to profit from this contribution.

Over the years, continued Russell's legal draft, Nova became solely responsible for the development and maintenance of the shared programs. Nova had been burdened with the responsibility for the overhead and expenses, including faculty salaries and insurance costs, while NYIT had been entirely relieved of such responsibility. Due to the unequal bargaining posture between NYIT and Nova, the 1975 oral agreement imposed disproportionate obligations on Nova.

In addition, in a 1982 employment agreement, Schure had been given an excessive package. His salary as chancellor of Nova University was $80,000 a year, in addition to his salary as president of NYIT. He received pension plan benefits, an automobile with all auto expenses paid by Nova, an entertainment expense account of $10,000 per year, and a housing allowance of $12,000 per year because as chancellor he was required to reside part-time in Broward County. Russell accused Schure of receiving substantial benefits when he instructed Nova to purchase computers from the NYIT Computer Graphics Lab at above-market prices. Another key issue Russell cited was the NYIT Board of Trustees' decision to demand payment of the exorbitant sum of $10,000,000 to dissolve the agreement. That payment was, in effect, a bribe. The NYIT members of the Nova Board of Trustees had consistently acted in NYIT's best interests, not Nova's, and used their position of influence to benefit NYIT, not Nova.

The plaintiffs, Nova University, had, over a period of several years, sought relief within the corporate structure of NYIT, but without success. Since the plaintiffs had suffered irreparable injury and had no adequate remedy at law, the legal document asked for the original 1970 agreement to be declared invalid and the 1975 oral agreement terminated. The brief argued that the acts of Alex Schure constituted adequate cause for terminating the exorbitant 1982 employment agreement.[16]

These legal challenges were dubious at best, especially the view, not expressed earlier, that the money from the shared programs that Nova paid to NYIT was illegal. Nova had never questioned the 1975 shared agreement or Schure's executive package as excessive until it began looking for a way out of the 1970 agreement. Had these legal issues ended up in court, it would have been difficult for Nova to challenge for cause the legality and the sanctity of the original contract. A contract was a contract, and Nova had agreed to the stipulations and paid Schure the designated sums for the entire fifteen-year period. It would have been difficult to explain in 1985 why suddenly the contract was invalid.

Of course, Nova had no desire to file the lawsuit, because it would have taken several years and would have cost the university thousands of dollars. It wanted to use the threatened lawsuit as leverage to persuade Schure to end the association. The defining moment came when Mary McCahill went to Schure's office and gave him a copy of the legal brief that Nova was going to file. She told him that Nova had someone waiting at the courthouse to file the brief immediately if he did not agree to end the federation. Schure read the document and allegedly said, "Make me an offer." Schure did not want to defend a lawsuit; it would have been disruptive and expensive for both parties.[17] The carrot/stick approach worked. Nova would pay off its debt to NYIT, take care of Alex Schure, and drop the threatened lawsuit. Schure agreed because he had tired of the relationship with Nova and did not want any more conflict.

NYIT and Nova quickly hammered out a final agreement that was signed on October 31, 1985. This document formally and legally ended the relationship between NYIT and Nova University. Nova agreed to pay its debts to NYIT with an immediate check of $250,000, and then nine payments of $125,000 each and a final sum of $875,000. The total of $2 million would be paid off by June 1988. As part of the agreement, Alex Schure resigned as chancellor of Nova, all NYIT trustees agreed to resign from the Nova board, and Abe Fischler and Mary McCahill left the NYIT board. Outside of the formal agreement, Nova stipulated that the university would pay Schure a full salary of $80,000 for one year and then half salary for five years, for a total of $280,000—an expensive buyout.[18]

One person on the Nova board, Tinsley Ellis, opposed the threatened lawsuit against NYIT. Ellis did not object to ending the association; he simply disliked the methodology. He thought any disclosures in court would embarrass Alex Schure and Nova University. Ellis said that Schure had allowed Nova to run its own programs and rarely interfered with the university's operation. Schure had come to the rescue at a time when Nova would have failed; he had been a very honorable man in his dealings with Nova and should not be demeaned in a legal action.[19] Fischler agreed with Ellis that Schure and NYIT had saved Nova on several occasions and that Nova would not be extant without their help. In that context, Fischler thought the original 1970 deal with NYIT was a good decision. Although there was some criticism of the generous payoff to Schure, Fischler thought it was a worthwhile cost as it helped free Nova from its federation with NYIT. The final understanding made certain that Schure and NYIT were paid back for their help and support.[20] In the final analysis, it appears that Nova repaid all of the money loaned to it by NYIT.

Nova University was on its own again. The school had weathered numerous storms from 1964 to 1985, and it appeared on many occasions that the university would not survive. But thanks to the tenacious leadership of Fischler and the board of trustees, a determination to succeed, and a series of saviors, Nova would now embark on twenty years of growth and prosperity.

6

Stabilization and Expansion
1986–1998

Nova University had finally extricated itself from what had become a restricting and controversial arrangement with the New York Institute of Technology (NYIT). Nova now had the freedom to chart its own course, but first had to put its financial affairs in order. The money from the Goodwin Unitrust had saved the day in the immediate term and allowed Nova to pay off some of its debt and open the law school, but money issues would continue to plague the university. In 1986, Nova's budget was in the black for the first time in its history, and the university moved confidently and enthusiastically into its first year unfettered by outside controls. The years from 1986 to 1998 would usher in a more stable era of growth and would set the stage for a period of extended success. The university was under the aegis of three presidents in those years: Abe Fischler, who left office in 1992, Stephen Feldman (1992–1994), and Ovid Lewis (1994–1997).

President Fischler recalled that the period from 1985 to 1992 demonstrated that Nova did not need a partner. The school could go it alone, and "the future was in our hands." To completely free itself from NYIT, Nova began paying off its debt and by 1992 had liquidated the debt. From 1986 on, Nova earned enough surplus money to expand its departments and develop new programs.

Fischler remained busy trying to keep the budget in the black and keep Nova moving forward. A typical day in the late 1980s included several daily meetings with his personal staff and weekly consultations with the administrative council. Because Fischler had performed almost all of the administration of the university by himself for many years, he needed additional executive support to run an independent and rapidly developing institution. Thus he increased the upper levels of his administration. Fischler explained that under his leadership the university was not organized in the traditional university style; rather, "it was organized as a business." The directors of the various centers reported directly to Fischler, but he saw his organization as more of a communications vehicle than a way of controlling how the directors ran their centers. Fischler did not want the faculty senate to have input on university decisions because he believed that "the academic senate is built on distrust and not on trust." In a business model, he thought, one should not allow the employees to make judgments on important matters. A benevolent dictatorship functioned more efficiently.

The president spent about 50 percent of his time in the community. "Part of that was friend making, part of that was giving visibility to the university, and part of that was trying to raise additional funds." Because Fischler thought the university president should be active in county affairs, he was on the board of directors of the chamber of commerce, the art museum, the Hollywood Medical Center, the Mailman Family Foundation, and the United Way. He wanted to make strong connections to the community and entice important people from downtown Fort Lauderdale to come out to see what Nova was doing.[1]

To increase public interest in Nova and to provide citizens with insight into world affairs, Stephen Goldstein, vice president for public affairs, set up the "Distinguished Speakers" series. The variety and excellence of speakers appearing in Fort Lauderdale would rival any university's speaker series in the nation. Beginning in 1980–1981 with news commentators Irving R. Levine and Douglas Edwards, the parade of celebrities and newsmakers from 1981 through 1988 astonished the local media. Noted politicians included former presidents Jimmy Carter and Gerald R. Ford; former secretaries of state Henry Kissinger and Alexander Haig; former secretary of defense James R. Schlesinger; Zbigniew Brzezinski, national security advisor to Jimmy Carter; Tip O'Neill, speaker of the U.S. House of Representatives; and Ramsey Clark, former U.S. attorney general. Also on the list were well-known writers such as playwright Edward Albee; authors James Baldwin, Kurt Vonnegut, Ellen Goodman, and Isaac Bashevis Singer. From television news came David Brinkley, Eric Sevareid, John Chancellor, Alistair Cooke of *Masterpiece Theater*, Diane Sawyer, and Charles Kuralt. Foreign visitors also graced the podium: Edward Heath and Harold Wilson, former prime ministers of the United Kingdom; Helmut Schmidt, former chancellor of West Germany; and Kurt Waldheim, former secretary general of the United Nations. Political commentators included William F. Buckley Jr. and George Will.

Covering more mundane matters were Miss Manners (Judith Martin) and gossip columnist Ann Landers. Controversial speakers included G. Gordon Liddy and Benjamin Spock. Other invitees were General William Westmoreland, actress Joan Fontaine, and opera singer Beverly Sills. This list does not come close to covering all the distinguished visitors who appeared in Fort Lauderdale, but it gives one some idea of the broad coverage and significance of the speaker's series. Nova was no longer intellectually isolated[2] and had been able to convince some of the most powerful personalities in the world to come to a relatively unknown university. Nova had an additional cultural impact on the community by sponsoring art shows, musical programs, a performance by the Fort Lauderdale Opera Company, and creative arts workshops.

In mid-June 1988, rumors persisted that the Florida state university system wanted to take over Nova. Those rumors proved reliable when the state legislature passed a bill that directed the Board of Regents, the administrative body for the state university system, to "investigate the feasibility of incorporating Nova University into the state university system" as the tenth state university. One legislator argued that Nova's law school and undergraduate programs were attractive and successful, and since Nova was already getting state funding for its liberal arts program, it made sense to purchase the university and incorporate Nova into the state system. Initially the idea would be for Nova to remain a separate institution, retain its autonomy and its property, and continue to offer innovative courses, but still be a semiautonomous part of the state system. Nova officials were less than enthusiastic about the idea. Abe Fischler had no comment, August Paoli felt "strongly" that Nova should remain private, and Tom Panza, a Nova attorney, declared, "Nova is not for sale."

Backers of the proposal asserted that Broward County had been underserved by the state in higher education and that local citizens deserved the presence of a state university. A positive factor for the state was that it would cost the Board of Regents virtually nothing to convert the already existing private school into a public university. The Nova Board of Trustees rejected the state's offer and expressed no interest in giving up the school's independent status. President Fischler commented that the school might lose its creative edge if taken over by the state: "I see nothing for Nova to gain if we were to become part of the state's system." Shortly thereafter, the State Board of Regents recommended that Nova remain private and independent. Some legislators thought the decision was a disservice to Broward residents, whereas trustee Ray Ferrero Jr. wanted to maintain a middle ground where Nova would be independent but still receive state money.[3]

In 1989, Nova University celebrated its "Quarter-Century Anniversary," the twenty-five years since its founding in 1964. President Fischler's report to the university and the community recorded the school's progress since 1964 and documented the impact that Nova had in each of its critical areas: teaching, research, community service, cultural affairs, and finances. Fischler commented that Nova was the second largest independent university in Florida, had awarded more than 20,000 graduate and undergraduate degrees, and offered degree programs in twenty-two states. He stressed Nova's innovative qualities and its ability to make education accessible to many students without compromising standards. In an attempt to promote Nova and boost morale, Fischler made clear that the financial impact Nova University had on Broward County was considerable. By 1989 it had become one of the largest employers in the county, with 886 faculty and staff and a payroll of $25.4 million. In twenty-three years, Nova had spent more than $332 million for goods and services, salaries, and construction. In 1986–1987, the university's revenues exceeded $46 million, the second year that the school posted a surplus.

Fischler touted Nova's advances in research in addictive and eating disorders, family violence, and neurological syndromes. The Oceanographic Center had made major discoveries in the assessment of coral reefs and coastal dynamics. The president expressed pride in Nova's community services, particularly the publicly funded not-for-profit mental health facility in the school of psychology.

In the future, Fischler expected Nova to capitalize on breakthroughs in teaching and learning through advances in technology while continuing its innovative curriculum. The university constantly stressed that "the student is the class" and that no student was lost in the crowd. Later on, this theme was developed with a thoughtful tag line for Nova publications: "Nova: Your Future, Your Terms."[4]

Law School

An important development for the university's future arose when Nova decided to move the law school from the Southwest Ninth

Avenue building to the main campus. The law school had been growing at a rapid pace since 1974, and in 1988 boasted some 770 students from twenty-two states and four foreign countries. Roger Abrams, the new dean of the law school, arrived in 1986 after earning his law degree at Harvard University and working for twelve years as a law professor at Case Western Reserve University in Cleveland, Ohio.[5] In 1988, the law school achieved an important academic distinction by being accepted into the prestigious Association of American Law Schools. Dean Abrams commented that the association accepted only the best schools and that this recognition was an important event for Nova. "It shows the world that we have arrived." What was really surprising about this honor, continued Abrams, "is that it is rare to be admitted the first time after applying."[6]

Nova law school had made progress in several areas since 1974. The school designed a new program called the Summer Conditional Program. The idea was to assist law students who did not score well on the Law School Admission Test (LSAT). The marginal students who did not score high enough on the LSAT but showed promise of being a high achiever were given the option of taking two law courses in the summer. If they scored a C-plus or better in the two courses, then they were admitted unconditionally to the law school. Ray Ferrero Jr. a member of the law school's board of governors, concluded that the law school made great progress from 1974 to 1989 and the school's reputation had improved.[7]

Nonetheless, the school still had a problem with its graduates passing the Florida bar exam. By 1989, the percentage increased to 79 percent, but Florida State, the University of Florida, and Stetson law schools had passing rates of about 87 to 88 percent. Nova, not pleased with its results, recommended better student preparation and looked at other ways to improve the scores.[8] Ron Chenail did a study on Nova law students in early 2000 to explain why they were not doing well on the bar. The study discovered that the one variable that predicted success on the bar exam was the student's grade point average (GPA) in law school. When a student's GPA dropped below a 2.5, the likelihood of passing the exam was not very good. The law school began to help the weaker students with their study skills, and the passage rate increased.[9]

In 1988, the school benefitted from a generous gift of $3 million from Shepard Broad. A legal and business pioneer in South Florida, Broad had given much of his time and resources to many charities and played a large role in the development of the area. An orphaned

Russian immigrant, Broad came to America in 1920. He graduated from New York Law School and moved to Miami in 1940. A founding partner in the Miami law firm of Broad and Cassel, he was a member of the board of governors of the Nova law school, a close friend of Ray Ferrero Jr., and had been a strong proponent of establishing the law school.

President Fischler called the $3 million gift especially welcome during the university's twenty-fifth anniversary: "It enables us to bring the law school back on campus, and that's important because of the synergy between the law school and the rest of the facilities on campus." The law school, no longer isolated on the east campus, would now be an integral part of the university and law faculty could interact more easily with the other centers. Since at this time there were only seven or eight buildings and several modular units on the main campus, the construction of the new law building marked a major step toward developing a sound infrastructure on the central campus. The planned three-story law center complex would include a library, academic and administrative wings, classrooms, and an extensive computer research center.

Dean Abrams commented that Broad's gift was "another important step in the growing recognition of the law center as a law school of the first rank." Fischler announced that the Nova Center for the Study of Law would be renamed the Shepard Broad Law Center of Nova University and would be housed in the newly constructed Leo Goodwin Sr. Law Building. The Goodwin building was completed and opened for use in 1992.[10]

Naming the law building created something of a conundrum for university officials. The Goodwin Unitrust had given $5 million to the law school, so the law school named the new, yet to be completed building the Leo Goodwin Sr. Law Building. To accommodate Shepard Broad's gift, the university decided to rename the law school for him. Thus, the Shepard Broad Law Center was located in the Leo Goodwin Sr. Law Building. The widow of Leo Goodwin Jr. was apparently none too pleased with the new arrangement. To appease her, in 1992 Nova administrators named a new dormitory—the fifth student dormitory built—the Leo Goodwin Sr. Residence Hall.[11]

Campus Construction

In 1988, the campus remained "very rustic" and to some visitors had the appearance of a wasteland with a "parking lot to nowhere." Ron

Chenail recalled that several programs were still housed in trailers, affectionately known as modular units.[12] The decision to build the new law building set off a five-year mini-construction boom on campus.

In 1990, the university added the Parker Science annex, but a more intriguing development concerned a man named Joseph (Joe) Sonken, who wanted to give money to the University School. Initially, Sonken wanted his gift to be used for a field house at the University School, but Abe Fischler persuaded him to contribute to the completion of an urgently needed classroom building for the University School. Sonken agreed to give half of the money from the sale of a piece of property he owned. The land sold for $750,000, so Sonken's gift amounted to $375,000. Construction began in 1986 and was stopped once due to lack of money. The University School eventually borrowed money from several financial institutions and completed the classroom building in 1988.

One problem with the gift was that Joe Sonken, a short, cigar-chewing Chicagoan who owned the Gold Coast Restaurant and Lounge in Hollywood, Florida, had a rather unsavory reputation. A 1980 Pennsylvania crime commission reported that his restaurant was a meeting place for mobsters. The report said that Joseph Bufalino, the head of a Pennsylvania crime family, held court in the Gold Coast Restaurant, often meeting with Frank Gagliardi, a member of the New York Gambino family. Sonken, who had never been identified as a mobster, denied that he had ever hosted anyone involved in organized crime. While in Chicago, he had been arrested twice for tax evasion, but both charges were dropped. He also had been arrested for running a gambling house, but that charge was also dismissed.

The *Miami Herald* published a cover story on Sonken's donation. Sonken said he was just a working man who wanted to give money to a worthwhile charity. "If I'm going to give it," he said, "I want to give it to somebody I thought was worthwhile. It's only money. You can't take it with you."

Joseph Randazzo, headmaster of the University School, said that Sonken viewed the contribution as a "reinvestment in the future of the Hollywood area for the good years he has had in Hollywood." Randazzo called him a friend of the university and said that the school knew "nothing of his past other than that he's a fine upstanding businessman in the community."

The Nova University Board of Trustees apparently came to the same conclusion since there was no opposition to the contribution expressed in the minutes of the board of trustee meetings. Nobody commented on Sonken's character and nobody spoke out against accepting his money. Abe Fischler said Nova needed the money, and although he admitted that Sonken was a shady character, he had never been convicted of any crime.[13] So Nova gladly accepted the gift.

In 1992, the university's first edifice, the Rosenthal Building, was expanded to include what the university had intended it to be in the beginning: a student union. Nova added a dining hall, a full kitchen, a bookstore, and administrative offices. These additions, long overdue, were hailed by student and faculty alike.

Two other major buildings came on line in 1994 (the Horvitz Building) and 1996 (the Maltz Building). Nova had planned for several years to erect a three-story central administration building with approximately 75,000 square feet of space to house the expanding central administrative staff.

Fischler began the fund-raising process for the new administration building and targeted William (Bill) Horvitz as a major contributor. Horvitz, president of Hollywood, Inc., one of the state's largest and most prestigious community development firms, had been an early supporter of the South Florida Educational Center and a longtime member of the board of trustees at Nova University. As Fischler explained the situation, Horvitz had not given the university much money from 1964 to 1988, so Fischler and others began to pressure him to part with some of his substantial personal wealth. Horvitz tentatively agreed to a gift of $1 million, but Fischler would not accept that amount since Horvitz had great wealth and Fischler needed a larger sum to pay for the administration center. After years of cultivation by Fischler, Horvitz raised the offer to $2 million, but Fischler wanted $4 million. Horvitz finally ended up giving $2 million, but only after Abe Fischler had left office as president.

One person close to the discussion of the gift said that Horvitz did not give the money to Fischler because he was concerned about Fischler's financial acumen. Stephen Feldman, who followed Fischler as president, claimed some credit for the final gift of $2 million, but Ovid Lewis, the fourth president of Nova, thought that Horvitz had given the money because of "constant pressure from Abe. Abe was after Horvitz all the time." Fischler did the groundwork and Feldman closed the deal.

John Santulli, then vice president for facilities management, remembered that the original architectural plan for the Horvitz Building called for a three-story building with 75,000 square feet so there would be room for expansion. When Stephen Feldman became president in 1992, he wanted to build the administrative center as inexpensively as possible, so the final product was two stories instead of three. The William and Norma Horvitz Administrative Building became the capstone of the new campus. The distinctive two-story building was organized around a spacious, dome-vaulted rotunda that gave visitors a sense that important activities were taking place at Nova. The center was dedicated on October 27, 1994. Other major donors to the Horvitz Building were honored for their contributions in the form of the Harry and Edith Gampel Rotunda and the Jack and Bernice LaBonte Board Room. Local corporations also supplied funding for the center. The banking community also made sizeable contributions, evidenced by the Wachovia Financial Aid Wing and the SunTrust Institutional Advancement Wing.[14]

By 1997, in need of additional office space, the university rented facilities in the University Park Plaza Shopping Center adjacent to the main campus that housed classrooms, a microcomputer laboratory, the Institute for Learning in Retirement (later the Institute for Retired Professionals), and the offices of licensure and state relations, grants and contracts, and continuing education.

Nova University needed a much larger footprint as it began to grow, and the psychology department, shoehorned into the Mailman-Hollywood Building, had expanded and needed more space. Frank De-Piano, then the dean of the Behavioral Science Center, reestablished a former acquaintance with Anna Maltz, the widow of Maxwell Maltz, as a possible donor. Maxwell Maltz, who passed away in 1975, was a brilliant plastic surgeon, author, and lecturer. His 1960 book *Psycho-Cybernetics* sold more than 30 million copies. Maltz discovered that as a practicing plastic surgeon, he could correct a person's facial scars but could not heal the patient without also eliminating the inner scars. A change in the person's self-image was more important than any physical changes achieved by plastic surgery. *Psycho-Cybernetics* was one of the first "think positively and you will do well" books designed to improve one's self-image.

When Maltz retired from private practice, he and his wife bought a house in Fort Lauderdale. He soon learned that the Behavioral Science Center was doing research in behavior modification and biofeedback. The ever-inquisitive Maltz spent quite a bit of time on campus, lecturing infrequently and discussing psychology with students and faculty. Anna Maltz continued to live in Fort Lauderdale after her husband's death and years later remembered her husband's interaction with Nova. She was invited to several campus events and enjoyed her association with the university. DePiano had cultivated her friendship over the years, and since she and her husband had no children, DePiano suggested that a good way to remember her husband was to put his name on a new psychology building.

Prior to his death, a businessman and psychologist named Max L. Hutt had promised money to Nova. DePiano contacted Hutt's widow and tried to put the two potential donors, Anna Maltz and Anne Hutt, together. The two women did not know each other, but they immediately bonded. Their names were similar, they were exactly the same age, and their husbands were both named Max. Feeling a sense of karma, both women committed to putting up a new structure devoted to psychology. The money became available when both women passed away within months of each other.

By the time the building was complete, the Maltz estate had become worth more than the Hutt estate, so the 68,000-square-foot center was called the Maxwell Maltz Psychology Building and contained the Hutt Wing. The first floor housed NSU's Community Health Center, with administrative and faculty offices and classrooms on the second floor. The Maltz estate also included works by the famous surrealist artist Salvador Dalí. Maltz had operated on Dalí's wife, and Dalí had given the paintings to Maltz.[15] The paintings are currently stored at NSU.

In the 1970s and 1980s, the university's physical plant and maintenance had been neglected. The problem that John Santulli faced, as did everyone at Nova, was a lack of funding. Santulli understood that Fischler had to take whatever monies he could find and plow them back into the academic programs. At the time, it was the correct decision and made sense—there was little other choice. Nova's position was that landscaping and maintenance were not high priorities. This left very little money for the physical plant, and Santulli could not do a lot of maintenance. He did the best he could with what he had. As Nova's fortunes improved, so did the landscaping and maintenance of the facilities.[16]

Baudhuin Oral School

Once the Fort Lauderdale Oral School moved on campus in 1984 and became established as part of Nova University, the school made significant progress. The university wanted to expand the purview of the school to include children with communication challenges, and in 1985, the Oral School opened its doors to children with autism. In the late 1980s, the Baudhuin Oral School entered into a contract with the School Board of Broward County to provide publicly funded special education programs to preschool children with autism and related disorders.[17]

In 1989, when the Oral School won accreditation from SACS, the inspection team praised the school's ability to provide each student with an individualized program and allow them the freedom to develop to their potential. The final report also lauded the utilization of the resources of Nova University, especially graduate students who were doing practicums in education, learning disabilities, speech-language pathology, counseling, and psychology.[18]

Proud of its accreditation, the Oral School broadened its services by adding a new wing. Nova dedicated the new building in 1991 to Jack and Bernice LaBonte for their generous support of the school. The new structure would house the LaBonte Institute for Hearing, Language, and Speech and would help achieve Nova's goal of having one of the most comprehensive speech-language pathology centers in the country.[19] Supporters of the Oral School, intent on further expansion, organized a capital campaign committee. Dolphins quarterback Dan Marino, who had a son with autism attending the Oral School, sponsored a luncheon that attracted 350 guests and raised $31,000.[20]

By 1994, the Baudhuin Oral School had emerged as a national leader in the fields of special education for students with hearing impairments, autism, or attention deficit disorder (ADD). The Baudhuin School had increased its numbers to 160 students, and the LaBonte Institute had enrolled some 245 graduate students and offered the country's largest master's program in speech-language pathology. The Baudhuin School and the LaBonte Institute, according to Jack LaBonte, enjoyed "a productive partnership that reaches a level of excellence far beyond what would be possible for either facility working alone" and brought positive publicity to the university.[21]

University School

At the same time that the Oral School prospered and progressed, the University School did the same. The University School was originally designated as a demonstration school or a lab school. In the lab school setting, Nova graduate students in education could do their teacher training by observing classes, learning teaching methods, and gaining practical experience. By the mid-1990s, the University School had grown to include the Lower School with prekindergarten through grade five, the Middle School with grades six through eight, and the Upper School, or high school, with grades nine through twelve. The school grew from a small demonstration school to a major college preparatory school with significant resources and well-rounded programs while remaining "true to the founding principles." The University School was an integral part of Nova University and became one of the then-sixteen centers in the university. It was not, as some observers believed, "affiliated" with Nova; rather, it was part of the university but had the autonomy to run its own programs.[22]

Hurricane Andrew

In a state known for severe hurricanes, it seemed inevitable that Nova University would feel the wrath of at least one major storm. That event occurred on August 24, 1992, when Hurricane Andrew paid an unwelcome visit to South Florida. At 4:55 a.m. that day, the National Weather Service provided a snapshot of the menacing storm. The strongest winds were around the eye, "cutting across south Dade [County] like a buzz saw blade." By that time, Homestead, Florida, had been swept by the storm's most intense winds, with gusts up to 140 to 150 miles per hour. Hurricane forecasters described the storm as "powerful, nasty, compact, speedy, and surprising." The area had never experienced such a severe storm. It was only the third Category Five storm to make landfall in U.S. history.

At Nova University on August 22, officials feared the worst, although none of the experts could be sure about the final track of the storm. Freshmen had just arrived on campus for the beginning of the fall term, and the university decided that the safest place for the students would be in the Leo Goodwin Jr. Residence Hall, a solidly built, recently completed structure. Brad Williams, vice president for student affairs, remembered telling the students to gather up their mattresses and pillows and huddle in the hallways until the storm passed. The *Nova Knight* reported that although the students were frightened, "some people in the dorm seem to have had too much fun." One student commented that "with all the partying going on, it was like we forgot what was going on outside. It was kind of cool. We got to know each other." President Stephen Feldman, newly arrived in Florida from Connecticut, had no experience in preparing for hurricanes. After hearing about storm damage on the campus, he ventured out to check on the students. When he got to the dorm, he found that the students "were great. They were having a hurricane party. They didn't care." The new building stood up well to the wind and rain with little damage.

Fortunately for Nova, the storm veered south at the last moment and spared the campus much of the catastrophic damage sustained in Homestead. Andrew uprooted many of the palm trees recently installed by Feldman, but the maintenance staff was able to replant the trees and they survived. Damage to the trailers was significant, and there was some flooding and downed trees and power lines, but overall damage was minimal. Nova had escaped what could have been a disastrous situation. Just a few miles to the south, Andrew had done an estimated $30 billion worth of damage, at the time the most expensive disaster in U.S. history. More than 250,000 people were homeless, people were cut off from their families, there were many power outages and a large number of injuries, and citizens faced the long, heartbreaking task of restoring life to normal.

Nova closed for four days while crews cleared downed trees and debris from the grounds. Administrators arranged for classes to begin and allowed students to make up for lost time. They offered assistance to any students or faculty who needed help. Elaine Poff, who currently works in enrollment and student services, was impressed by Nova's quick response as the university became a family to those students who had recently arrived on campus and who had been so rudely displaced.[23]

The Stephen Feldman Presidency: 1992–1994

As early as 1990, Abe Fischler had begun to contemplate stepping down from office after twenty-two years (1970–1992) as president. At age 63, he decided that he had done what he had come to Nova to do. "I built a university that had stability, that I knew would make it," he said. He was also a little tired and knew the school needed new blood, new leadership. In his 1991 resignation letter to the trustees, Fischler wrote that it had been a "most rewarding and exciting twenty-six years at Nova University," and he had been "proud to have been a part of building an educational institution for the 21st century." Fischler planned to take a one-year sabbatical before resuming his research as a professor at Nova.

In a personal interview and in his letter of resignation, Fischler spelled out all of the accomplishments of his administration: a balanced budget for six years in a row (1986–1992) and the financial stabilization of the institution; the merger with NYIT; acquisition of the University School and the Oral School; an increase in student enrollment from 57 to 10,600, making Nova the second largest private university in Florida; the emphasis on technological development and innovative course offerings; expansion of the Oceanographic Center; new dorms, with the Goodwin dormitory under construction; renovation of the Rosenthal Building; the eventual completion of the Horvitz and Sonken Buildings; accreditation of the law school, which would soon be on the main campus with a new facility almost completed; moving the business school to the main campus; and, most important to Fischler, his development of the concept of clusters and distance education, which changed the face of American education. Fischler had few regrets about his tenure in office, although he believed that he had too frequently hired the second in command after an administrator had retired instead of bringing in new talent, and he thought he should have spent more time placing Nova's achievements before the public.[24]

In an interview with *Nova News,* Fischler said that he would miss dealing with 1,200 to 1,300 unique personalities and "having to cajole and coerce them into keeping the ship moving in a common direction. I won't miss the pressure of the office or attending so many functions as the university's representative." When asked about the negative press Nova had received in the past, Fischler admitted that in the beginning the university tried to oversell what it could deliver— Nova could not be the MIT of the South. Fischler noted that there was a negative reaction to off-campus learning because society was reluctant to accept a new concept. Nova offered bona fide education, he said, by "bringing it to people and utilizing the best instruction. It was a threat to the establishment. Today, much of what we are doing is being done by many other institutions and Nova is not considered 'way out.' Other universities are catching up to us."[25]

When his resignation became effective on July 31, 1992, colleagues, city and state officials, the board of trustees, and friends congratulated Fischler on his accomplishments. Jim Farquhar said, "One of the greatest things I did was to ask Abe to serve as chief executive officer. It's not always possible for academicians to cross the lines into administration. . . . I don't think Nova would have developed as it did without his leadership." Farquhar, in retracing Fischler's history with the university, said that Fischler mainly wanted to teach and do research, but agreed to be president for a couple of years in a time of need. "That turned into twenty-two years."

Mary McCahill, the first woman to serve as chairman of the board of trustees, admired Fischler's courage and vision and his successful incorporation of innovative delivery methods into education, which made quality education accessible. The *Fort Lauderdale Sun-Sentinel* concluded that Fischler's "adventuresome imagination and tenacious competitive instinct" were his primary tools for success. Ron Brown, although he often disagreed with Fischler, said he kept things rolling when it seemed impossible for Nova to survive. Fischler exhibited the kind of inspiring leadership and the dedication and intensity that made Nova successful. Brown added, "Otherwise it [Nova] would not be here. There were so many times that it could have disappeared. And there were times that he kept it going by shifting things from one pocket to another. Smoke and mirrors." In appreciation of Fischler's services, the Davie Town Council, by proclamation, renamed Southwest 30th Street, from College Avenue to University Drive, as Abraham S. Fischler Boulevard.[26]

There were, of course, detractors who, despite Fischler's yeoman service, thought he had outlived his usefulness. His opponents declared that he had not been a stellar financial wizard, and after twenty-two years the university needed a change in leadership.

The university launched a nationwide search for Fischler's successor. The board of trustees hired a search firm and appointed a committee to field applications, interview candidates, and reduce the number of viable candidates to five. Ovid Lewis was not hopeful that Nova could find an outstanding candidate. He said that Nova was still relatively unknown, had experienced financial difficulties, and was not in a position to attract the best people.

Stephen Feldman, who would become the committee's choice, arrived on campus for an interview on January 24, 1992. Feldman had dinner with Ray Ferrero Jr. and David Rush, the chairman of the search committee, and August Paoli. The following morning, Feldman met with Fischler. They discussed educational philosophies, and Fischler tried to determine if Feldman would be a good fit for Nova. A committee from Nova then visited Western Connecticut State University, where Feldman served as president. The group spoke with faculty, student leaders, and administrative personnel and reported that all recommendations were "very, very good." Ray Ferrero Jr. and Abe Fischler added their recommendations to those of the search committee, and the board of trustees offered Feldman a four-year contract. Feldman would assume his duties as president on July 1, 1992.

At the time, Feldman seemed a logical choice. He was a sitting president with eleven years in the post, so he had administrative experience and a strong business background suitable for a business-oriented school like Nova. Although Feldman came from a more traditional academic background, the committee felt he recognized that distance learning was a major component of Nova and had already been doing research in the field.[27]

After a lengthy discussion with his wife, Feldman accepted the job. He had done due diligence in researching Nova and was impressed with the implementation of its successful distance-learning program. Feldman liked Nova's inventive way of giving people an opportunity to earn a degree and recognized the university's success with the law school, the Oceanographic Center, the University School, and the Oral School. Feldman viewed Nova as an interesting and eclectic mix of different ideas and different institutes, both traditional and nontraditional. He admired the board of trustees for its business orientation and concluded that the school had been run in a businesslike way. As an independent institution, it had more flexibility and leeway in making decisions. Feldman knew about the past financial difficulties, but thought the school was now on sound footing and had tremendous potential. Broward County was a large and fast-growing county with its own airport, and Nova was the major educational institution in the county. For Feldman, as with Nova, his decision to come to Fort Lauderdale seemed a sensible decision.

Stephen Feldman, like Fischler, grew up in Brooklyn, New York. Born in 1944, he attended New York City public schools and matriculated at the City University of New York (CUNY) with an MBA and PhD in business, specializing in finance. He was a professor of banking, finance, and investments at Hofstra University from 1969 to 1977 and the coauthor of *The Handbook of Wealth Management*. In 1977, Feldman became dean of the business school at Western Connecticut State University and in 1981 became president of the school.

When Stephen Feldman accepted the office of president at Nova, he knew he needed to make the transition from running a public university to presiding over a self-determining private university. The new president realized that in public universities, the trustees were more political; in private universities, they were more business oriented. Feldman believed that "the business of education is business, the culture was a corporate culture. Nova would expand when it

Figure 6.1 Stephen Feldman, PhD, president, 1992–1994. (By permission of Nova Southeastern University Archives, Fort Lauderdale, Florida.)

defined itself as a business, its students as customers and the world of higher education as the competition." If the school managed its affairs efficiently, it would succeed.

Feldman believed that Nova needed to work hard to raise money for a road system on the campus, new dorms, and new buildings for classrooms. Feldman hoped to expand the size of the campus by one-third and to set up an endowment. Also on his wish list: better technology, expanding the undergraduate college and overseas programs, improving the landscaping to recruit new students, a good bookstore on campus, and more favorable press coverage for Nova.

During Feldman's abbreviated two-year tenure as president, he determined that as a CEO, he needed to spend more time with the trustees and businesspeople in the community and less time with students and faculty. He devoted much of his day to strategizing about the future, meeting with deans, raising money, and consulting with the administrative staff, most frequently with the vice president for development. He wanted to attend as many community events as possible because image and publicity went hand in hand and he wanted the public to be aware of what was going on at Nova.[28]

With a serious decline in undergraduate enrollment in 1992–1993, the university immediately set up an admissions council to coordinate with financial affairs, public affairs, and student life to make the university more attractive to potential enrollees. In addition, Nova coordinated marketing strategies and held a university-wide open house in 1995 that attracted more than 1,000 visitors. The university also tried to keep the tuition as low as possible so it could compete with the University of Miami, which was more expensive than Nova, and Florida Atlantic University, a much cheaper option than Nova. Feldman felt that it was "tucked in nicely between the two."

Feldman and the board of trustees wanted to tie Nova more directly to the people of Florida, so they chose an interesting group of citizens to recognize by awarding them honorary degrees in the 1994 commencement exercises. All had Florida connections. The list included Lawton Chiles, governor of Florida; Joycelyn Elders, the first African American U.S. surgeon general; Gloria Estefan, a Hispanic singer and community activist; Janet Reno, a Florida native and U.S. attorney general; and Don Shula, coach of the Miami Dolphins.

During his presidency, Feldman made most of the decisions on his own, leaving many of the details to his administrative staff. Feldman respected former President Fischler and had no objection to having him on campus. He later regretted that he did not consult Fischler more often, because the former president had such great knowledge of the school's history. Fischler indicated that while Feldman did contact him from time to time, they were not close and he did not offer much advice to the new president. During Feldman's time in office, his vice president for academic and student affairs was Ovid Lewis, the former dean of the law school. Lewis recounted that things went smoothly between him and Feldman, although there was no close personal relationship. The president usually requested that Lewis be present when there was an academic component to the meeting, so Lewis handled that part of the portfolio, discussing important issues with the deans and the faculty. Feldman rarely interfered with Lewis in his handling of that responsibility.

In April 1994, Lewis tendered his resignation effective December 31, 1994. When asked why he wanted to leave his post, Lewis said he never felt like he was an administrator. He loved teaching and wanted to get back to his first love. Feldman, who depended heavily on Lewis's academic expertise, wrote his vice president a letter, saying, "If I had a choice, I would reject your resignation and would force you to continue in this position." Feldman lauded Lewis for his remarkable contribution to the university over the past fifteen years, and noted that under his leadership the school had grown and prospered. He added that Lewis would be "sorely missed."[29]

One of President Feldman's early goals was to develop the physical plant while improving the landscaping and the general appearance of the campus. Alex Schure once wryly pointed out in the early years the campus bespoke poverty, and others ventured the opinion that even in the early 1980s it still looked much like an airfield. Feldman knew that first impressions were important. If the university looked like a first-class operation, then people would assume it was. If it looked fourth rate, they would assume it was fourth rate. The appearance of the campus was important to those visitors considering enrolling in Nova and to those contemplating giving money to the university. When the Horvitz and the law school buildings were constructed, Nova made certain that while the emphasis was still on the functional, the overall aspect of the structures would be more aesthetic and appealing to the eye.

The board of trustees supported Feldman's vision for a more attractive campus despite the lack of funding. Arvida, a Florida resort and real estate development company, advised Feldman that the best way to achieve success cheaply was to put in some grass and line the entrance, driveways, and circumference of the campus with trees. Feldman purchased trees wholesale and planted more than 800, mostly palm trees. Everyone seemed pleased with the campus transformation, and now Nova looked more like a real university. The staff and trustees took pride in the spruced-up appearance and said they felt more of a sense of community. The psychological impact of such a change is hard to gauge, but it certainly helped in recruiting students and faculty. Feldman asserted that the landscaping did not change the academics, but it created a better image for Nova, and in the early 1990s, that was a significant step forward. Feldman's ideal of a more aesthetic campus came to fruition in later years.[30]

Feldman had such a short tenure at Nova University that he did not have enough time to achieve many of the very ambitious goals he discussed when he took office. He participated in two major developments that overlapped presidential terms at Nova. He was on board when the agreement for the Miami Dolphins football team to move its practice facility on campus was finalized, but he was not part of the initial planning. Feldman participated in the planning stage for the merger with Southeastern University of the Health Sciences, a momentous decision that altered the future of Nova in many ways, but he was no longer around when the merger was completed.

Miami Dolphins Training Facility

In 1988, the Robbie family, owners of the Miami Dolphins professional football team, hired Eddie Jones as president of the football franchise. One of Jones's first tasks was to upgrade the training facility for the Dolphins. The team had trained at St. Thomas University for many years, but the location had become, according to Jones, "deplorable." The team did not have a lot of money to build a new facility, so Jones tried to get public money to erect the training center, but this attempt failed.

Jones's fortunes changed during a casual meeting of the board of governors at the Oral School. Dan Marino, the team's successful quarterback, was a member of the board. At the end of the meeting, board chairman Jack LaBonte thanked Marino for his help in raising money. LaBonte said, "You are helping us, what can we do for you?" Marino replied that the Dolphins needed a new training facility and asked LaBonte to call Eddie Jones to set up a meeting. LaBonte and Jones met and began discussing a possible move to the Nova campus.

LaBonte contacted Abe Fischler and asked if he had any interest in having the Dolphins locate their training facility on the Nova campus. At first Fischler said he did not have the time to work out an agreement, but LaBonte said he would broker the deal with the Dolphins. Fischler thought it would be a great idea but would be interested only if it did not cost Nova any money.

Eddie Jones of the Dolphins wanted a deal done as soon as possible, because in the era of free agency in football, a team could not be competitive without a first-class training facility. The team also needed a dormitory near the training center where the players could live. Nova would be a good fit as the team would later be able to use the Rolling Hills Hotel for a dormitory; it was one mile from the training center and had bus service to the campus.[31]

By February 1992, negotiations had proceeded apace, and since the Dolphins needed a training facility immediately, the conversations were put on the fast track. Jack LaBonte, the dominant force in the negotiations, had strong support from Dan Marino and Earl Morrall, a former Dolphins quarterback and the mayor of Davie. The Dolphins wanted Nova University to take the lead in planning, developing, and constructing the training center.[32] The original proposal called for Nova to build the facility, which the Miami Dolphins would then lease. The Nova University Board of Trustees agreed to explore the proposal so long as there was no cost to the university. To begin with, ten acres of Nova property on Southwest 30th Street were set aside for the Dolphins facility, and on May 30, 1992, the board of trustees ratified an agreement with the Miami football team.[33]

The final contract called for the university to build a facility that would initially cost $8.2 million. The Dolphins contributed $3 million, and the university sold $5.2 million in bonds. The team paid off the $5.2 million bond issue and agreed to pay Nova a yearly lease fee for use of the land and the facility. The lease agreement was for forty years. If the team ever abandoned the site and no other National Football League team could be found to replace the Dolphins, the university would take over the facility. The Dolphins paid all tax obligations and upkeep for the facility as if they owned it, although the buildings and the land were still owned by Nova University and would always belong to Nova University.

The Dolphins received a state-of-the-art training center and the university received a long-term lease, with the Dolphins initially paying $145,000 per year in leasing fees—a nice source of extra income for the university.[34] The new Dolphins training center included a main building of 56,400 square feet, with a two-story structure housing the team's executive offices, coaching and operations staff, and the training facilities. The bleachers could seat 1,000 spectators. The team later added 10,000 square feet for administrative offices and a highly visible pressurized air-conditioned bubble facility to allow for team practice in inclement weather.[35]

The benefits to Nova were considerable. The ribbon cutting for the new center on July 11, 1993, generated a great deal of publicity and visibility. Because the team was very successful and popular at the time, the new arrangement connected the university with the larger South Florida area. Feldman praised the relationship, as both the Dolphins and Nova University were dedicated to the area's vitality and economic growth and both institutions were committed to excellence. Nova was not as well-known as it could have been, so the two entities had agreed that whenever the Dolphins facility was mentioned, they had to call attention to the fact that it was located on the Nova campus. The training camp in the summer brought some 1,500 to 2,500 spectators to the campus each day for the team's twice-daily practices. Dolphins players helped Nova with its fund-raising and in other public activities. The Dolphins held football camps for kids at the training center, and the university occasionally used the facility's meeting rooms for social events.[36]

By any assessment, the deal with the Dolphins helped Nova. Nova needed the publicity, and it received the on-campus facility and the recognition at no cost. Nova had new practice fields and the Dolphins' help when it needed to raise money, but there were now ten acres of land unavailable for university development and expansion.

After completing the deal with the Dolphins, in a totally unexpected move, Stephen Feldman abruptly resigned as president of Nova on June 13, 1994. This was the second occasion in the university's history (Warren Winstead was the first) when a president had suddenly given up his position. University documents do not provide many details about the circumstances of Feldman's departure.

On June 8, 1994, in his annual performance review before an executive session of the board of trustees, the board determined that Feldman would not receive a "favorable review." This negative evaluation had the effect of dismissing him from the presidency. At the same meeting, the board appointed Ovid Lewis as interim president.[37] Apparently Feldman had asked for a vote of confidence during his annual review, but the board of trustees refused to give it to him. Feldman said that he left because he "succumbed to the call of private industry." He subsequently became vice president of Ethan Allen, a home furnishings and design company.

Why did the Nova board end Feldman's employment with the university? Some observers believed that Feldman had been the wrong hire and was simply not the right man for the job. He had to follow Abe Fischler, who had been president for twenty-two years. Fischler had been innovative and experimental and had built up a large group of loyal supporters. Nova was still in a transition period, and it is always difficult for a new leader to come in and promote a new agenda for any university. For Feldman, Nova was a different culture, much different from a public university. Feldman came from a traditional university where all the resources flowed through the president's office, and he did not change his modus operandi sufficiently to fit into a different type of school.

Feldman apparently did not have a good relationship with the faculty since he did not visit with them as often as they desired, and his interaction with the board of trustees may have been strained because of the way he viewed his authority. Two of his closest colleagues saw him as being too imperious as a leader. One person recalled Feldman explaining his way of running the university: "If I say it's green, even if it's yellow, I expect [my] employees to say it's green." Another incident had Feldman saying, "See that picture on the wall? If I say I don't like that, by tomorrow they will have it down."

Ovid Lewis did not see Feldman as part of the community of scholars and believed that his approach to governing—ruling by directive and edict rather than by consensus and persuasion—hurt his effectiveness as a leader. It appeared that Feldman, while personable, articulate, and intelligent, had simply not connected with the local community and after two years still seemed like an outsider. He had perhaps alienated some of Nova's most prominent backers with his haughty behavior, but all of this is conjecture. Whatever the circumstances, by June 13, 1994, Stephen Feldman was no longer president of Nova University.[38]

The Ovid Lewis Presidency: 1994–1997

As discussed earlier, Ovid Lewis had been dean of the law school and worked with Stephen Feldman as vice president for academic and student affairs. With Feldman's abrupt departure, Nova University was in a quandary. The university faced the very important SACS reaccreditation process and the beginning of the fall term without a president. The board of trustees had to act swiftly and concluded that it did not have time to conduct a national search. If the board intended to hire from within, there were few alternatives. Ovid Lewis was the logical choice. He had years of administrative experience as dean of the law school and as vice president; he was well-respected and "a proven commodity." He had worked closely with Feldman, knew more about the inner workings of the institution than anyone else, and would provide continuity.

One issue the board had to consider was Lewis's earlier declaration that he wanted to retire at the end of 1994. He stated that he did not consider himself an administrator and did not like fund-raising. The board was therefore unsure how Lewis felt about becoming president in 1994. When members of the board approached him about the job, Lewis reasoned that he had no choice but to accept the position, although it was not something he longed to do. He recalled, "What else were they going to do? This guy's [Feldman] going to be leaving. We're going to have a vacuum here. So I did agree to accept the position." Lewis viewed himself as an interim president because "I did not plan to stay on for very long."

The Nova Board of Trustees, on June 8, 1994, appointed Ovid Lewis as interim president. While Lewis had already stated that he did not plan to stay in the position for long, he strenuously objected to the interim title. The use of "interim" suggested that he was merely an acting president, and the title would undermine his authority and limit his long-term plans. Lewis refused to take the post unless he had the title of president of Nova University. The board of trustees removed the interim tag and Ovid Lewis became the fourth president of Nova University.[39]

When Ovid Lewis took over as president, he did not have many long-range goals. His first priority was to recruit "the best possible directors for the various programs." Lewis thought it was important for the university to hire "people who were more effective than we are, who are brighter. Sometimes administrators don't want to do that; they don't want to have competition as such, but I think it's good." Lewis knew that excellent directors could bring in top-notch faculty. He concluded that he accomplished his purpose by attracting such superior leaders as Joseph Harbaugh as dean of the law school, Donald Riggs to head up the library, and Randy Pohlman, who spoke the language of area business leaders, as dean of the business school. Harbaugh instituted the successful evening program for the law school.

Figure 6.2 Ovid Lewis, JSD, president, 1994–1997. (By permission of Nova
Southeastern University Archives, Fort Lauderdale, Florida.)

In 1997, Donald Riggs began planning a long overdue new library facility, which was approved by the board of trustees in 1998.[40] Riggs was also able to restructure and streamline several administrative positions.

President Lewis expected Nova to increase its support and services to the local community. Since South Florida had one of the largest retirement communities in the country, he saw a profound need to improve care for the elderly and organized a gerontology task force to develop the curriculum in gerontology. Nova set up the School of Social Sciences, which included the Institute for Service to Families to provide mediation services. Eventually the school offered an MA in gerontology and an MS in human services administration, along with new courses in death and dying as well as health and nutrition. Later, the School of Social Sciences evolved into the School of Social and Systemic Studies, which offered courses in conflict analysis and resolution, which used negotiation, mediation, and facilitation as an alternative to litigation.[41]

Shortly after assuming office, Lewis sat for an interview with a local journalist. Described as a "brilliant and eclectic lawyer, scholar, and educator," Lewis spoke briefly of his personal philosophy: "Do good. Avoid evil. Make the world a better place; be empathetic." He spelled out his role as president: "The name of the game is cooperation and synergy." Each program should be the best that it can be, and then all of the various programs should work together for the benefit of the university. Lewis favored academic cross-fertilization as he thought it counterproductive that every center seemed to be operating independently of one another. The computer science program should help all the other disciplines in their use of technology. The computer experts followed the president's suggestion by first developing the electronic classroom to enhance computer-based learning, and then creating a technological marvel, the virtual classroom. Lewis encouraged the law school to work closely with psychology and the medical school, and also share knowledge with other disciplines. He applauded the university's focus on distance education and its commitment to the idea that education should not be bound by time or place.

Lewis was mainly interested in the acquisition of knowledge, not just information. Knowledge enabled one to understand and use the information acquired. He proposed creating an institute on learning and an institute on pedagogy. The emphasis would be to analyze in-depth the learning process and then teach people how to learn and how to understand.[42] Lewis never got around to creating these institutes, but it gives one a sense of him as an academic and a scholar rather than an administrator.

Lewis's first major responsibility was to guide Nova through the important SACS reaccreditation process. Lewis knew that the inadequate library facilities would be a problem. SACS had previously urged Nova to do a better job of linking budgeting and strategic planning, especially resource allocation. To satisfy SACS's concerns, Nova set aside more funding for the library and to support planning strategies. Nova set up guidelines for grant proposals to be rated by priority and available funds. Lewis managed to organize the campus for the inspection team, and the entire process went very smoothly. In 1998, Nova gained regional reaccreditation for another ten years.[43]

Lewis next focused on Nova's overseas programs. He closed the fledgling program in Bogotá, Colombia, because, although it made money, it did not meet any of the required SACS criteria for accreditation. He faced a similar problem with the Panama program. The Panama Center did not have a full-time faculty or a library, required by SACS, so Lewis went to Panama to check out the program. The director, Martin Taylor, whom Lewis described as "a very strange fellow," met Lewis at the airport, handed him a revolver, and said, "Here is your gun." Naturally the scholarly and genteel Lewis was shocked at the necessity for packing heat and said his experience in Panama "was the closest thing to a western movie he had ever seen."

Lewis recognized that Taylor, who spoke fluent Spanish, had developed a strong board of advisors and made money for the university by attracting students from the Panama Canal Authority and the U.S. troops garrisoned in the area. However, when the United States began the process of turning the canal over to Panama and the U.S. Army Southern Command pulled out, the Panama Center did not have enough students to survive and the program closed down.[44]

During the Lewis era, improvements in the physical layout of the university included opening of the Center for Psychological Studies and the Community Mental Health Center. The University School, with strong support from Lewis, was selected as a National Blue Ribbon School of Excellence by the U.S. Department of Education and opened a school sports center. The Fischler Center for the Advancement of Education, still one of Nova's major moneymakers, moved to new quarters in North Miami Beach.

Remembering the founders' contributions to the progress of the university, Lewis inaugurated the Alumni Silver Medallion Award, given to the alumnus whose service and achievements added to the university's quality of life. Mickey Segal, who was retiring, was selected for her work with the Family Center, the Oral School and the University School. Lewis said, "Mickey will be missed, but she will never be forgotten. She has been the heart and soul of the Family and School Center. Childhood education would have been dramatically different in the nation had we not been blessed by Mickey's brilliance." Her father, A.L. Mailman, was posthumously awarded the President's Community Award for his work in mobilizing support for the university.[45]

Lewis constantly referred to Nova as a "university of professional schools" that needed to expand both the numbers and quality of its undergraduates. He praised the flexibility of the university, both in its desire to tailor courses to meet the student needs and its ability to make decisions without the hindrance of an entrenched bureaucracy.

On a typical day, Ovid Lewis would arrive early at his office and spend much of his time, at least twice weekly, meeting with deans. Lewis liked to have the deans discuss their agendas and activities with the other deans so that everyone knew what new proposals had been made. This was part of his theory of synergy: if you got the leaders talking about what they were doing, other centers might get involved in the new proposals. Lewis met with his cabinet at least once a week and had constant communication with the board of trustees. His meetings with the board were essentially informational. "You had to dance with the trustees, but they were virtually invisible," he said. Lewis viewed most trustee boards as rather passive; they met only once every two months for a couple of hours and the president usually had his suggestions accepted by the group.

As president, he was always available for meeting with students and faculty. He recalled that he "managed by walking." He thought it essential that students and staff saw the president and got to know him. It was very important that "you be visible and they know that you're concerned about them and their education." Unlike his predecessor, he often attended student gatherings and invited student organizations in to lunch with him. Lewis was aware that the students had frequently petitioned for a student union. He understood that the university had to provide social amenities to attract new students to the campus, and once students enrolled at Nova, the university had to maintain and expand those facilities.[46]

Student Activities Under President Lewis

Nova students and staff realized that the social situation on campus was not what it needed to be. The campus newspaper had long advocated for a student union, but Nova administration had other priorities. Some of the impetus for change came when Brad Williams was hired in 1989 to head the division of student affairs. He immediately noticed that there was no sense of a university, no spirit of unity or any cognizance of campus tradition. Students did not identify themselves as Nova students; their sense of place was tied to the law school or business school. They were law students, not Nova students. Williams set out to change this attitude.

When Williams began his job, there was little to work with in terms of equipment or student interest. Eventually, with constant effort, Williams organized the students into intramural volleyball and flag football teams. He was finally building a sense of community.

Williams decided to sponsor a "welcome back" party at the beginning of the 1989 fall term. He served food, decorated the area, put up posters, and hired a band. Williams was discouraged when only four people showed up. The following Monday, a student named Gina DeGiovani came by his office and asked if she and some of her friends could set up a beach party. Williams consented and promised to support the effort. That next Saturday, some 130 students showed up for the party. Williams then realized that social gatherings worked better if the students, not the dean, planned the event. His job was to encourage them to organize activities on their own.

On another occasion, a student named Rob Armstrong, an energetic young entrepreneur who acted as a deejay at some of the parties, proposed that Nova develop a campus radio station. Williams pronounced it a great idea and within a few years the radio station, later called Radio X (88.5 FM), had evolved from a dorms-only station to one that broadcast to all of Broward County.[47]

Brad Williams thought that developing fraternities and sororities on campus would contribute toward a greater unity of the student body while affording members new social outlets. He hired a young Scott Chitoff as the graduate assistant in charge of developing a fraternity and sorority system. When Chitoff began his difficult task, there was little knowledge of or interest in fraternities or sororities among the 550 to 600 undergraduate students since there had never been any Greek letter organizations on campus. Chitoff pitched a tent with a sign announcing "Greek Life at Nova," which elicited a strong response. Nova inaugurated the Greek system in 1993, and by 2012 there were eleven fraternities and sororities. Of these eleven, there were three Pan-Hellenic sororities, three fraternities, two Hispanic organizations, and three historically African American fraternities.

The hardest task for Chitoff was to persuade commuter students to get connected to the school and to return to campus after class for social activities, athletic contests, and games. He organized events like a twenty-four-hour softball game, homecoming celebrations, and concerts.[48] The university made some strides toward creating a social fabric on campus, but it was not until enrollment increased and the school had successful athletic teams that students had a sense that they were Nova students. By 2011, the social programs had expanded to the point where there were ninety-five staff members in the Division of Student Affairs.

From 1987 through 1998, Nova's athletic programs advanced from a minor presence on campus to an integral part of the university. In 1990–1991, Nova University joined with seven other NAIA schools to form the Florida Intercollegiate Athletic Conference (FIAC). In 1992, the FIAC changed its name to the Florida Sun Conference (FSC). That same year, the men's soccer team finished 11-5-3, and in 1993 the Knights baseball team and the women's volleyball team both won their first-ever Florida Sun Conference championships. In 1994, Nova added softball as its fourth intercollegiate women's sport, and one year later augmented the program with women's soccer. Women's basketball became the sixth women's sport in 1998. That same year, the softball team collected its fourth straight FSC championship. The university remained a member of the NAIA, but as the number of teams increased, the athletic director began discussions about becoming an NCAA Division II member.[49]

President Lewis approved of the athletic teams' progress and was cognizant of the students' concerns and goals. He had the same interaction with the university staff as he had with students. At the end of the academic year, he would send a nice note and a small gift to thank people for their hard work and achievements. Lewis also managed to send out birthday cards to everyone. "I thought it was important that they know they counted," he said.[50]

By the middle of 1998, Ovid Lewis had begun counting the days until he could retire. He resisted going to public events and community meetings. He would occasionally visit some civic clubs, like the Rotary Club, and made short appearances at other groups, but he "did not particularly enjoy it," he said. Lewis revealed that he would have been much happier if he had remained dean of the law school.

Lewis, as was his wont, often understated his abilities, but it was generally recognized that he was not as good an administrator as he was an academic. Everyone agreed that he was a brilliant scholar and a true academician. Ed Simco called him "a very bright individual, very capable, very knowledgeable, and not against innovation, but still sound in the academics." Virtually everyone liked and respected Ovid Lewis, but he always preferred to write and think and grew tired of administrative duties that did not interest him. In May 1997, Ovid Lewis agreed to step down as president of Nova Southeastern University on January 31, 1998.[51]

Despite his desire to leave administrative worries behind, Ovid Lewis made significant contributions to Nova University. He increased the size and prestige of the law school, providing it with able and stable leadership. As vice president for academic and student affairs, he strengthened the liberal arts program, gave significant aid to the computer center and computer science, and worked hard to expand distance learning at Nova. While vice president, he actively participated in the dramatic merger with Southeastern University of the Health Sciences. Lewis was the point person in the SACS reaccreditation effort, and he saw Nova become the largest independent college in Florida. Under his leadership, Nova increased funding for the library and opened the first dental school in the country in twenty years. Nova either completed or dedicated more than $70 million in construction during his reign. Lewis worked assiduously to expand social and athletic opportunities for students and continued to encourage them in their academic pursuits.

Ovid Lewis never gave up on his grand desire to spread knowledge and learning. After his retirement he ventured the opinion that the business mentality had become too strong at Nova and overshadowed the academic side of things. He remembered one trustee coming up to him after a meeting and chiding him for "using such big words." Taken aback by the trustee's pronouncement, Lewis explained that he just "tried to use the appropriate terms." It was just this sort of anti-intellectual attitude and lack of sophistication that distressed Lewis.[52] Nonetheless, when his university called him to serve in a time of uncertainty, he twice rose to the challenge and gave the best that he had.

7

Merger with Southeastern University
of the Health Sciences
1994

A momentous event that dramatically altered the university's history occurred in 1994 when Nova University became affiliated with Southeastern University of the Health Sciences to form a new institution, Nova Southeastern University, Inc. The new arrangement added a medical school, college of pharmacy, college of optometry, college of allied health, and college of medical sciences to the Nova campus.

The merger between Southeastern and Nova University began with the vision of Morton (Mort) Terry, a medical student at the Philadelphia College of Osteopathic Medicine (PCOM). Arnold Melnick, a close friend and classmate, would later join him in Miami to help realize Terry's dream. There were only five medical colleges of osteopathic medicine in the United States, and when the two young doctors of osteopathy (DOs) graduated in 1945, there were few internship possibilities.

As Melnick and Terry began their careers, a medical degree in osteopathic medicine was denigrated and not accepted by most MD or allopathic medicine programs. Allopathic medicine, practiced in the great majority of hospitals in America, is a system of medicine that combats disease by using remedies such as drugs or medicine. Osteopathic medicine is based on the theory that diseases are due chiefly to loss of structural integrity, which could be restored through manipulation of the musculoskeletal system. DOs also prescribe drugs and perform surgery. Osteopathic physicians tend to treat patients holistically.

Figure 7.1 Morton Terry, DO, chancellor, Health Professions Division, 1994–2004. (By permission of Nova Southeastern University Archives, Fort Lauderdale, Florida.)

Stanley Cohen, an educator, had extensive contact with medical students and was one of the earliest members of Mort Terry's staff. He described osteopathic physicians as "hands-on" people, more oriented toward family practice. They believe in sitting down with patients and listening to them, because they know that the patient's description of their symptoms would help with diagnosis. The emphasis is on humanism, compassion, and empathy for patients. DOs use traditional medicine, but also utilize manipulation of the neuromuscular system.[1]

When Melnick and Terry began their practice, many MD programs in the country discriminated against osteopaths. Some allopathic hospitals did not allow DOs to practice, nor could DOs visit their own patients when they resided in an allopathic hospital. The Dade County Medical Association prohibited MDs from "consulting or consorting" with DOs. Those violating the rules could be penalized or ostracized.

Mort Terry decided to move to Miami, Florida, where he built a very successful internal medicine practice. He collaborated with other osteopathic physicians in the area and established an osteopathic hospital, Biscayne Osteopathic General Hospital, a 100-bed general community hospital founded in 1953. In 1960, the privately owned hospital moved to North Miami Beach, was renamed the Osteopathic General Hospital, and became a not-for-profit institution.

As osteopathic medicine made perceptible strides in the Miami area, Mort Terry anticipated the day when he could establish an osteopathic medical school in Florida. His attempt to get financial aid from the state legislature failed, so Terry recognized that creating a Florida-based osteopathic medical school would have to be a private endeavor. He focused his time and effort on accomplishing that goal. In spite of many financial and political barriers that thwarted his plan to build an osteopathic medical school, Terry doggedly forged ahead. He refused to accept defeat and viewed challenges as learning opportunities.

In 1979, Terry, as chairman of the Osteopathic General Hospital board, arranged for the sale of the hospital to American Medical International (AMI) for $12 million and put that money into a foundation to create an osteopathic medical school. In 1980, Terry contacted his old friend Arnold Melnick, who had recently retired as a practitioner in Philadelphia, and asked him to help launch the new medical college. Terry initially told Melnick that as founder, it would be more appropriate for Terry to be dean of the new college rather than president, but Melnick protested, saying, "With your business sense, with your drive, and with your desire to get the school started, you should be president." So Terry became the president. Melnick agreed to be dean of the college and moved to Miami in June 1980.[2]

Starting a medical school with limited funds and virtually no outside support would be a daunting task for a team of experts, let alone for two doctors with a lot of chutzpah and little else besides an unrelenting desire to reach their goal. Because Terry began his medical school as a private institution—the Southeastern College of Osteopathic Medicine (SECOM)—he did not have to jump through all the hoops that would have been required if a state university wanted to set up a medical school. The time it took to establish a medical school was, on average, five to ten years; Terry and Melnick did it in a little over one year. With the assistance of a secretary and a finance officer, the two men began by planning the curriculum and hiring some faculty. The only people available were DOs who practiced locally. Most were willing to use their free time to instruct the new students. Terry and Melnick used a renovated auxiliary building across from the Osteopathic Hospital for classrooms, labs, and offices. They later added two buildings to house a library and auditorium.

The two founders, known as risk takers, decided to open their medical school in the fall of 1981 with an initial class of forty students. The state and the American Osteopathic Association (AOA) objected, telling them that they should start with fifteen to twenty students in the first group and slowly build the number over the years. Terry and Melnick ignored the admonitions and enrolled forty students the first year, increased the number to sixty in the second year, accepted a class of eighty students by the third year, and ended up with 100 students in the fourth-year class. By 1981, as promised, SECOM had enrolled its first class and was open for business, a remarkable achievement. The venture succeeded in part because Mort Terry was a very persuasive, influential, intelligent, hard-working leader. SECOM graduated its first class in 1985 and in the same year received accreditation from the AOA.

When American Medical International (AMI) decided to close the osteopathic hospital it had purchased in 1979 for $12 million, Terry repurchased the five-story hospital for the bargain price of $4 million. The building needed refurbishing, but now SECOM had sufficient space to expand.

As SECOM slowly developed its medical college, some hospital administrators complained that they could not find enough pharmacists in South Florida and asked if SECOM could start a pharmacy school. There were only two pharmacy schools in the state, one at the

University of Florida (UF) and one at Florida Agricultural and Mechanical University (Florida A&M) in Tallahassee, but none in South Florida. A new school of pharmacy had not been created in the United States in the previous eighteen years. Terry was undeterred. Within fifteen months, with the able assistance of Frederick (Fred) Lippman, a practicing pharmacist and a member of the state legislature, SECOM created a board of overseers, organized a new pharmacy school, and in 1987 enrolled its first class.

Shortly thereafter, SECOM began planning a college of optometry since there were none in the state of Florida. The new college was quickly established and began training new optometrists and receiving financial assistance from the state of Florida. The state had been paying from $6,000 to $8,000 a year to support Florida residents who were being trained in Houston and Memphis, the nearest schools of optometry. It did not make sense for the state to support an external school, so the state legislature took the money that went to Houston and Memphis and used it to support students at the SECOM College of Optometry. The extra money helped SECOM solidify and enlarge the fledgling school, and since there was a critical shortage of pharmacists, the state also supplied money to train students in that profession. Terry had foreseen the need for more opticians and pharmacists and moved promptly to fill the void.

With the College of Osteopathic Medicine, the College of Pharmacy, and the College of Optometry, SECOM met the state requirements for university status and became Southeastern University of the Health Sciences.[3] With the success of the first three colleges, Terry began to think about founding other health profession colleges. In the early 1990s, Southeastern introduced the College of Allied Health, which had programs for physician assistants, occupational therapists, and physical therapists. Next, SECOM developed the College of Medical Sciences, home of the school's interdisciplinary PhD faculty. The faculty in this college provided all the basic science courses needed by the other four colleges and also developed degree programs of its own, such as a master's degree in medical sciences. Terry argued that basic sciences were the same; each student in all four colleges had to learn microbiology, physiology, and pathology. Rather than have each college hire an anatomy professor (or a biochemist or a microbiologist), Terry would hire an anatomy professor to teach anatomy classes in each of the colleges. After all, a course in anatomy was essentially the same whether it was taught to a physician or an optometrist. Terry's system of assembling a basic science faculty to cover all the courses reduced the cost of education; his system was replicated by medical centers all over the country.[4]

Now that Mort Terry had established a successful medical center, he began to consider retirement and worried about the future of the institution. "I wanted to find another university to merge with, to create a partnership that would make both institutions stronger." In late 1989, the dean of the College of Medicine at the University of Miami met with Terry and his group, but the two universities did not reach an agreement. Terry then sounded out Nova University as a possible partner. Abe Fischler had known Terry slightly, and the two men discussed the possibility of a merger. Fischler expected Nova to control the new school, and at the time Terry did not want to be in a position of inferior authority.

A merger decision for Southeastern remained in abeyance until Terry was invited to attend the presidential inauguration of Stephen Feldman on the Nova University campus. Feldman had already visited the Southeastern campus and knew a little about Terry's institution. He and Terry had gotten along well, but had not talked about a merger. The exact details of the conversations that occurred during the inauguration vary according to the source. There is general agreement, however, that at the investiture, Terry wrote down on the back of the inauguration program eleven points as guidelines for a possible merger with Nova University. Terry handed the program to David Rush, a trustee of both Nova and Southeastern, who would play an important role in getting the two sides together. Rush took the program to Robert (Bob) Steele, the vice chairman of the Nova Board of Trustees, and Ray Ferrero Jr., then chairman of the Nova Board of Trustees, and asked them to look at the proposal. Rush said, "If you're interested, let's do it." David Rush took the idea to Feldman, and the new chief executive responded favorably.

Ray Ferrero Jr. brought the concept to the Nova Board of Trustees, and it made sense to them. Southeastern had an endowment of around $35 million, its medical school and other colleges had been accredited, its buildings were paid for, and the university was debt-free. Southeastern earned around $3 million a year, and its future seemed assured since it had many more applicants for medical school than it could accept—3,000 applicants for 100 openings. Southeastern's training emphasized geriatrics, rural medicine, and minority medicine—important niches for family medicine in South Florida. Employment projections in the health care industry showed an increase of 50 percent in the next fifteen years.

Southeastern was eager for a merger since it probably could not grow without an affiliation with an established university. While osteopathic medicine had been unfairly criticized in the past, by the 1980s the profession was accepted in allopathic hospitals, and a large number of Southeastern graduates did their residencies in MD programs. What was not to like? Southeastern University had exactly what Nova needed—cash, stability, and a medical center that would potentially earn significant sums of money in the future.

The Nova board wisely decided to expedite the process as much as it could. There was some opposition to a merger: a few Nova trustees feared that the medical school would control the new university, and on the Southeastern side were misgivings about connecting with a school that had been fiscally unstable. The positive aspects of the deal, however, outweighed the few naysayers.[5]

Formal merger discussions began in late March or early April 1993. Mort Terry was heavily involved in the talks and nothing was agreed to without his approval. Arnold Melnick was one of the primary participants for Southeastern; Nova was represented by Ovid Lewis, Joel Berman (the university's attorney), and Feldman. Melnick and Terry trusted and liked Ovid Lewis, who worked on most of the academic issues. Melnick had to report all details to Terry, while Lewis furnished the facts to Feldman, Ray Ferrero Jr., and the Nova Board of Trustees. No final decision would be made without agreement from the two major players, Terry and Ferrero. The other representatives worked out the details of the agreement.

When Melnick came to the table, he had three major requirements before consultations could proceed. He and Terry wanted the new university's name to be Nova Southeastern University; this was presented as a nonnegotiable item. After a brief discussion, everyone agreed to that provision. Melnick also wanted Southeastern to have representation on the new board of trustees for the combined universities. Both sides agreed that Southeastern would have five members on the Nova Southeastern University (NSU) board for a limit of ten years. The Health Professions Division (HPD) would have its own advisory board, and Nova could have representation on that board. Terry would be chancellor of HPD at NSU, with Arnold Melnick as provost. Terry would have his own budget but would use Nova's accounting system and would report to Feldman. The HPD was designed to be semiautonomous, and the deans of the various colleges would report to Terry, the chancellor. Melnick's third request was that all Southeastern employees be blended into the Nova University retirement system. That too was accepted by everyone. Southeastern's employees were taken care of; none were fired.

The final transaction took nine months because there were other complicated aspects to the bargaining, including blending the by-laws, reconciling retirement plans, and keeping psychological studies at Nova University and not the HPD. One interesting aspect of the merger was Southeastern's insistence that the HPD not be allowed to award any allopathic or MD degrees. Southeastern agreed to sell its southeast Miami campus and move to the Nova campus. The old campus buildings were never sold, but instead were rehabilitated, and the Fischler School moved its headquarters there. Other issues resolved were faculty and staff salaries (Southeastern's salaries were significantly lower than Nova's), faculty status, redistribution of over-head costs, and fringe benefits.

Southeastern University was happy to move to the Nova campus and agreed to pay to build the new medical center. The merger was a win-win for both schools. Nova had the land but could not afford to build a medical center. Southeastern had the money but needed the land and the affiliation with Nova. Southeastern selected the architect and construction company and agreed to pay $25 million to erect a building to house the HPD. Southeastern also agreed to spend $5 million for a parking garage, $1 million for moving expenses, and $1 million for equipment. John Santulli recalled that the final cost for the new medical campus was around $40 million. Both sides agreed to split the legal costs. The formal agreement became effective on January 1, 1994. The flexibility of both private institutions allowed the merger to proceed in a rapid and orderly fashion. This decision was yet another example of Nova University taking a measured risk. The Nova board approved the final agreement and plan of merger on September 27, 1993.

For its part, Nova spent $3.175 million to purchase twenty-one acres of land on the campus periphery. The site was contiguous to the original campus and the HPD had a separate entrance. When the initial building was completed in 1996, Southeastern moved its entire medical center from Miami to the Nova Southeastern University campus.[6]

Shortly before the merger, Terry and Melnick decided they wanted to extend the size and reach of the new Health Professions Division and were considering either a veterinary or a dental school. Terry favored a dental school, although no new dental schools had been built in the United States in the previous twenty-six years and some nine schools had closed in recent years. Everyone felt that Mort Terry was crazy to start a dental school in light of the recent closings. Terry, however, had done his due diligence. He discovered that most of the dental schools had closed due to mismanagement and loss of federal funds. He also learned that half of the U.S. population had no access to dental care, there was no dental school in South Florida, and there was a large and growing population in need of increased dental services.

A report from the Dental College Task Force confirmed Terry's views. The study concluded that since there would be a significant number of applicants for admission to a school of dentistry, the school could charge $25,000 a year or higher for tuition. The Dental College Task Force saw numerous opportunities for new revenue with the large underserved patient pool in South Florida and voted unanimously to recommend establishing a college of dental medicine. Ray Ferrero Jr., after viewing the study, was convinced that it was a good idea and urged the board of trustees to go forward with it. Some board members warned that it would cost a lot of money and would take several years to build, but Terry and Ferrero brushed them aside. As Ferrero later commented, "It turned out to be a great decision." The new dental school building was built and paid for by the Health Professions Division and admitted its charter class in August 1997. The College of Dental Medicine now has approximately 3,000 applications for 125 to 130 openings, as well as 300 dental chairs reserved for serving a large number of indigent patients in South Florida.[7]

The new Health Professions Division immediately prospered. As soon as the various schools opened, the number of students increased every year. By September 1994, there were 104 new students in the College of Optometry, and the occupational therapy program had forty-eight new students. This boded well for the future of the merger. By 1995, HPD had a health maintenance organization (HMO) type of university health service for employees and families and opened the HPD Broward County Center. A new pharmacy was completed in May 1998 as HPD grew and developed new facilities and new programs. When the new health complex opened on June 22, 1996, there were six buildings with 900,000 square feet of usable space on twenty-one acres. The physical plant and the 1,600-car parking garage were adjacent to the five-story administration building, which housed the administrators for all the colleges and a cafeteria. The assembly building housed ten auditoriums (one with 500 seats, one with 250 seats, and eight with 120 seats) that would accommodate

1,750 students. The laboratory and library facilities were opened, and finally, HPD constructed the clinical building, the Sanford L. Ziff Health Care Center, which housed the primary care practices. One year later, the HPD added a structure for the dental school.[8]

The new arrangement with Nova University helped Southeastern University of the Health Sciences because it was now affiliated with a university, had a medical complex contiguous with the Nova campus, and could grow and expand as part of a major university. There was a huge upside for Nova. The new buildings and the medical center assets were worth around $60 million. This infusion of new money bolstered the university's bottom line. Nova Southeastern University now had a good credit rating and could borrow money whenever necessary. Even as late as 1994, Nova's finances were still uncertain, but with the advent of the medical school, NSU would be able to earn sums of money that the original founders could not have imagined. Fred Lippman indicated that the HPD contributed some $5 million to $6 million a year to NSU's coffers.

Nova Southeastern University was now a full, comprehensive university. Some called it a multiversity. NSU's newfound status enabled it to attract better-quality students, like the premed and prelaw students who wanted to attend medical or law school on the same campus. The original concept of the university had undergone a dramatic and irrevocable change. It was now a much different and more diverse university from what it had been just three short years prior to the merger and drastically different from the Oatmeal Club's original concept. NSU could provide medical and health care services to the entire county and finally earned the prestige it lacked in the past. As Ray Ferrero Jr. said about the merger, in this case one plus one did not equal two; rather, one plus one equaled ten. The new coalition demonstrated once again the opportunistic nature of a flexible administration at an independent university. Certainly Nova was in a much better economic situation in 1994 than in 1970 or 1985, but it would not have seen such dramatic growth from 1998 to the present and would not have been able to broaden its mission without the Southeastern merger. Nova no longer needed saviors; now it needed supporters.

SACS immediately recognized the official name change to Nova Southeastern University and continued Nova's accreditation after the merger with Southeastern. The SACS approval was essential for the ultimate success of the newly merged institutions. SACS did indicate that NSU would have to complete a self-study and achieve reaffirmation of accreditation within five years.[9]

Fred Lippman called the agreement a "great symbiosis," as both schools were born and bred as underdogs. Nova had been derided and demeaned because it invented distance education. Southeastern had been vilified because it created a school of osteopathic medicine and did not train "real" doctors. Mort Terry and others at Southeastern saw in Nova a group of like-minded people who were innovative fighters and believers in what was right.[10]

All of the achievements by SECOM and the new Health Professions Division could not have been accomplished without Mort Terry's leadership and vision and Arnold Melnick's assistance. When Terry passed away at age 82 on January 11, 2004, he received numerous accolades from colleagues and friends. Ray Ferrero Jr. called Terry a valued friend and colleague and praised him for leaving behind an extraordinary professional legacy that would continue to live on through the colleges and numerous programs that comprised NSU's Health Professions Division. Ferrero said, "There are few people in life who have done as much for their profession and medical education than Dr. Morton Terry." Other members of the Health Professions Division lauded his integrity, loyalty, humanity, motivation, and respect for what was right.[11]

With the merger with Southeastern a fait accompli, Nova cast its eyes to the future. Nova would never be the same, both in name and in its objectives. A university that began in 1964 as a vision of a group of Fort Lauderdale businessmen had been changed beyond their imagination. From 1998 on, NSU would embark on a journey of remarkable growth under a new and hard-driving leader, Ray Ferrero Jr.

8

The Ray Ferrero Jr. Presidency

After Ovid Lewis's retirement, the NSU Board of Trustees had the responsibility of choosing the school's third president since 1992. Under these circumstances, the designation was easy since the new leader was already on campus and was more familiar with the institution than any other candidate. Ray Ferrero Jr., a distinguished attorney, had been a member of the Nova University Board of Trustees since 1984 and served as chairman from 1988 to 1995. In 1997, he was chairman of the executive committee and the finance committee and had a thorough knowledge of NSU's recent history.

Some board members approached Ferrero in 1997 to see if he had any interest in becoming the new president. Ferrero said he would be willing to discuss the matter. He knew that NSU had great potential but believed the school had lost direction in the previous few years, and he thought he knew a successful way forward. Ferrero's interest was contingent on two conditions made prior to formal discussions. He had to clear the matter with his wife and his law partners, and he needed enough time to close his law practice. He also had to be certain that all board members, not just a few, favored his candidacy. The NSU board agreed to those terms, and on May 17, 1997, chose Ray Ferrero Jr. as president-elect to assume office at the conclusion of Ovid Lewis's term on July 1, 1998.

On December 1, 1997, the board of trustees decided that Ovid Lewis would leave office six months earlier than originally agreed upon. He would vacate the office on January 1, 1998, instead of July 1, 1998, and would receive a leave of absence and a sabbatical

Figure 8.1 Ray Ferrero Jr., JD, president, 1998–2010; chancellor, 2010–present. (By permission of Office of Publications, Nova Southeastern University, Fort Lauderdale, Florida.)

at full pay to carry him through December 31, 1998.¹ Ferrero would assume the mantle of the presidency on January 1, 1998. It is unclear exactly what role Ferrero played from June 1997 until January 1, 1998. The *Miami Herald* claimed he had been running the university from June 1997 while continuing his role as vice chairman of the board of trustees.

In selecting Ferrero, the trustees had made a wise choice. Not only was Ferrero intimately acquainted with the university, but he also helped guide it through several difficult patches: the end of the merger with NYIT, the association with Southeastern University of the Health Sciences, Stephen Feldman's resignation, and other key events. He had been on the board of governors for the Shepard Broad Law Center since 1978 and had a thriving law practice as a partner in the Fort Lauderdale firm of Ferrero, Middlebrooks, and Carbo. As former president of the Broward County Bar Association and the Florida bar, he was well connected and well known around the state.

When NSU announced Ferrero as the new president, there were protests from some in the academic community. Critics said that NSU had not conducted a national search, that Ferrero had no academic background, and that he did not want faculty to be included in the process of shared governing. William D. Horvitz came to the defense of the hire: "He comes to us as a known quantity, rather than bringing in some educator from a far-off field who doesn't understand the way this school works."² The board of trustees decided that it would be more practical and safer to select one of their own, especially someone with Ferrero's skills and experience.

Like Abe Fischler and Stephen Feldman, Ray Ferrero Jr. was born in New York City. He attended public schools in Queens through high school and received his undergraduate degree in business administration from St. Johns University in 1955. Ferrero's father was a first-generation Italian American; his mother was one generation removed from Europe. His parents taught him strong values, a solid work ethic, and an interest in education. Ferrero remembered that his parents "encouraged us to obtain the best education possible, believing that with an education you could accomplish anything. They taught us to respect the worth of people, irrespective of where they came from or who they were." From 1955 to 1957, Ferrero served his country in the U.S. Marine Corps, leaving the corps as a captain. He earned a JD degree from the University of Florida law school in 1960 and after a short stint in Miami began practicing law in Fort Lauderdale in 1963.³

When Ferrero took the reins of the newly reorganized university, NSU was the largest private independent university in Florida, with fifteen colleges, a student enrollment of 15,500, an annual budget of nearly $200 million, and some 1,800 faculty, staff, and administrators.[4] Ferrero's first report to the board of trustees on January 26, 1998, emphasized his desire to work out more partnerships with private and public universities. Ferrero gave fulsome praise to the dual admission programs that had been established at NSU, as they led to a marked increase in undergraduate applications and in the quality of the students.[5]

Ferrero, described by the *Miami Herald* as a "robust, ferocious fireball," listed his main goals as president: to increase fund-raising efforts, seek out new grants and scholarships, create endowed chairs, and lobby his educational ideas before the Florida legislature. He wanted to lift the university back to the cutting edge of distance-learning technology, a concept Nova pioneered in the 1970s but had somewhat neglected in recent years.[6]

Ferrero's formal investiture as president occurred on November 6, 1998, during what the university called the "Celebration of Excellence." In his first state of the university address, Ferrero spoke to more than 900 faculty, students, and alumni. In leading NSU into the new millennium, the president recognized that Florida would experience an enormous demand for education at the college and postgraduate level in the next ten years. The number of new students would overload the system, and there would not be enough state resources to take care of all the new applicants.

Ferrero proposed an alternative to the traditional means of providing education. Instead of building new public universities at a huge cost to the taxpayers and continuing the "needless duplication of programs"; Ferrero recommended a statewide collaborative effort among public and private institutions to increase educational resources. Independent institutions like NSU should be considered as equal partners with the community colleges and the state university system in meeting the challenges of higher education. The Florida Resident Access Grant, worth $1,800 per student in 1998, had been designed by the legislature to defray the cost of educating Florida citizens in private schools. Ferrero insisted that it would be much cheaper in the long run if state taxpayers were to financially supplement independent institutions for taking in some of the students desiring an education in Florida.[7]

When Ferrero became president, he faced what he believed to be an underperforming institution. He thought that some elements within the university were malfunctioning or nonfunctioning and perceived that some employees had not grown with the university. He felt there was no overall blueprint for NSU's future, and as a result, the university had not realized its full potential.

Ferrero, in attempting to change NSU's direction, held a series of meetings with staff, faculty, and the board of trustees to discuss the university's direction and how it would get there. First of all, NSU would remain a private not-for-profit university. Ferrero's new plan envisioned NSU collaborating more with private and public institutions and public corporations. Ferrero wanted to reach out to the eastern part of Broward County and hoped to become the county's university. He constantly stressed that NSU needed to branch out and "be more visible in the state from the standpoint of being a valuable asset for the education of Floridians."

Ferrero understood, perhaps more than any of his predecessors, that NSU lacked a core physical infrastructure. He recognized that previous presidents simply did not have the wherewithal to build new structures, but now NSU needed superior facilities to house the university programs. Instead of increasing NSU's endowment, Ferrero decided to embark on a huge building program. From around 2000 to 2011, NSU built almost 2,000,000 square feet of facilities and by 2012 developed a physical plant that would meet the institution's needs for the foreseeable future.[8]

As Brad Williams and others noted, at this particular time Ray Ferrero Jr. was the best man for the job. Observers saw Ferrero as more aggressive and visionary than past presidents, and they knew that with his personality and contacts, he would rally people in favor of the university.[9] Ferrero had a plan to lift NSU into a higher echelon in university circles and immediately set out to bring in a team that would work toward that goal.

Ferrero began his tenure at NSU with four major appointments that would prove crucial to the success of his presidency. First and perhaps most important, he persuaded George Hanbury, then the city manager of Fort Lauderdale, to accept the position of executive vice president. As Ferrero pointed out in his announcement, Hanbury had worked in city managerial positions for thirty years and would do an excellent job of managing a new "city," namely NSU. This choice would prove to be momentous as Ferrero and Hanbury made an excellent team. Ferrero would articulate a vision, and Hanbury would make it happen. Three other crucial selections were John Scigliano as vice president for academic affairs and technology and executive provost. Scigliano had been instrumental in creating one of the first online graduate programs in the United States. Ferrero chose Fred Lippman as executive vice chancellor and provost of the Health Professions Division. Finally, Norma Goonen, a first-generation Cuban American, took over as dean of the Farquhar Center for Undergraduate Studies.[10] The appointment of these capable and professional subordinates allowed Ferrero to concentrate on the big picture.

A typical day for President Ferrero began at five a.m. He worked at home for an hour or two and arrived at his office at 7:30 a.m. His day was filled with strategic planning and meetings with staff, faculty, and visitors. Several nights a week, he attended university-related events and met constantly with potential donors. Ferrero said that university presidents always had to be thinking about fund-raising and "friend-raising." He was usually one of the closers in the quest for a gift because a donor "wants to look the president in the eye and understand the gift is going to be meaningful and going to be appreciated."[11]

Ferrero tried to improve the flow of communication between the central administration and the various centers, and he wanted to forge a consensus—a shared vision—on the future of the university. He held town hall meetings with faculty, staff, and students to ascertain their views of NSU's future. Ferrero opposed a faculty senate, but he did consult with the dean's advisory council and the faculty advisory council.

Ferrero believed in having continuing contracts for faculty and strongly opposed tenure for any faculty other than the law school— the ABA required tenure for law faculty as part of accreditation. He believed that there was no longer a fear of a professor losing one's job for unpopular and controversial comments, and if there were a threat, the faculty member always had legal recourse. In Ferrero's opinion, professors with tenure often became too comfortable in their job, did not keep up with the literature, and had a tendency to stagnate. He believed that a secure lifetime university appointment offered less incentive to perform at a high standard.

Several of NSU's full-time faculty aired some vigorous complaints about conditions at the university. They expressed anxiety about job security. They argued there was not enough time for research and that faculty did not have enough input into university governing and decision making. The professors carped that teaching loads were too high, there was no clear-cut grievance policy, and too many part-time teachers were being hired to save money. The faculty's primary concern was job tenure, and they concluded that the only way to protect their positions and have their grievances resolved was to form a union. The faculty felt they needed greater job security due to the capricious nature of contracts, which varied widely from center to center. They asked NSU's Board of Trustees to recognize them as a chapter of the United Faculty of Florida.

When recognition from the NSU Board of Trustees was not forthcoming, the faculty applied to the National Labor Relations Board, which authorized a faculty vote on whether to join a union—in this case, the United Faculty of Florida. Only full-time faculty members were eligible to vote. Nova administrators pointed out that the use of adjunct and part-time faculty allowed a private university the flexibility it needed to thrive financially and that the faculty's fears of job security were groundless. "Why should they be concerned about job security if there's no history in this university of that being as issue," asked President Ferrero. When the vote was taken, a majority of the faculty voted against the union.[12] The negative vote did not end the controversy, however; some faculty still worried about their jobs, and some continued to gripe about a lack of faculty input into university decisions.

Alvin Sherman Library, Research, and Information Technology Center

The university library had been neglected over the years and needed immediate improvement. The library had been housed in various buildings all over the campus and its holdings, it was generally agreed, were inadequate. President Abe Fischler, lacking sufficient funds, did not see a need to build a large facility; it would be a waste of money since technology would soon enable researchers to read books, journals, archival materials, and other resources online.

When Ray Ferrero Jr. took office, an idea promoted by Samuel Morrison, then director of the Broward County Library System, had been making its way through the administrative levels. The concept was for Broward County and NSU to build a new library as a joint-use facility. Morrison said that the idea originated with Donald Riggs, who had previous experience in building libraries and had been appointed as NSU's vice president for information services and university librarian. Morrison and Riggs began discussing the idea in the late 1990s, but nothing was done until Ferrero became president. Ferrero dusted off the concept and began talking to key people to see if a joint-use facility might solve NSU's need for a new library.

Morrison believed that the general public, small business owners, and researchers should have access to a major university collection. Riggs and Morrison set out to persuade the Broward County Board of County Commissioners that this joint venture would be a great thing to do.[13] The two sides had a common goal: the county needed a new library in the western part of the county, and NSU wanted to consolidate its various libraries into a larger building. They realized that an alliance would enable them to achieve an objective that neither entity could afford on its own.

Frank DePiano gave much of the credit for the proposal's implementation to Ray Ferrero Jr., who had the credibility and influence to bring everyone to the table. Ferrero turned to George Hanbury, who, as the former city manager, had inside information about how the county commission functioned and the technical knowledge to work out a final contract. Hanbury recalled that Ferrero asked him to lead the effort to get approval of a unique proposal: a private not-for-profit university with a public library.

Hanbury visited each of the county commissioners and explained that the county would get a major research library that would be open 100 hours per week, unusual for the public sector. All county residents could get a library card and have full access to the collections, databases, and library services. There were many hurdles to overcome, and negotiations went on for six months. The politics of sharing revenue, facilities, and a parking garage between public and private entities made the discussions difficult, but the two parties eventually decided that the county would pay half of the construction cost of the library and a parking garage.[14] Ferrero, Hanbury, John Santulli, Tom Panza, and others received credit for pulling off the deal, but none of it would have been possible without input and support from Morrison and Riggs.

On December 14, 1999, the NSU Board of Trustees and the Broward County Board of County Commissioners unanimously approved a forty-year agreement between Broward County and Nova Southeastern University for the construction and operation of a joint-use 325,000-square-foot, full-service library, research, and information technology center to be built on NSU's main campus. The university would supply the land and be responsible for building construction.

The project included a 1,525-space parking garage. The new library was a demonstration of a new kind of partnership between a private university and a public entity. The building would have five floors, four of which would be built out, with space for more than 1.4 million volumes, a 500-seat auditorium, and two exhibit galleries, along with twenty electronic classrooms and Internet access with 1,000 user seats.

Donald Riggs judged that the new facility would enable Broward County and NSU to serve their users more effectively and that both entities would realize benefits that neither could achieve alone. Ray Ferrero Jr. called the new building "the intellectual center of our community" and welcomed all county residents to use the facility. Broward County was responsible for 40 percent of the annual operating costs for the first four years. After that, the library would electronically tally the number and types of users and apportion the operating costs accordingly.[15]

Ground was broken in early 1999, and the building was completed and opened for use on October 8, 2001, just fourteen months after work began and less than two years from inception to completion—by any standard, a remarkable achievement. The final cost of the largest library building in Florida: $43 million. When completed, the new library also featured the Rose and Alfred Miniaci Performing Arts Center, children's and young adult sections, wireless Internet access, a cafe, 700 computer workstations, study rooms, meeting rooms, and multimedia rooms. This would be the first jewel in Ferrero's building program, and it set the standard for future facilities.

More than 7,000 spectators attended opening ceremonies on December 8, 2001. Visitors were given guided tours of the library; children were treated to a special book reading. President Ferrero remarked that he was thrilled to see "our vision become a reality, and in an even grander form than we ever imagined. This incredible new library will impact the lives of thousands of people in and around the university and the community." Florida Education Secretary Jim Horne lauded the joint venture as a "shining example of the way government and the private sector ought to cooperate." He saw the library as a portal to knowledge and culture and encouraged students "to blaze their own electronic trails."

Most visitors were interested in the electronic classrooms, first pioneered by Nova in 1985. The "e-classrooms" contained the most cutting-age computer equipment, providing instant access to the Internet using wireless technology while erasing some of the traditional boundaries of learning. There was also a special e-classroom designated for children under twelve.[16]

In 2003, the library received a gift of $7 million from longtime South Florida real estate developer Alvin Sherman. A highly decorated World War II pilot, Sherman flew thirty-five combat missions and received the Distinguished Flying Cross. He formed the Development Corporation of America (DCA), which specialized in low-cost, single-family detached homes, and became a leader in the south Florida real estate market. A witness to NSU's beginnings, Sherman was impressed by NSU's rapid growth and excellence, especially for an independent university. Ferrero, the main cultivator of Sherman's friendship, gratefully accepted his gift. It would benefit the university and all county citizens, as libraries, said Ferrero, are the "center of learning for all of us and serve as a bridge to the past as well as to the future." In recognition of Sherman's generous gift, the library was named the Alvin Sherman Library, Research, and Information Technology Center.[17]

The joint-use library venture has had some financial problems over the years. Difficult economic times forced the Broward County Board of County Commissioners to cut back on the county's annual funding. Despite the cuts, the library at NSU has managed to stay open the agreed-upon 100 hours per week. As of 2011, the library has issued 60,000 library cards to county residents. The main benefit to NSU was a new high-tech library that is both functional and aesthetically pleasing. The library strengthens the university's ties to the community and encourages people to visit the NSU campus to discover the opportunities it offers.[18]

Business School

The school of business had a more difficult road to success than the law school. The business school, then known as the Center for the Study of Administration (renamed the School of Business and Entrepreneurship in 1982) first taught students in 1971. From 1971 to 1982, the school's offices and classrooms were scattered throughout the campus; they were housed in modular units prior to moving to better facilities on the east campus. The center offered graduate programs in business, human resource management, and public administration. The center developed one of the few weekend MBA programs for working professionals in the United States.

The business school had some difficulty raising money in its formative years. In 1987, the Glenn and Lucy Friedt Family Foundation agreed to give $1 million for a building to house business courses. The amount was contingent on Nova matching Friedt's gift. Although the university targeted wealthy businesspeople in the area, in March 1991 President Abe Fischler informed the Friedts that Nova had been unable to raise the matching dollars stipulated in the agreement.[19]

Although the business school did not receive large sums of money in its early years, those large donations were soon to be realized. The business school had become a leader in distance learning, with more than forty off-campus U.S. and international locations. Positive changes in the school occurred after Ovid Lewis chose Randolph (Randy) Pohlman as dean. Pohlman earned a PhD in finance from Oklahoma State University, had been dean of Kansas State University's college of business administration, and worked as a senior executive for Koch Industries, the second largest privately held company in the United States. Pohlman became dean in July 1995 and began putting his corporate, academic, and entrepreneurial experience to work.

Pohlman helped revamp the MBA program and promoted executive training programs for area corporations. When Pohlman resigned after fourteen years as dean, the school had grown from 1,300 to more than 6,000 students, had expanded its program offerings, and the students enjoyed learning in the new 261,000-square-foot Carl DeSantis building. Dean Pohlman was succeeded by Michael Fields, who earned a PhD in marketing from the University of Arkansas and had been dean of the college of business administration at Central Michigan University.[20]

As dean, one of Pohlman's first tasks was to raise funds for a new building on the main campus. Fortunately, generous donors in the area helped Pohlman realize his goal. One such benefactor was H. Wayne Huizenga. Described as "one of the greatest deal makers of the twentieth century," the self-made entrepreneur had an unprecedented business career, having created three Fortune 500 companies. He developed Waste Management, Inc., into the global leader in the waste industry; he was CEO of Blockbuster Entertainment before selling it to Viacom for $8.5 billion in 1994; and he was the founder of AutoNation, Inc., at the time the world's largest public automobile dealership. He brought major league baseball to South Florida as chairman of the Florida Marlins. He owned the Florida Panthers of the National Hockey League and the Miami Dolphins of the National Football League.

The Horatio Alger Association recognized Huizenga for his numerous business achievements and charitable donations. He is a five-time recipient of *Financial World Magazine*'s CEO of the Year award, and in 2005 Ernst & Young honored him with its World Entrepreneur of the Year award. Huizenga's community involvement included membership in many civic organizations, such as the Salvation Army, the Boys and Girls Club of Broward County, and the Florida Council of Economic Education. The Huizenga Family Foundation gave $1 million each to the United Way of Broward County, a Broward County homeless shelter, and an African American research library in Fort Lauderdale.[21]

Huizenga became interested in Nova because of its roots in Broward County, the business school's entrepreneurial theme, and his friendship with Ray Ferrero Jr. In September 1999, Huizenga and his wife, Marti, donated $4 million to NSU to help finance a new building that would return the graduate school of business to the main campus in Davie.

Both Ferrero and Pohlman acknowledged the Huizengas' leadership and generosity. Ferrero was satisfied that the new link with the business community on the east side of Fort Lauderdale would go a long way in making NSU Broward County's university. Pohlman declared that the relationship between the Huizengas and the school was a natural fit, "as both had built their success upon a belief in entrepreneurship and innovation in business." In Huizenga's honor, the business school was named the H. Wayne Huizenga School of Business and Entrepreneurship. The gift was made without any conditions, and Huizenga did not request that the school be named for him. In 2011, Huizenga and AutoNation pledged a significant gift for the Pathway Scholars program to benefit students who are financially or otherwise disadvantaged.[22]

The total cost of the new business school building was estimated at $14 million. Huizenga's gift was important, but there were other significant contributors as well. Carl DeSantis, founder and chairman of Rexall Sundown, a leading developer, manufacturer, and marketer of vitamins, nutritional supplements, and other health products, came up with $2 million. The new building housing the H. Wayne Huizenga School of Business and Entrepreneurship was named the Carl DeSantis Building. August Urbanek, a financier and member of the NSU Board of Trustees, contributed $1 million; the university named the Entrepreneur Hall of Fame Gallery after him. Harris W. "Whit" Hudson, vice chairman of the board of AutoNation and Republic

Services, gave $2 million for the Hudson Center of Entrepreneurship and Executive Education. Leonard Farber, a decorated World War II vet and developer of more than forty-five shopping centers, donated $1 million for the Leonard and Antje Farber West Hall.[23]

The university broke ground for the DeSantis Building and the H. Wayne Huizenga School of Business and Entrepreneurship on January 24, 2002. At that time, the school had more than 2,000 students and 9,000 alumni and offered master's and doctoral programs. The Hudson Center of Entrepreneurship and Executive Education made nondegree executive education programs available to interested businesspeople. In addition to the weekend MBA program, the doctoral division enabled students to earn degrees in business administration, international business, and public administration.

The DeSantis Building opened in spring 2004 and added a second gem to the campus. Dean Pohlman said the building "meets the needs of the future with cutting-edge technology for our students, yet honors the past and those who have helped us get to where we are today." The 261,000-square-foot, five-story facility is built around a central three-story courtyard enclosed in a glass atrium. The 2,000-square-foot marble entrance, surrounded by columns and glass walls, is a spectacular introduction to the building. The imposing columns, the cherrywood furniture in the classrooms, and the overstuffed leather chairs and couches strewn throughout give the appearance of an upscale office building. Business major Keith Dixon pronounced the arrangement as "very conducive for learning." The new structure included general-purpose classrooms, compressed video and teleconferencing classrooms, a lecture theater, computer labs, conference facilities, and administrative and student offices. The building is also home to NSU's Graduate School of Computer and Information Sciences.[24]

Over the years, the business school has done an excellent job of offering educational advancement for individuals working full-time. Zeida Rodriguez, who now works as a recruiter for the business school, earned an MIBA, a master's degree in international business, in the weekend program. She took two classes of two hours each on Friday night, and then came back all day Saturday for eight hours. She was in class for a total of twelve hours during the weekend. Zeida liked the small classes and the ability to keep working while pursuing a degree, and she appreciated the contacts she made with other full-time workers.[25]

Charles Shirley went to work for SunTrust Banks in Fort Lauderdale and was one of the first students in the executive MBA program.

He concluded that the course content was challenging and that the material encompassed the same ground that a traditional MBA course would cover. Shirley appreciated that some of the teachers were active in their professions and could give real-life examples of things he needed to know. He would often apply what he learned in class to his work back in his office. He valued his experience at NSU, kept in touch, and ultimately became president of the alumni association.[26]

Like Charles Shirley, Paul Sallarulo gained valuable knowledge in the business school. He received a graduate degree in business while working full-time. It gave him the confidence to become an entrepreneur. Proud of his degree and his special connection to NSU, Sallarulo later became chairman of the board of the Huizenga School and currently is on the NSU Board of Trustees.[27]

In these three cases, the business school did its part to help each individual advance his or her career. In return, the school received long-term commitments from its former students.

At the time of this writing, in 2012, the Huizenga School of Business is one of the larger business schools in the country, serving more than 6,600 bachelor, master's, and doctoral students and offering fourteen MBA programs, including conflict resolution and global management, as well as a master's in accounting and public administration. All courses offer flexible formats: students can choose full-time, part-time, days, evening, weekends, online, or a combination of those options.

The school's mission continues to be individual personal growth and professional development in business, academia, government, and nonprofit organizations. The success of the courses is realized when students apply their knowledge to create value in their respective businesses. To assist their students and faculty in acquiring this knowledge, the Huizenga School invites world-class businessmen such as T. Boone Pickens, Jack Welch of General Electric, and Mike Jackson, CEO of AutoNation, to share their experience and ideas.

An important new department in the business school was the Huizenga Sales Institute. When asked what skills their employees lacked, several Florida businesses replied that sales training was a serious need. In response, the Huizenga School opened the Sales Institute on the third floor of the DeSantis Building. The institute spans 8,200 square feet of space and includes sixteen mock sales rooms with video-conference capabilities. The new courses include an MBA in sales and an MBA in sales management.[28]

Athletics: 1998–2012

The NSU sports programs continued to grow, and one of the most significant changes occurred in 2002, when the school was granted full NCAA Division II membership. The National Collegiate Athletic Association (NCAA) is a voluntary organization of about 1,600 schools committed to maintaining athletics as an integral part of the educational experience. Division II is one step above NAIA, but does not require the huge amount of money and large stadiums necessary for participation in NCAA Division I. NSU remained a member of the Sunshine State Conference (SSC). President Ray Ferrero Jr. expressed pleasure at being part of Division II but did not anticipate that NSU would expand to Division I due to its low undergraduate enrollment and the prohibitive cost of building up the necessary athletic resources.[29] In July 2003, Michael Mominey was promoted to director of intercollegiate athletics at NSU. He added women's rowing and reinstated men's cross-country and women's tennis.

Brad Williams, worried about students connecting with NSU's sports teams, decided that a new mascot might be in order. When quizzing students about the current nickname, the Knights, he found that 41 percent of them did not know the athletic team's moniker. Williams put together a school spirit task force to increase knowledge of and participation in sports. A contest for a new school mascot garnered 447 entries. The final choice was narrowed to two—the sharks and the stingrays—and 83 percent of the student body voted for the sharks. Williams approved of how the contest created interest and energy on the campus. The students liked the new mascot so much that they raised money to have a Swedish sculptor build a shark statue, which now stands outside the Don Taft University Center.[30] NSU's new symbol gave the university community a sense of identity and helped unify the campus.

The athletic programs at Nova went on to national prominence in several sports. The women's golf team won four straight national championships (2009–2012). In 2009, the NSU women's rowing team won the Varsity 4 title at the 2009 NCAA Division II national championships. In 2008, the women's softball team was ranked number two in the country and the men's golf team won two SSC titles. In 2012, the men's golf team finished first in the Division II championships. By 2012, the sports facilities had been upgraded and included a new natatorium, a baseball complex, a new basketball arena, a soccer complex, and other venues. In 2010, Ray Ferrero Jr. boasted, "For the past five years, all sports, men's and women's, have seen the overall grade point average for NSU student athletes exceeding 3.0, and they are graduating in time. That is huge."[31]

The crowning achievement for students and athletes was the long-awaited, urgently needed university center. The complex took fifteen years from planning to fruition. Construction began in fall 2004, and the structure opened its doors in August 2006. The planners thought it would be a good idea to put the new complex, the campus energy center, next to the library, the intellectual center of the university, as the student center would create a sense of community. The center's location was designed so that students from the dorms would pass through the center on their way to the library. The 366,000-square-foot multipurpose facility would be a centerpiece of the Davie campus. The 4,500-seat sports arena/convocation center allowed NSU to host concerts, special events, lectures, and conferences. The new building would be the focal point for student life and redefined the university's interaction with students, faculty, and the surrounding community.

The new facility contained a performing arts theater, the student information center and card office, the student development and activities offices, the Flight Deck Lounge, the student union, and a food court. The design incorporated a modern health and fitness club with a gym, racquetball and squash courts, and a rock-climbing wall. NSU's certified athletic training staff housed its sports medicine services in what was known as the RecPlex.[32]

In 2009, three years after the completion of the center, Don Taft, a South Florida businessman, donated money to NSU, which renamed the university center as the Don Taft University Center. At Taft's request, NSU declined to reveal the amount of his gift, but said it was in the "multiple millions" and was one of the largest donations the university has received. George Hanbury said Taft was the epitome of the old saying "you make a living by what you get, but you make a life by what you give." Thanks to the influence and generosity of Don Taft and the Taft Foundation, NSU became the permanent home of the Special Olympics Broward County.[33]

Student Activities

While the Don Taft University Center was a wonderful campus addition for students, President Ray Ferrero Jr. and NSU also moved

swiftly to meet the housing needs of incoming students. NSU increased
its on-campus living capacity by erecting the $45 million high-rise
Commons Residence Hall in 2007. The university wanted to grow its
undergraduate population, and the new coed dorm, with 525 beds,
met the need.[34] NSU also upgraded living quarters for graduate students. In 2007, NSU purchased the Rolling Hills Hotel for $12 mil-
lion. It consisted of one seven-story tower and one three-story tower,
which were converted into a plush graduate residence hall with 373
beds. A renovated pool and the frequent Shark Shuttle service to campus, one mile away, made this an ideal choice for graduate students.
By 2011, approximately 1,500 students lived in campus dorms.[35]

Ferrero and others have emphasized that one future objective for
NSU is to increase its undergraduate population to achieve a better balance with graduate students, perhaps eventually achieving a
sixty-forty split without reducing the number of graduate enrollees.
Since the professional programs are oversubscribed, any growth at
NSU would more logically take place at the undergraduate level. Provost Frank DePiano said new undergraduates at NSU should expect a
much more personal education, with smaller classes and more interaction with faculty than one would find at a large public university.
NSU has developed a $21 million scholarship fund to help defray the
cost of the private institution. DePiano expects NSU to recruit higher-
performing students without denying access to qualified students.
Increasing the undergraduate pool to 5,000 would create a critical
mass on campus to generate more energy and extracurricular activity.
Undergraduate enrollment had grown to around 2,600 by 2011, but
everyone agrees that the number needs to be higher. NSU has the capacity, facilities, and desire to enlarge the undergraduate population.

Since increasing undergraduate enrollment was one of his major concerns, Ray Ferrero Jr. pointed out that the new library and
classroom buildings, the upscale student housing, and the university
center created a campus environment that should be attractive to undergraduate students. Another factor in persuading new students to
enroll at NSU was increasing the course offerings in the Farquhar
College of Arts and Sciences and transferring the undergraduate business program to the business school. Ferrero wanted to keep tuition
($20,000 for undergraduates in 2011) within reach of most students
while maintaining NSU's place between FAU (approximately $4,300
per year) and the University of Miami (more than $35,000 per year).
Frank DePiano cited the dual admissions program as an important
option that gave new students an advantage in entering the dental,

medicine, or law programs. Students who meet the qualifications with test scores or SATs will be admitted to NSU with a reserved spot in the graduate school of their choice. After successfully completing the undergraduate requirements, usually in three years, they would then enter the professional school.[36]

To attract new undergraduates to NSU, the university increased its advertising budget in state newspapers, sponsored open houses, and organized campus tours for interested families. One recruiter revealed that the most difficult issue in selling NSU was the cost, but the new campus facilities, the dual admission program, the large number of available majors, and the location helped overcome that issue. President George Hanbury pointed out that potentially 4,000 recruiters (students, staff, and faculty) were already on university grounds and would be organized to recruit for the entire campus, not just for individual centers.

By 2011, social opportunities for students had increased exponentially: there were 241 student organizations on campus, fraternities and sororities, high-quality recreational facilities, a superior student union, new dorms, and the possibility of working on the student paper, *The Current*, radio station Radio X, or SharkFINS (Fun and Interesting News for Students), the weekly student e-newsletter. The Office of Campus Recreation operates the RecPlex and sponsors intramural sports and group fitness. There is also the Office of Student Disability Services and the Office of Career Development, which gives career consulting and job search assistance. In 2000, to enable students to move around campus more efficiently, the university launched a fleet of four new sixteen-passenger shuttle buses called the Shark Shuttle, with "Wave and Ride" services to all forty permanent buildings on campus.[37] All of these improvements helped make a student's time at NSU more productive, more enjoyable, and more fulfilling.

NSU also reached out to its alumni to help publicize the school. Not much had been done with the alumni association in Nova's early years, but as the number of graduates multiplied, the university has made more of an effort to stay in contact with alumni and bring them up to date on happenings at NSU. The university sends out alumni newsletters, sponsors alumni chapters around the country, and mails invitations to campus events. NSU alumni, however, are scattered all over the world, and some have never even seen the campus, so it has been difficult to raise money from alumni of a school less than fifty years old.[38] NSU has made improving alumni relations a major objective.

The school continues its dedication to a diversified campus. In fall 2010, women accounted for 63 percent of the student population. Minorities made up 67 percent of the undergraduate population and 54 percent of the graduate enrollment. The *Princeton Review* rated NSU one of the top universities in the nation for diversity, and the U.S. Department of Education considers NSU the top university in the nation for diversity. For many years the school has been highly ranked in the number of master's and doctoral degrees awarded to African Americans. In 2011, *The Hispanic Outlook in Higher Education Magazine* certified NSU as the top institution in the nation in the number of doctoral degrees awarded to Hispanics.[39]

Oceanographic Center

The Oceanographic Center continued to do significant research. In 1998, the U.S. Congress established the National Coral Reef Institute (NCRI) at NSU. NCRI's objectives included the protection and conservation of coral reefs around the world through assessment, monitoring programs, and research on restoration. In 2000, President Ray Ferrero Jr., continuing his support of the center, appointed Richard (Dick) Dodge to succeed Julian (Jay) McCreary as dean of the Oceanographic Center. Dodge oversees research efforts in physical oceanography and biological and environmental sciences, as well as educational activities. The center offers programs in marine environmental science, marine biology, coastal zone management, and biological sciences.

Dodge, an expert on coral reefs, commented that these are trying times for ocean life and the land environment, with global climate change, El Niño, pollution, overfishing, and overuse of resources creating myriad problems. To help save endangered ocean life, Dodge received a research grant from the National Oceanic and Atmospheric Administration (NOAA) to put damaged coral in underwater nurseries, regrow it, and transplant it back in damaged reefs. Initial transplant experiments have shown great promise. Coral reefs, explained Dodge, are one of the oldest ecosystems on the planet and an invaluable part of the ocean's infrastructure. Since coral reefs serve as home for 25 percent of all marine life and Florida has 84 percent of the coral reefs in the United States, it is imperative that the reefs be preserved and protected.

In January 2010, the U.S. Department of Commerce announced that the Oceanographic Center would receive $15 million in federal stimulus money to build the largest coral reef research center in the United States: the Center of Excellence for Coral Reef Ecosystems Research. NSU agreed to match that grant. There were 167 applicants for the grants and only twelve received funding, with NSU being one of only two to receive the full $15 million award. The 86,000-square-foot, five-story building opened in September 2012 at a final cost of $50 million. The new building features a dramatic architectural design and a number of eco-friendly aspects, including motion-sensor and solar-powered lighting, rainwater collection and reuse, and native-plant landscaping. The center has created new academic jobs, employed additional graduate students, and produced 300 construction jobs. The Center of Excellence for Coral Reef Ecosystems Research will have a "transformational effect on coral reef research" and enable the Oceanographic Center to attract new faculty and students. In 2012, the Oceanographic Center leads NSU with approximately $50 million—over 75 percent—of the total NSU extramural grant funding. The center now has more than 200 graduate students and offers five master's degrees.[40]

Shepard Broad Law Center

In its thirty-eight years of existence, the law school has had a lasting influence on South Florida and the legal community. Many judges and state and elected officials were included in its alumni Gallery of Achievement. By 2010 the school had grown in enrollment to around 1,263 students, with 53 percent women and 30 percent members of minority groups. Of the sixty-six full-time faculty, there were twelve African Americans, five Hispanics, two Asian Americans, and thirty-three women. Three unique master's programs were designed to educate non-lawyers on complex issues that they might encounter in their professional work. The school offered an MS in health law for practitioners, an MS in education law for teachers, and a degree in employment law.

The law school has continued its Alternative Admission Model Program for Legal Education (AAMPLE), a special admissions program for students with limited credentials. The school has worked assiduously to recruit a diverse community of scholars, especially in the Hispanic community, which had been underserved in previous years.

The law school's performance on passing the Florida bar exam has been raised to where NSU graduates now consistently rank third or fourth in the state. Some law faculty believe that the school has become too large and will not improve the quality of its students until it raises the admission criteria and lowers the number of admissions each year. While almost all faculty favor the AAMPLE program, the lower admission standards hurt the school in national rankings. Nonetheless, insiders claim that the school educates its students well, and morale at the law school is high.

In recent years, the Shepard Broad Law Center added other special programs, such as joint degrees with schools in the European Union, in which students are licensed to practice in both the EU and the United States. There were also cooperative programs in business, psychology, and dispute resolution. Each new student has the opportunity of spending one semester in the Law Center's clinical program in business, dispute resolution, criminal justice, and environmental law.[41]

Health Professions Division

Fred Lippman, the current chancellor of the Health Professions Division (HPD), was an early confidant of Mort Terry and Arnold Melnick and has been with SECOM and HPD almost from the start, having served in a number of administrative capacities. He succeeded Arnold Melnick as provost in 1998 and became chancellor in 2004. He knows as well as anyone about HPD's extraordinary growth since it became part of NSU. The colleges have expanded in the number of students and programs, but perhaps more important, there has been a tremendous expansion of basic research and research publications in recent years. Lippman reported that he has concentrated on creating more effective and innovative academic and clinical programs for the students. As part of that goal, in 2001 the NSU College of Osteopathic Medicine (NSU-COM) signed a landmark ten-year agreement with the North Broward Hospital District that would provide additional clinical opportunities for NSU-COM students at the district's four hospitals. Lippman also focused on sharing knowledge and interdisciplinary research among the six colleges, believing that the physician, pharmacist, and other specialists should work together to coordinate patient care and treatment.[42]

In less than two decades, HPD has developed into a multidisciplinary health center. With modern facilities, the division has redoubled its commitment to innovation and community development. The College of Health Care Sciences offers physician assistant programs on campus and in Fort Myers, Jacksonville, and Orlando. Both the occupational therapy and physical therapy programs have enlarged their offerings. The nursing school, now a separate college, began allowing registered nurses (RNs) to earn a master's of science in nursing (MSN) and continued to attract students for its bachelor of science in nursing (BSN).

The College of Dental Medicine is currently housed in a 70,500-square-foot, three-story building containing 171 modern dental operating units. The college remains committed to helping indigent and underserved patients. The College of Medical Sciences has sustained its role as the provider of all basic and medical science education for the other division colleges. The College of Optometry, founded in 1989, remains the only college of optometry in Florida. The college conducts a wide range of research in ocular disease, and its Eye Care Institute enables the general public to receive eye care.

The College of Osteopathic Medicine now has a public health program available to students and continues its emphasis on a holistic approach to healing and on family physicians and their role in rural and underserved communities. Each medical student completes a required three-month rotation in a rural practice. The Area Health Education Center (AHEC) supplies funding and electronic access to NSU's medical library for those physicians working in rural areas.

After the devastation of Hurricane Katrina in 2005, NSU-COM mobilized a university-wide relief effort. The medical center performed primary and follow-up care to victims with chronic illnesses and acute injuries sustained during the storm. On an annual basis, NSU-COM students are also sent on medical missions to foreign countries—Ecuador, Haiti, Jamaica, Peru, and others. The health care contingent provides medical stations for pediatrics, general medicine, dermatology, and other specialties. Although not acting as physicians, students benefit from this hands-on experience. Taylor Hathaway, a medical student, commented on his time in Jamaica: "This experience gave us . . . a great chance to gain firsthand experience with patient care, not just as observers, but as medical care providers, under the supervision of physicians."[43]

The College of Pharmacy concentrates on drug-use review and medication therapy management in a rapidly changing field. The HPD operates five multispecialty health care centers, including a women's health care center, in both Broward and Miami-Dade County. These

centers furnish patient care not offered by other local health care providers. The NSU health care system has more than 300,000 patient
visits yearly to the communities it serves.[44] The HPD, which arrived
on campus in 1994, has been a major addition to NSU, adding prestige to the university and enabling NSU to serve the community in a
way it never could before.

Mailman Segal Center for Human Development

The current Mailman Segal Center for Human Development's history
goes back to 1972, when Marilyn "Mickey" Segal developed early
learning programs in the community. Segal was one of the first educators to emphasize the importance of learning in a child's formative
years, which are critical for development. Desirous of an early childhood center that would serve as a teaching and research facility and a
model for quality child care, Segal set up the Family Center in 1975.
The focus of the Family Center expanded in 1983 when the Baudhuin
Preschool (formerly the Fort Lauderdale Oral School) was relocated
to campus and became a unit of the Family Center.

Initially working with children with hearing impairments, the
Baudhuin School expanded to include children with learning disabilities, attention deficit disorders, and autism. By 1988, the school had
contracted with the School Board of Broward County to provide free
services to children with the educational eligibility requirement of autism. The Baudhuin Preschool, with 157 children with autism in its
care, is one of the only preschools nationally accredited by the National Association for the Education of Young Children for children
with autism spectrum disorders.

In 2001, Jim and Jan Moran donated $3 million as a challenge
grant for the Family Center to expand its outreach programs, to build
a new, larger facility to house all Mailman Segal Center programs currently on campus, and to increase its programs so that more families
in the community can benefit from its services. The Moran gift was
part of a $12.5 million project to build a 110,000-square-foot center
on five acres adjacent to the campus, ultimately known as the Jim and
Jan Moran Family Center Village. The new edifice, which opened in
2003, is a nationally recognized demonstration and training facility.

One half of the Moran Family Center building is devoted to the
study of autism; the other half offers programs in parenting, early
childhood, and early brain development. There are specially designed

family rooms and outdoor play spaces to encourage families and the 1,000-plus children to play and learn together. The center also goes into at-risk communities in surrounding areas to offer parenting classes, child development programs, and training and professional development to its community constituents. In collaboration with other NSU centers, the Mailman Segal Center for Human Development offers academic classes in early childhood, autism, and applied behavior analysis. In 2010, after thirty years of focusing on children and families, the center is now composed of three institutes: the Early Childhood Institute, the Parenting Institute, and the Autism Institute.[45]

University School

With the University School (prekindergarten through 12th grade), the Mailman Segal Center for Human Development (birth to five), the undergraduate Farquhar College, the professional schools, and the Lifelong Learning Institute (formerly the Institute of Retired Professionals), NSU had met the original founder SFEC's vision of cradle-to-the-grave education. The university achieved, in less than fifty years, the creator's dream of an integrated learning experience.

President Ray Ferrero Jr. liked the concept of a campus-based school, "a university school within a university." Ferrero described the University School as having a very nurturing culture and praised it as a fine prep school whose graduates attended some of the best universities in the nation. One hundred percent of its graduates have gone on to college. Although there were already several collaborative programs with NSU, Ferrero encouraged more interdisciplinary interaction between the University School and NSU programs, especially with the Oceanographic Center and the College of Arts and Sciences.[46]

While the school has expanded in terms of facilities and students—as of 2011 there were 1,900 students enrolled—Jerome (Jerry) Chermak, headmaster since 1999, continues to emphasize the school's original pedagogy: to base instruction on the student's learning needs, interests, and abilities. Chermak, concerned about the development of individuals and their values beyond academics, encourages extracurricular activities such as sports, music, art, debate, theater, and community service. Recent expansion at the school includes a 70,800-square-foot performing arts center, the Epstein Center for the Arts with a 750-seat auditorium, an art gallery, and band practice rooms.[47]

Nadine Barnes, currently the director of the Lower School, said that the teachers begin language instruction at a very early age. The Lower School introduces students to current moral issues during Cultural Unity Week, which teaches children about tolerance, acceptance, and name-calling. According to Barnes, it is important to help young students overcome reading and learning problems and social disabilities. She recalled one second-grade student who was barely reading and exhibited psychological problems. A complete psychological workup, with assistance from experts in the field from NSU colleges, remedied his problems, and he ended up attending Harvard University.[48]

International Studies

In recent years, NSU bolstered its international programs and expanded into new countries, focusing on its Latin American neighbors. In previous years, international exchange programs were just an afterthought. NSU signaled its long-term investment in a greater international presence with the appointment of Anthony J. DeNapoli as executive director of the newly created Office of International Affairs (OIA). DeNapoli, who began his new job on August 18, 2010, coordinates and facilitates existing and new international programs and works with NSU's colleges, schools, and centers to increase the number of affiliations with foreign institutions. DeNapoli also coordinates and expands existing services for on-campus and online international students, as well as students who are earning NSU degrees in countries around the world.

DeNapoli is heavily involved with NSU's growing and constantly changing international partnerships in the Bahamas, Belize, China, Colombia, Costa Rica, the Dominican Republic, Ecuador, Greece, Italy, Jamaica, Puerto Rico, South Korea, Spain, Malaysia, Mexico, and Great Britain. NSU is also working on agreements with Brazil and Argentina. NSU students and faculty, as of 2010, were engaged in projects in more than fifty-four countries, with students from 106 nations taking NSU classes at the main Davie campus or in clusters in their own countries. There are approximately 1,200 international students residing and studying on the NSU campus. Of the international students on campus, 76 percent are taking graduate courses, primarily in business and health sciences. Most of them are supported through scholarships or government aid from their home countries; for example, the Saudi Arabian government funds sixty Saudi students.

Before foreign students arrive in Florida, the Office of International Affairs gives them a pre-arrival orientation, which they can complete online. They attend an additional orientation session when they arrive on campus and a series of workshops throughout the year. Assisting foreign students in their adjustment to U.S. life and culture can prove difficult. One of the sensitive issues the OIA faced was providing Muslim students proper food and a time and place for prayer. NSU welcomes its Saudi visitors because it gives NSU students a chance to interact with Muslims and understand their religion and culture. OIA stresses the need for ethnocentric Americans to understand other cultures and religions.

NSU also recognizes the value of faculty exchanges and the interchange of research and ideas. Most faculty return from their time abroad reenergized and ready to share their experiences. The university is belatedly developing study-abroad programs for undergraduate students, who may spend a semester in such locations as Rome or London. This outreach will benefit U.S. students, who will need to understand the rest of the world to function effectively in the twenty-first century.[49]

Abraham S. Fischler School of Education

The Abraham S. Fischler School of Education, an early pioneer in field-based distance education, is located in an 18-acre, four-story building in North Miami Beach and serves more than 15,000 students annually in many states and several foreign countries. The school offers dozens of programs in the field of educational leadership, "almost all delivered through high-quality distance education techniques perfected after more than thirty years of experience." A wide array of degrees is available: bachelor, master's, and doctoral degrees, as well as educational specialist and teacher certification. Students have several course format options: online, campus based, site based, off campus, or a combination of these. Doctoral programs include educational leadership (the very same course the school began with some forty years ago), health care education, human services administration, special education, and many others.[50]

From 2000 to 2012, NSU pushed for increased technology for the entire university. President Ferrero, expanding on Abe Fischler's early concept of distance education, said NSU would solidify its reputation as a "brick and click" university. The brick part was reflected in the new library, business school, and Don Taft University Center. The click part, or technology and distance learning, would always be emphasized. As technology improved, NSU adapted online delivery formats for students dispersed nationally and internationally. By 2003, NSU offered 2,700 online courses and twenty-eight online degree programs. Ferrero and others predicted that student interest in distance education would only increase as the general population became more engaged with telecommunication technologies. By 2007, distance education represented 42 percent of NSU's fall term enrollment. By 2012, most major U.S. institutions, including Ivy League schools, had adopted similar forms of online education.

Ferrero, responding to ongoing criticism of online education, defended the distance education programs as academically rigorous. He maintained that they would always be an important part of the NSU curriculum because they provide a valuable service to society: reaching those who might otherwise be shut out of an education.[51]

There has been some discussion about the efficacy of online education. Practitioners have found that many students like a "blended" course—some online work and some face time with the instructor. Other students prefer live classes, while many enjoy the convenience and efficiency of a purely online course. Many adult students prefer the option of a cluster class so they can attend live classes near their home on night and weekends. Two big advantages of the cluster courses are that students can get a top-notch professor and the courses are convenient for full-time employees. Since the university's costs for off-site courses are low, both the student and the provider benefit.

The cluster courses and live classes offer an exchange of ideas and personal communication between professor and student. Online courses typically lack the nuance, dialogue, and eye contact between professor and student (although the virtual classroom and video-conferencing software are rapidly overcoming these problems). Both Anthony DeNapoli and Susan Atherley, who teach online and live courses, say that while there are distinct advantages in a live class, the online course can be done well. As Ferrero and Fischler have often reminded people, education is neither place nor time bound.

NSU has rapidly developed its in-state, off-campus cluster programs by buying or renting buildings all over Florida as student service centers. NSU has major education centers in Jacksonville, Orlando, Tampa, Fort Myers, West Palm Beach, and Miami, where students receive person-to-person courses without having to leave their hometown. The major centers offer courses at all levels in business administration, health professions (physical and occupational therapy and nursing), education, psychology, and other fields. Each center has a director, staff, and classrooms. These service centers are efficient and profitable.

The service center in Miami is a representative example. It has 70,000 square feet of classroom and meeting space with videoconferencing and Internet access in every room. There are forty-six "smart" classrooms, three computer labs, and two compressed video suites. The degrees available at the Miami location include a bachelor's degree in education and business; a master's degree in business administration, education, and mental health counseling; and a doctorate in educational leadership and organizational leadership.[52]

Cultural Outreach

Under President Ferrero's leadership, NSU continued being a good community servant and forged new relationships with community groups. When several board members from the Museum of Art Fort Lauderdale approached Ferrero about a possible affiliation, he responded favorably: "I think a university, if it has the capacity, should be part of the community, have outreach, and support important community assets." Ferrero thought NSU would bring a lot to an affiliation with the museum and that NSU's support would give the public and museum supporters confidence for the future and allow the museum to grow.

On July 1, 2008, the Museum of Art Fort Lauderdale became part of the expanded creative campus of NSU when the two institutions agreed to a merger. Cooperative programs between NSU and the museum would further enrich educational programming in the visual arts. In essence, with the merger, the museum lost its identity as a separate entity, though it kept its name. NSU owns the land and the museum building and has full financial oversight over it. NSU did not pay anything to merge the two but did accept the museum's liabilities. This move gave NSU another presence on the east side of town and enabled it to increase the undergraduate population by offering more fine arts courses.

Founded in 1958 as the Fort Lauderdale Arts Center, the museum is located in downtown Fort Lauderdale in a 75,000-square-foot facility. The museum is known for its collection of contemporary Cuban art and its successful high-profile exhibitions, including "Saint

Peter and the Vatican" and "Tutankhamun and the Golden Age of the Pharaohs." From 2003 to 2008, more than 1.5 million visitors have enjoyed the museum's exhibitions. Executive director Irving Lippman praised the merger, saying the two entities would become sites "for innovation in the arts, a catalyst for new ideas, and a hub for cross-disciplinary collaboration." Ray Ferrero Jr. called the association a complement to the cultural and learning experiences NSU delivered to the community and to its students and faculty.[53]

NSU has added to its community involvement with the concept of the NSUCommuniversity. Its purpose is to initiate and develop public/private relationships that address the needs of Broward County citizens. NSU students and faculty have partnerships with the Broward Education Foundation, the Urban League of Broward County, the Broward Alliance, the United Way, and other organizations. In addition to community service provided by the Health Professions Division, the Oceanographic Center works to preserve natural resources and NSU students participate in America Reads, a federally sponsored work-study program that gives undergraduates the opportunity to tutor elementary school students who have reading problems. Between 1999 and 2002, 150 NSU students helped approximately 750 Broward County schoolchildren in thirty schools. While aiding others, NSU students derive valuable hands-on experience and leadership training that they can apply in their future endeavors.[54] These collaborative efforts between the private and public sectors are examples of what President Ferrero promised the university would do when he took office.

The Distinguished Speakers Series, under the aegis of the Farquhar College of Arts and Sciences, continued its tradition of hosting leaders who are prominent in their fields. Two of the more notable visitors were His Holiness the 14th Dalai Lama of Tibet and Nobel Laureate Archbishop Desmond Tutu. These proponents of peace appeared on campus within two days of each other. The Dalai Lama, who also visited the campus in 2004, spoke to faculty, students, and the public on February 23 and 24, 2010, discussing "The Effect of Compassion on the Global Community."[55] Tinsley Ellis, one of the invitees to a private session with the Dalai Lama, recalled being instructed not to touch him: "So I didn't touch him—but he came and hit me in the back and asked how I was doing. He was very personable."[56]

Archbishop Desmond Tutu arrived on February 26, 2010, to present a lecture entitled "Good vs. Evil: Human Rights or Humans Wronged." Archbishop Tutu had been awarded the Nobel Peace Prize in 1984 for his long and unyielding fight against apartheid in South Africa. Don Rosenblum, dean of the Farquhar College of Arts and Sciences, welcomed the archbishop to NSU, saying, "His message of engaging in peaceful resolution to address conflict and oppose injustice is especially relevant to our students," and they will gain personal insights and inspiration by listening to him.[57]

Other recent lecturers have upheld the high standards of the series. They include Eliezer (Elie) Wiesel, another recipient of the Nobel Peace Prize; writers Kurt Vonnegut and Salman Rushdie; former secretary of defense Robert S. McNamara; Geraldine Ferraro, the first woman nominated for vice president by a major political party; and Ehud Barak, the former prime minister of Israel. Other orators included Gloria Steinem and John Kenneth Galbraith. For a slice of controversy, the university also invited Spike Lee and Jack Kevorkian to speak. It is significant that an academic institution such as NSU has devoted time and money to host such eminent and notable personalities. NSU clearly understands the importance of having these world-class speakers impart their wisdom and experience to students, faculty, and the community at large.

Retirement of Ray Ferrero Jr.

Ray Ferrero Jr., who had aggressively guided the university since taking over in 1998, had been gratified by NSU's accelerated growth in terms of students, buildings, courses, and faculty from 2000 until 2011.[58] After thirteen years at the helm, however, Ferrero decided to retire. Possible reasons for his decision were the expiration of his contract in 2011, some health problems, and having accomplished much of what he set out to do. Ferrero knew that an experienced successor, George Hanbury, was ready to take over.[59]

When administrators, colleagues, and former students were asked to describe Ferrero's personality and evaluate his presidency, responses were uniformly positive. Colleagues described the silver-haired president as a hands-on leader who read voraciously, quickly got to the point, and asked a lot of questions. They portrayed him as a power broker whose connections to the highest tier of South Florida's legal, business, and civic institutions opened numerous doors for NSU. Fred Lippman characterized Ferrero as a doer: "A thorough thinker . . . an administrator who finishes a task." Abe Fischler credited him with developing the campus infrastructure and said that Ferrero "believes in community cooperation, and he has demonstrated that."[60]

Other comments paint a rather clear picture of Ferrero as president: "He's a very strong leader with a very strong personality." "Ferrero collected information, made a battle plan, and then marshaled his forces." "A good word to describe him would be determined." "He gets things done." "If an opportunity presented itself and it made sense, he took advantage of it."

Many observers saw Ferrero as a true visionary who turned what originally was a war-surplus landing strip into a credible university. One of his greatest strengths was his ability to partner with a variety of people and institutions, both public and private. When most administrators hit a wall, observed a friend, they would stop, but "Ray hits a wall and finds a way around it, over it, under it, rebuilds the wall, remodels the wall." A strong supporter of the university thought that the "growth and development of NSU is a result of the charisma and forcefulness of Ray Ferrero Jr." A dean who worked with Ferrero over the years liked that he knew faculty names and was willing to have lunch with students and get their views on important issues. An alumnus referred to Ferrero's "remarkable recall" and his ability "to go through ninety different things going on at the university without ever missing a beat." Another person who worked closely with Ferrero called him the "catalyst" who moved things along. His background in law and business and his familiarity with the university enabled him to move ahead with great dispatch.

There were, of course, some detractors. A few members of the faculty viewed him as somewhat arrogant, a person who did not suffer fools gladly, and when at work, demonstrated a limited sense of humor. Others pictured him as a taskmaster who ran roughshod over any opposition. People respected him, but some of his close associates admitted, "It was difficult to say no to Ray Ferrero Jr." When a powerful leader is determined to achieve success, there will always be those who disagree with his goals and methods, and there might be a few bodies strewn along the way, but in the end, Ray Ferrero Jr. made his mark.

Overall, praise for Ferrero was fulsome. Administrators in particular realized the difficulty of moving forward in an academic setting and recognized his intelligence and ability to get things done.[61] That, as Ferrero himself might say, was the bottom line.

On December 7, 2010, the NSU Board of Trustees approved a leadership succession plan. Effective January 1, 2010, Ray Ferrero Jr.

would become university chancellor and CEO, and George Hanbury would become university president and chief operating officer. The board also stipulated that in 2011 Hanbury would assume the role of CEO when Ferrero's term expired.

It is clear that in his thirteen years as president and chancellor, Ferrero enjoyed his work. When he began his time in the Horvitz Building, he asked himself three questions: "Would I enjoy being president? Is the timing right both personally and professionally? And do I think I would make a difference?" The answer to all three questions was yes. In 2008, Ferrero told a reporter, "The last ten years here have been among the most rewarding in my life."[62]

During his time as president, NSU had become a very different place from the university he inherited. Enrollment increased 68 percent in the previous ten years, and the number of degrees awarded during the same period grew by 77 percent. In 2011, with 28,741 students enrolled in courses both on and off campus, NSU was the nation's seventh largest private not-for-profit research university and the largest independent institution in the Southeast. One of Ferrero's early priorities was to bolster the school's undergraduate population; from 1998 to 2008, undergraduate enrollment increased 32 percent.

From the outset, Ferrero knew that NSU did not have the kind of facilities it needed, so he focused on that area to the point where more than two million square feet of construction projects were completed during the last years of his tenure. The most notable new structures are the Alvin Sherman Library (Ferrero said, "It's one of the things I am most proud of."), the Don Taft University Center, the DeSantis Building, student housing in the Commons and Rolling Hills, and the new central energy plant that expanded the energy output on campus.

As the founders predicted many years ago, NSU had become an economic powerhouse in Broward County. In 2011, NSU was the second largest private employer in the county, and its statewide economic impact in 2008 was $1.4 billion. Ferrero had achieved what his predecessors found difficult. Not only was NSU in the black, but it was also a very successful financial entity. In the longtime tradition of the school, Ferrero displayed his skill as an administrator and entrepreneur, limiting his investments to "measured risks." He took advantage of new opportunities, such as the Alvin Sherman Library, and made decisions with due diligence.

Two areas that garnered much of his attention and were a central part of his vision were diversity and community interaction. NSU, as noted earlier, has won many accolades for its diversity, and this continues to be a top priority. From 2004 to 2009, the number of minority students in undergraduate programs increased by 19 percent, in graduate programs by 28 percent, and in professional degree programs by 35 percent. Ferrero pointed out that NSU "is an institution that gives everyone an opportunity."

Ferrero always had a personal penchant for interaction with other universities and particularly with local community organizations. NSU's outreach helped make Fort Lauderdale more dynamic and energized. His merger with the art museum, his support of the NSUCommuniversity, and the public service performed at the various university centers speak volumes about Ferrero's zeal to help others. On a personal level, Ferrero was a member of many city and county organizations, such as the United Way and Chamber of Commerce, and he was chairman of the Broward Alliance, the county's official public-private partnership for economic development.

Ferrero expanded the university's presence statewide with student educational centers all over Florida. He advocated for increased international exposure for the university and demanded updated technology. He also presided over vast improvement in the three As: academics, athletics, and attitudes. He remained steadfast in his desire to improve academic excellence both for students and faculty. The President's Faculty Research and Development Grant Program supported hundreds of faculty proposals. Athletics progressed and developed with new sports teams, a new facility, and excellent student athletes. The attitude at NSU has changed from the early days when people were defensive about the underdeveloped campus and resented the derisive remarks about Nova's off-campus courses. Today, staff, students, and faculty are pleased with their campus and proud of their university.

On Ferrero's departure from his thirty years of service, Ronald G. Assaf, current chair of NSU's Board of Trustees, praised his contributions: "Ray Ferrero's vision has transformed NSU from a small niche university into one of the country's largest private not-for-profit universities. He is that rare combination of a pragmatic visionary."

As he took his leave, Ferrero commented on his time at Nova: "That's what we do here. We change lives. And NSU certainly changed mine. There are not too many people who are blessed, and this has been a blessing. I was given the greatest opportunity that anyone could have."[63]

Plate 1 Shepard Broad Law Center. The law center is housed in the Leo Goodwin Sr. Hall. (By permission of Nova Southeastern University Archives, Fort Lauderdale, Florida.)

a

Plate 2 Miami Dolphins Training Facility. (By permission of Office of Publications, Nova Southeastern University, Fort Lauderdale, Florida.)

Plate 3 Maxwell Maltz Psychology Building. Home of the Center for Psychological Studies. (By permission of Nova Southeastern University Archives, Fort Lauderdale, Florida.)

Plate 4 Health Professions Division, Terry Building. (By permission of Nova Southeastern University Archives, Fort Lauderdale, Florida.)

d

Plate 5 Alvin Sherman Library, Research, and Information Technology Center. (By permission of Nova Southeastern University Archives, Fort Lauderdale, Florida.)

Plate 6 Carl DeSantis Building, H. Wayne Huizenga School of Business and Entrepreneurship. (By permission of Office of Publications, Nova Southeastern University, Fort Lauderdale, Florida.)

f

Plate 7 Don Taft University Center. (By permission of Nova Southeastern University Archives, Fort Lauderdale, Florida.)

Plate 8 Center of Excellence for Coral Reef Ecosystems Research. (By permission of Office of Publications, Nova Southeastern University, Fort Lauderdale, Florida.)

h

9

The Hanbury Era
2010–Present

In December 2009, as discussed in Chapter 8, NSU came up with a leadership succession plan for when Ray Ferrero Jr. retired. Effective January 1, 2010, Ferrero would become university chancellor and chief executive officer (CEO), and George Hanbury II would become president and chief operating officer (COO). On June 30, 2011, when Ferrero's contract expired, Hanbury would then become president and CEO. Ferrero would retain his title as chancellor but would no longer be CEO. Hanbury would assume leadership of the university and would be the only person reporting to the board.

The NSU Board of Trustees designed the succession plan to create a smooth transition from Ferrero to Hanbury. Board of trustees chairman Ronald Assaf expressed enthusiasm "in knowing that the strategic direction and opportunity for transformational change will continue in good hands." The NSU board had worked closely with Hanbury during the previous twelve years and felt he was "uniquely qualified to be the next CEO of NSU." Once again, NSU declined to perform a national search and instead chose a known quantity. Hanbury responded to his selection: "I am humbled and honored to receive the confidence of the board to lead the university as President Ferrero's successor." He praised Ray Ferrero Jr. as a mentor over the previous twelve years and credited his leadership in guiding NSU to "educational preeminence."[1]

George Hanbury began his career at NSU in September 1998, after eleven years as city manager for the city of Fort Lauderdale. He had become friends with Ray Ferrero Jr., who approached him

Figure 9.1 George L. Hanbury II, PhD, president, 2010–present. (By permission of Office of Publications, Nova Southeastern University, Fort Lauderdale, Florida.)

about working at NSU. Ferrero needed an experienced hand to assist in planning the new infrastructure and other campus projects. Hanbury protested that he was not an educator, but Ferrero insisted that there were many similarities between running a city and a university. Hanbury finally agreed to come on board since he had accomplished much of what he wanted to do in the city and "thought it would be an interesting career change after thirty years of public service to go into another noble career working for a private . . . university." Hanbury signed on as Ferrero's partner and senior operating officer.[2]

Hanbury grew up in Virginia, the youngest of three children born to Adah and Emmette Hanbury. Early on, his mother encouraged him to attend college and inspired him to earn his doctorate. She said that education was the secret to freedom and would give George the power to undertake whatever he wished to do.

Hanbury earned his bachelor's of science degree in business administration from Virginia Tech University and his master's in public administration from Old Dominion University. He earned his PhD in public administration from Florida Atlantic University. During his thirty-year career, Hanbury worked as an assistant city manager in Norfolk, Virginia, and as city manager of the cities of Portsmouth, Virginia; Virginia Beach, Virginia; and Fort Lauderdale, Florida.

In 1974, as city manager in Virginia Beach, Hanbury urged police officers to earn a college degree and offered to pay for their books and tuition at a school called Nova University. He had heard of Nova but had no specific knowledge about what kind of school it was. After researching the school, he discovered that the faculty were highly credentialed and had practical experience. The concept of bringing the classroom to the student at a convenient time and place intrigued the young city manager. So when he arrived in Fort Lauderdale, Hanbury was already familiar with NSU's purpose and philosophy.

Hanbury came to NSU committed to being active in the community. He had a deep-seated belief in working for the common good, serving on the boards of the Museum of Art Fort Lauderdale, the United Way of Broward County, the Library Foundation of Broward County, the finance committee of the First United Methodist Church of Fort Lauderdale, and the business development board of Palm Beach County. As COO and CEO of NSU, Hanbury devoted much of his time in continuing NSU's outreach to the community that Ray Ferrero Jr. promoted so effectively.[3]

George Hanbury was formally installed as the sixth president of NSU on April 21, 2011, during a ceremony attended by students, staff, faculty, alumni, and members of the community. Ronald Assaf, chair of the NSU Board of Trustees, lauded Hanbury as a man who had the "vision to take NSU to the next level of excellence." Ray Ferrero Jr. called Hanbury "a proven leader at NSU for more than a decade." Hanbury, in his acceptance speech, said he was honored to undertake the responsibility the board of trustees had entrusted to him. He told his audience that the occasion of his inauguration was an opportunity to refocus the university's mission and unveil a new vision: NSU's Vision 2020.

In his speech, Hanbury presented eight core values to guide the university into 2020 and beyond: academic excellence, student centered, integrity, innovation, opportunity, scholarship/research, diversity, and community. He called his agenda a "shared vision" and spoke about "one university" because he wanted NSU to grow as an institution, not just as individual colleges. Hanbury thought NSU's major purpose should be to foster academic excellence, intellectual inquiry, leadership, research, and commitment to community through the engagement of students and faculty members in a dynamic, lifelong learning environment.[4]

George Hanbury became the president and functioning CEO on July 1, 2011, and began his pursuit of a positive future for NSU. Hanbury had an advantage with future negotiations because of his long experience in city management and his previous work on behalf of NSU. He felt he could easily deal "with multiple cultures, multiple backgrounds, and multiple personalities."

A typical day for the new president usually begins around 5 a.m., when he gets into the pool for a brisk swim. He arrives on campus between 8 and 9 a.m. and spends his day meeting with staff, administrators, faculty, and students. Hanbury has a regularly scheduled luncheon with students one day a month. At night his schedule is full of public functions. He wants to be seen at athletic and other student events on campus and must attend meetings of various community organizations. As was true for previous presidents, 30 percent of Hanbury's time is spent building relationships with potential donors.

One of the first items on Hanbury's agenda is to increase the law school's national standing by correcting the weakest areas. Second, he recognizes that in today's global economy, it is important for students to experience some form of education outside of the United States and wants to expand the school's international programs. Another area of need is the centralization of some of the university functions. For too long each center had its own computer systems, registration, marketing, applications, and admission policies. Many of these services could be centralized, providing a huge savings with a single database and shared administrative expenses. The unification would only be service oriented, and each center would continue to control its academic decisions. Hanbury is aware that he has to be careful not to divert too much power to the central administration as that could destroy the innovative and independent tradition the centers have enjoyed over the years. Hanbury argues that NSU has too many different brands and wants one "single, clear vision of the university." He emphasizes that there is but one NSU, not eighteen separate colleges. [5]

High on the president's list is to expand the university's endowment, currently around $52 million. A larger endowment would enable NSU to set aside more money for scholarships, new faculty, and research. To increase the endowment, NSU has embarked on a $100 million capital campaign. Hanbury admits that the goal will be difficult to achieve, but he will be a "cheerleader for the university" and the point man in raising the money. Another goal is to build a public hospital for central Broward County. The proposed hospital would be located next to the Health Professions Division and integrated with the medical school, all of the health professions, and the university itself. Hanbury has put forward his single shared-vision "2010–2020 Business Plan," which defines a new era at NSU. The plan includes specific performance measures, both quantitative and qualitative, and will be constantly monitored for necessary corrections and additions. While ambitious in scope, Hanbury believes NSU's goals can be met by 2020.

Inspired by Thomas Jefferson's plan for founding the University of Virginia, which he called his "academical village," Hanbury has his own master plan for an academical village. The university owns half of the University Park Plaza Shopping Center in Davie as a limited partner and plans to develop a for-profit, mixed-use project that would be integrated into the campus. NSU would transform thirty acres of the shopping center into three million square feet that include multifamily residential units, the NSU bookstore, a hotel-conference center, residential units, offices, retail, space for research and biotechnology, the aforementioned hospital, and a medical office building. The concept would tie the for-profit shopping center into the not-for-profit university, combining academics, research, and business. The final product could have an economic impact of more than $1 billion. The academical village is representative of NSU's focus on entrepreneurial success to bolster its academic programs.

The new president is satisfied with NSU's status as a NCAA Division II athletic program, because the university has always emphasized the "student" part of student athlete. NSU athletes' GPAs average above 3.0, and Hanbury is proud of that accomplishment. He wants NSU to concentrate on sports in which they can excel and where there is the possibility of gaining a national reputation, as with the women's golf team. He revels in the scientific achievements at the new National Coral Reef Institute at the Oceanographic Center. He views it as a center of excellence for coral reef preservation and marine biology and believes that the new research center will attract students from all over the world who are interested in preserving the ecosystem for future generations.

Perhaps Hanbury's major goal, and one that is advocated by Ferrero and just about everyone else at NSU, is a significant increase in the undergraduate enrollment. Only 20 percent of NSU's students are undergraduate (a total of about 5,500: 2,500 traditional first-time college students and 3,000 career students), and only 2,500 of those students reside on campus. The NSU Board of Trustees has determined that any great university must have as its foundation a high-quality undergraduate program. Hanbury would like to double the number of undergraduates and to that end is planning more scholarships, better recruiting, and more advertising. Hanbury wants prospective students to understand the value of an NSU education and foresees more dorms, faculty, classrooms, and science and physics labs for undergraduates.

Hanbury believes it is essential that NSU upgrade the quality of its undergraduates. Currently, the average GPA of entering day students is 2.6; for some of the career students it is around 2.0. By 2014, Hanbury expects that all entering students will require a minimum GPA of 3.0 for admission. The current retention rate for undergrads from the first to the second year is 64 percent, and the graduation rate is 47 percent. Those numbers could be improved with higher entrance requirements. An increase in the number and amount of scholarships, better marketing, and a low tuition rate should also lead to improvement in those scores. NSU has also adopted a tutoring program for undergraduates and emphasizes learning critical skills such as analyzing material, writing effectively, and making cogent oral presentations.[6]

President Hanbury strongly believes that independent universities like NSU should shoulder more of the burden of educating Florida's high school graduates. The Independent Colleges and Universities of Florida (ICUF), an association of thirty-one private, not-for-profit higher education institutions based in Florida, noted that independent colleges awarded 26 percent of the state's bachelor degrees. Students who received the Florida Resident Access Grant (FRAG) cost the state less than 1.5 percent of its higher education budget. A study by the Florida Council of 100 found that for each $1 million appropriation to ICUF institutions for undergraduate education, Florida gets 155 bachelor-degree graduates, whereas each $1 million appropriated to state universities produces only nineteen bachelor-degree graduates.[7]

To improve communication with students and the academic community, Hanbury has created a Facebook page called the President's Fan Page. He has also organized his own presidential Web page. On both pages, the president responds to questions from students, faculty, and staff; promotes NSU events; and presents information about NSU's vision and mission and the state of the university.[8]

President Hanbury wanted more interaction with the faculty, so he organized the President's Faculty Symposium. It meets once a month, and Hanbury has ensured maximum attendance by offering beer, wine, and cheese. The goal of the symposium is to promote kinship, intellectual discussion, and camaraderie. The discussion topics must be academically rigorous, have wide appeal, and be of current interest. A recent presentation focused on the legal aspects of child abuse and led to a national symposium at NSU sponsored by the ABA.[9]

During his presidency, Hanbury has made it a special objective to recognize major contributors to NSU's drive for excellence. He supports the Celebration of Excellence, NSU's premier event, which acknowledges NSU's accomplishments in the past year and praises those individuals whose leadership, generosity, and support provided the foundation for university growth.[10]

In October 2011, in an effort to increase giving, the university announced the Ambassadors Board, whose mission is to enlist widespread support for the university's development efforts and to serve as ambassadors to NSU's constituencies. Hanbury recognizes that NSU's 143,000 alumni have been neglected in the past and learned that the alumni giving rate was less than 2 percent. After a survey found that 96 percent of NSU graduates were proud of their degrees, he is now sending more information about NSU activities to alumni and is traveling to alumni chapters around the country to encourage support.[11]

Like Ray Ferrero Jr., George Hanbury is supportive of community service. When Best Colleges Online rated NSU as one of the top twenty colleges in the nation committed to community service, Hanbury welcomed the accolade: "We participate in a myriad of community service projects ranging from protecting local marine life to hosting health care assessments and nonprofit walks and runs on our main campus." In addition, the Carnegie Foundation for the Advancement of Teaching classified NSU as one of 115 elite colleges and universities in the United States demonstrating outstanding community engagement.

In 2012, the National Council for Accreditation of Teacher Education (NCATE) granted accreditation without qualifications to NSU's Abraham S. Fischler School of Education. This accolade meant that in addition to regional accreditation by SACS, NSU's program had been vetted at the highest level for quality and for the ability to produce effective, high-achieving educators. NCATE's 2012 decision reversed the one in 1979 to deny accreditation to Nova's school of education. This decision was additional evidence of the university's significant progress. Furthermore, as Hanbury pointed out, NSU was the only private university that housed Special Olympics on its campus. More than 1,000 runners participated in the 2011 Sallarulo's Race for Champions 5K run/walk and raised funds to benefit 800 local Special Olympics athletes.[12]

The Future of NSU

At the date of this writing, Nova Southeastern University has a very promising future. After all of its struggles to survive, the school has entered a lengthy period of stability and growth. The professional schools are filled to capacity and are forced to turn down many qualified applicants. The physical infrastructure has improved dramatically in the past twenty years and meets the university's current needs. Financial prospects are good: the 2012 budget is close to $600 million, and the university's economic impact on Broward County is some $1.5 billion. There are, however, some significant issues that need addressing.

First and foremost, NSU needs to develop a strong, highly qualified group of undergraduate students. The inverted pyramid of 80 percent graduate students and 20 percent undergraduates could be modified without reducing the number of graduate students. A total of 5,000 undergraduates on campus would provide the critical mass that provost and executive vice president for academic affairs Frank DePiano desires. The 5,000-student goal might not be reached unless the school can significantly increase scholarship money. That goal might be difficult unless NSU increases its endowment above the current $52 million, a low figure for a university of NSU's size. Raising the endowment to $150 million would elevate the university's stature in the eyes of decision makers, policy makers, *U.S. News and World Report,* and other relevant analysts. The $100 million capital campaign is a step in the right direction, but for the most part, except for specific, individual gifts, NSU has not been as successful as it hopes to be in raising money from its alumni and supporters.

Many observers see George Hanbury as the right man to lead NSU into the future and describe him as the stable influence NSU needs during turbulent times and an economic downturn. His goal, as expressed in "Vision 2020," is to elevate the school to a new level of recognition. Supporters applaud Hanbury's desire to aim high and for his positive attitude about having NSU recognized by CEOs, educational leaders, accrediting agencies, and the mass media as a university of prominence and preeminence. NSU has the capacity, flexibility, and desire to move forward.

If Hanbury is to take NSU to the next level, he needs to resolve three ongoing problems. One is the lingering image of Nova as a diploma mill. Hanbury says the only way to overcome that view is through superior performance and good marketing. Another issue is the fact that NSU is simply not well known around the nation, within Florida, and even in Broward County. Ray Ferrero Jr. thinks that has significantly changed, especially since NSU has a wide outreach in the state and local community. The professional schools have been successful, and NSU is finally building up a large alumni base to spread the word. Nonetheless, NSU still needs to tell the story of its rise to success and promote its centers of excellence, such as the Oceanographic Center and the Jim and Jan Moran Family Center Village.

Another important issue noted by many people interviewed for this book is what they perceive to be NSU's long-term identity crisis. As one observer noted, the university still does not quite know what it wants to be. NSU has tried to be all things to all people, but might be better served by concentrating on its strengths. According to several other interviewees, the school also needs to return to the old innovative, creative way of thinking that characterized its beginning. One person noted that there was a saying in the old days: "You can't get through the word innovative without seeing Nova." A few critics say that today the school is less innovative and is essentially doing what everybody else is doing. Others conclude that NSU is too entrepreneurial and should concentrate more on the quality of its education.

Astute observers pointed out that NSU's success had never really been defined as achievements by the university; rather, the honors went to individual units. The very things that helped Nova succeed—the entrepreneurship and each tub on its own bottom—are now holding the school back. NSU is an institution of interdependent parts but without much of a unified core. NSU must understand how it defines success and find a common bond that binds the university community together. NSU has been on a long quest in searching for its identity, and this question needs to be answered: exactly what is this university about?[13]

On December 19, 2011, MIT announced a new academic program that allows anyone, anywhere to take MIT courses online. Students earn an official certificate of completion for demonstrating mastery of the subject. Things had now come full circle. Nova Southeastern University, which began with the goal of becoming the MIT of the South, now had the satisfaction of seeing one of the best institutions in the country adopt the format of off-campus, online education that it pioneered in 1974.[14]

George Hanbury seems to be on track to answer these questions about NSU's identity and the school's future. Although, as of this writing, he has been in office only eight months, his strong emphasis on centralization and "one university" has gained supporters. He has an upbeat and positive view of the university's future—and why not? When one views the extraordinary story of Nova's struggle from a storefront on East Las Olas Boulevard through numerous crises that would have destroyed just about any institution to its current success, why would one not predict a positive future? NSU's history is much like a Horatio Alger story. Alger wrote "rags to riches" stories about young boys rising from humble backgrounds and their struggle against adversity to achieve success through moral fortitude, hard work, determination, and courage. Like one of Alger's youthful protagonists, Jim Farquhar, the Forman brothers, and many of the early founders and leaders of Nova Southeastern University overcame adversity and hardship on numerous occasions and ultimately achieved success. The school has lived up to its founders' promise of creating a cradle-to-the-grave educational system. NSU looks forward to its future, and its future is bright.

Notes

1. The Beginning

1. Mormino, *Land of Sunshine, State of Dreams: A Social History of Modern Florida*, 24, 25, 30.

2. *Rocky Mountain News*, June 12, 1967; Abe Fischler's interviews with W. Tinsley Ellis and Robert Ellyson; Stuart Synnestvedt, *Education, Science, and Technology Center of South Florida*, February 24, 1961, NSU Archives.

3. Abe Fischler's interview with Robert Ellyson.

4. *History of Broward County Public Schools*, n.d., no author, p. 1, NSU Archives.

5. *Miami Herald*, January 17, 1984; Abe Fischler's interviews with Hamilton Forman, A.D. Griffin, James Hartley, and W. Tinsley Ellis; *Miami Herald*, January 17, 1984.

6. Abe Fischler's interview with Hamilton Forman and Jim Farquhar; *Miami Herald*, October 2, 1977.

7. Grunwald, *The Swamp: The Everglades, Florida, and the Politics of Paradise*, 5, 106, 134–140.

8. Wagner, *The History of Davie and Its Dilemma*, 19, 21, 29.

9. Abe Fischler's interview with Jim and Ann Farquhar; *Miami Herald*, October 2, 1977.

10. Joe B. Rushing to the SFEC, February 23, 1961, NSU Archives.

11. SFEC Executive Committee minutes, February 5, 1962 (hereinafter referred to as SFEC minutes).

12. SFEC minutes, February 12, 1962; Joe Rushing, *Outline of South Florida Education Center for Science and Technology*, February 23, 1961, NSU Archives.

13. *Fort Lauderdale News*, March 1, 1963.

14. *Miami Herald*, March 19, 1961.

15. SFEC minutes, February 12 and 26, 1962, and March 5, 1962, NSU Archives.

16. Abe Fischler's interview with Hamilton Forman; SFEC minutes, April 23, 1962.

17. *Miami Herald*, October 2, 1977.

18. *Miami Herald*, October 2, 1977; Abe Fischler's interview with Jim Farquhar.

19. Abe Fischler's interview with Hamilton Forman.

20. Ibid.

21. SFEC minutes, April 6 and 16, 1962, and May 7, 1962.

22. SFEC minutes, May 28, June 11, June 25, and July 2, 10, 16, and 23, 1962.

23. Nova University News Release, September 20, 1967; *Nova High School*, undated newsletter, NSU Archives; SFEC minutes, October 16, 1962.

24. SFEC minutes, July 30, October 16, and November 5 and 12, 1962; Articles of Incorporation, U.S. Treasury Department, November 13, 1962, NSU Archives.

25. *NovaTech*, vol. II, no. 1, March 1965, p. 1; author's interview with Abe Fischler.

26. SFEC minutes, May 7 and 28, 1963; A.B. Wolfe to Governor Farris Bryant, December 21, 1962, NSU Archives.

27. SFEC minutes, December 10, 1962, January 3, February 12, March 26, and May 7 and 28, 1963; *NovaTech*, vol. II, no. 1, March 1965, p. 1.

28. Agreement between the Broward County Board of Public Instruction and the SFEC, 1963, NSU Archives.

29. Author's interview with Tinsley Ellis.

30. Abe Fischler's interview with Hamilton Forman.

31. Abe Fischler's interview with Robert Ellyson.

32. SFEC minutes, May 27, September 5, and October 15, 1963.

33. Ibid.

34. Author's interview with Tinsley Ellis.

35. SFEC minutes, February 24, 1964; author's interview with Abe Fischler.

36. SFEC to Warren J. Winstead, May 14, 1964, NSU Archives; SFEC minutes, August 20, 1964; James Dwight Leonard, *Nova University: Setting the Pace in Education for 25 Years*, unpublished manuscript, NSU Archives, 7; *Chronicle of Higher Education*, vol. II, no. 2, September 27, 1967; author's interview with Abe Fischler.

37. Biographical sketch of Warren J. Winstead, October 1964, NSU Archives.

38. Author's interview with Abe Fischler.

39. SFEC minutes, August 20, 1964, and February 26, 1965.

40. SFEC minutes, August 13 and October 1, 1964.

41. Abe Fischler's interview with Tinsley Ellis.

42. Hall of Fame/Inventor Profile. "Louis W. Parker." http://www.invent.org/hall_of_fame/117.html (accessed January 21, 2012).

43. *Hollywood Sun-Tattler*, May 11, 1970.

44. Abe Fischler's interview with Tinsley Ellis.

45. Warren J. Winstead, "Educational Concepts." *Novatas,* vol. 1, no. 1, October 1964; Leonard, *Nova University: Setting the Pace in Education for 25 Years,* p. 7; *Time,* June 30, 1967.

46. SFEC minutes, August 13, 1964; Certificate of Incorporation, Nova University of Advanced Technology, Inc., December 4, 1964, Office of the Florida Secretary of State, NSU Archives.

47. SFEC minutes, May 15, July 8, July 22, and August 20, 1964; Nova University News Release, September 20, 1967.

48. Abe Fischler's interview with James Hartley.

49. SFEC minutes, August 13, 1964; author's interview with Tinsley Ellis.

50. SFEC minutes, September 17, 1964.

51. SFEC minutes, September 17, 1964; *NovaTech,* vol. 2, no. 1, March 1965.

52. Nova University, *President's Annual Report, July 1, 1965,* NSU Archives; Leonard, *Nova University: Setting the Pace in Education for 25 Years,* p. 9.

53. Leonard, *Nova University: Setting the Pace in Education for 25 Years,* p. 9.

54. SFEC minutes, August 20 and 27, and September 24, 1964; *Architectural Concepts on the Master Plan for Nova University,* NSU Archives.

55. Abe Fischler's interview with A.D. Griffin; SFEC minutes, June 1965.

56. Abe Fischler's interview with Tinsley Ellis; SFEC minutes, October 1 and 22, 1964.

57. SFEC minutes, November 5 and 19, and December 3, 1964.

58. *President's Quarterly Report to the Board of Trustees, First Quarter, Fiscal Year 1966,* NSU Archives.

59. SFEC minutes, January 7 and 21, 1965.

60. SFEC minutes, December 17, 1964; Abe Fischler's interview with Robert Ellyson.

61. *The Impact of Nova University on Broward County,* report by Hunter Moss and Company, Miami, Florida, September 15, 1965, NSU Archives; *President's Annual Report, 1965,* NSU Archives.

62. SFEC minutes, January 7, 21, 28, 1965; *President's Annual Report, 1965,* NSU Archives.

63. Author's interview with Tinsley Ellis; Leonard, *Nova University: Setting the Pace in Education for 25 Years,* 10–11; SFEC minutes, June 1965; Herman E. Spivey, *Nova University 1968,* pamphlet in NSU Archives, 4–5; *President's Annual Report, 1965,* NSU Archives.

64. SFEC minutes, December 17, 1964, and January 7, 1965; Leonard, *Nova University: Setting the Pace in Education for 25 Years,* 10–11; *Time,* June 30, 1967; *Royal Dames of Nova University,* pamphlet in NSU archives.

65. Spivey, *Nova University,* 15–18.

66. SFEC minutes, January 28, 1965.

67. SFEC minutes, January 21 and 28, February 4 and 22, and July 1, 1965.

68. Leonard, *Nova University: Setting the Pace in Education for 25 Years*, 11–12.

69. Abe Fischler's interview with Robert Ellyson; *Fort Lauderdale Tattler*, April 7, 1973; author's interviews with Abe Fischler and Tinsley Ellis.

70. Nova University News Release, September 20, 1967; author's interview with Tinsley Ellis.

71. Nova University News Release, September 20, 1967; *Miami Herald*, May 22, 1967.

72. Ibid.

73. Abe Fischler's interview with James Hartley and Tinsley Ellis.

74. William S. Richardson to Arthur Wishart, Nova University, August 13, 1965, NSU Archives.

75. *Fort Lauderdale News and Sun-Sentinel*, March 29 and May 31, 1969; *Miami Herald*, April 3, 1967; *Pictorial Life*, Summer 1968; Abe Fischler's interviews with Hamilton Forman and Tinsley Ellis.

76. Warren J. Winstead to Stanley A. Emerson, May 12, 1969, NSU Archives; *Fort Lauderdale News*, April 17, 1969.

77. Nova University News Release, September 20, 1967, NSU Archives.

78. *Miami Herald*, September 1967.

79. *Your Questions Answered, Nova University, September 1967*, pamphlet in NSU Archives.

80. Nova University News Release, September 20, 1967, NSU Archives; *Fort Lauderdale News and Sun-Sentinel*, September 24, 1967.

81. Author's interview with Abe Fischler.

82. NSU News release, September 20, 1967.

2. The Opening of the University

1. News releases, Nova University, September 20, 1967; *Time*, June 30, 1967.

2. *Miami Herald*, September 26, 1967; Goldstein, *The Search for Nova University: An Essay on Its First Twenty-five Years, 1964–1989*, 1–2.

3. *Miami Herald*, August 27 and September 26, 1967; February 27, 1968.

4. Goldstein, *The Search for Nova University: An Essay on Its First Twenty-five Years, 1964–1989*, 4–5.

5. *Chronicle of Higher Education*, vol. II, no. 2, September 27, 1967.

6. *Miami Herald*, September 6, 1968; Winstead's report to the Board of Trustees, September, 1968, NSU Archives.

7. Board of Trustees minutes of Nova University, July 15 and August 26, 1968.

8. Bogorff, *The Leo Goodwin Institute for Cancer Research of Nova University, 1969–1980*, n.d., 1–4; *Hollywood Sun-Tattler*, February 3 and March 5, 1969; *Miami Herald*, January 24, 1969; Board of Trustees minutes, July 15, 1968.

9. Merger agreement with Nova University and the Leo Goodwin Sr. Institute for Cancer Research, Inc., 1972, NSU Archives; Bogorff, *The Leo Goodwin Institute for Cancer Research of Nova University, 1969–1980*, 5–8.

10. Abe Fischler to Kerrigan, March 31, 1975, NSU Archives; minutes of the Nova University Executive Committee, March 31, 1975, NSU Archives.

11. Bogorff, *The Leo Goodwin Institute for Cancer Research of Nova University, 1969–1980*, 6–8; *Hollywood Sun-Tattler*, July 19, 1972.

12. John C. Barker, executive secretary of SACS, to Warren Winstead, December 13, 1968.

13. Abe Fischler, *Chronological History of Nova University's Search for Accreditation*, November 29, 1973, NSU Archives; *Miami Herald*, December 15, 1971; *Novocrat*, May–June 1971, vol. 6, no. 2; Abe Fischler to Gordon W. Sweet, November 22, 1969, and January 13, 1970; Board of Trustees minutes, November 3, 1969, December 10, 1971.

14. *Hollywood Sun-Tattler*, January 30 and June 17, 1968, July 3, 1969, February 23 and June 1, 1970; *Miami Herald*, June 1, 1970.

15. Board of Trustees minutes, May 20 and 27, 1968; Abe Fischler's interview with Robert Ellyson; *Hollywood Sun-Tattler*, January 17, 1968, June 1, 1970; *Miami Herald*, June 1, 1970.

16. Author's interview with Ed Simco.

17. Board of Trustees minutes, August 28, 1968.

18. Goldstein, *The Search for Nova University: An Essay on Its First Twenty-Five Years, 1964–1989*, 7–13.

19. Report to the Nova University Board of Trustees, April 22, 1969; *A Year of Decisions: A Report to the University, 1969*, NSU Archives.

20. Abe Fischler's interviews with Tinsley Ellis, James Hartley, Robert Ellyson, and Jim Farquhar; author's interview with Abe Fischler.

21. Board of Trustees minutes, May 26, 1969; *Fort Lauderdale Sun-Sentinel*, June 7, 1969; *Miami Herald*, August 4, 1969; Abe Fischler's interviews with Tinsley Ellis and Robert Ellyson; author's interview with Abe Fischler.

22. J. Stanley Marshall to Jim Farquhar, May 15, 1969, NSU Archives; author's interview with Tinsley Ellis; Board of Trustees minutes, May 15, 1969.

23. Board of Trustees minutes, May 26, 1969; Kenneth R. Williams to Warren Winstead, May 26, 1969. NSU Archives.

24. *Fort Lauderdale News*, May 27, 1969.

25. Ibid., June 6, 1969.

26. Ibid., July 2, 1969.

27. *Miami Herald*, August 3, 4, 1969; Abe Fischler's interview with Tinsley Ellis.

28. *Hollywood Sun-Tattler*, August 5, 1969; *Miami Herald*, August 5, 1969.

29. Author's interview with Abe Fischler.

3. The Abraham Fischler Presidency

1. Abe Fischler's interviews with Jim Farquhar, Robert Ellyson, James Hartley, and Tinsley Ellis; author's interview with Abe Fischler; Board of Trustees minutes, August 25, 1969.

2. *Hollywood Sun-Tattler*, May 17, 1970; *Fort Lauderdale News and Sun-Sentinel*, May 17, 1970.

3. Board of Trustees minutes, July 15, 1968, May 26 and July 21, 1969; *Fort Lauderdale News and Sun-Sentinel*, August 16, 1970; Alex Schure to Warren Winstead, June 12, 1968; Warren Winstead to Alex Schure, August 29, 1968, and Alex Schure to Warren Winstead, September 4, 1968.

4. *Fort Lauderdale News and Sun-Sentinel*, August 16, 1970; *Fort Lauderdale News*, July 5, 1975; *Gold Coast Pictorial*, November 1973.

5. Board of Trustees minutes, June 25, 1969.

6. Abe Fischler's interview with Alex Schure; author's interview with Abe Fischler.

7. Abe Fischler's interview with Alex Schure; author's interview with Abe Fischler.

8. Official document of the merger of NYIT and Nova University, July 1, 1969, NSU Archives.

9. Abe Fischler's interview with Hamilton Forman; *Gold Coast Pictorial*, November 1973.

10. Author's interviews with Tinsley Ellis and Abe Fischler; Abe Fischler's interviews with Tinsley Ellis, Robert Ellyson, and Hamilton Forman.

11. *Fort Lauderdale News and Sun-Sentinel*, July 1 and 9, and August 16, 1970.

12. Author's interview with Tinsley Ellis; Abe Fischler's interview with Hamilton Forman; *Gold Coast Pictorial*, November 1973.

13. Abe Fischler's interview with Robert Ellyson; Abe Fischler's statement to the Board of Trustees, April 25, 1978, NSU Archives.

14. Author's interview with Abe Fischler; *Miami Herald*, September 6, 1970.

15. Author's interview with Abe Fischler; *Gold Coast Pictorial*, November 1973; *Miami Herald*, September 6, 1970.

16. *Fort Lauderdale News and Sun-Sentinel*, September 6 and 10, 1970.

17. Official invitation to the inauguration of Abe Fischler and his inaugural address, NSU Archives; Honorary degree to Alex Schure, NSU Archives; *Miami Herald*, October 5, 1970; *Nova University News*, vol. 4, no. 2, Fall 1970.

18. Investiture of Alex Schure as chancellor of Nova University, November 15, 1970, NSU Archives.

19. Board of Trustees minutes, February 16, 1973.

20. Author's interview with Abe Fischler; Leonard, *Nova University: Setting the Pace in Education for 25 Years*, 25–26.

21. Author's interview with Abe Fischler and Ed Simco.

22. *Miami Herald*, September 28, 1971.

23. Abe Fischler's interviews with Al Mizell, Phil DeTurk, Hamilton Forman, Robert Ellyson, John Scigliano, and Tinsley Ellis; author's interview with Abe Fischler and Ed Simco.

24. Author's interview with Abe Fischler and Tom Panza; Abe Fischler's interview with Hamilton Forman; Gordon W. Sweet, SACS, to Richard Morland, June 4, 1973, NSU Archives; *Nova Knights Newsletter*, November 21, 1983; *Miami Herald*, March 4, 1982.

25. *Cincinnati Enquirer*, January 28, 1978.

26. *Cincinnati Enquirer*, January 28, 1978; *Nova University, Inc. vs. The Cincinnati Enquirer*, U.S. District Court, Southern Division of Ohio, 1978.

27. *Miami Herald*, July 14, 1979; author's interview with Abe Fischler.

28. *Marketing Reconnaissance Report*, prepared by the Barton-Gillet Company, April 1983, NSU Archives.

29. *Chronicle of Higher Education*, November 3, 1980, 13–14.

30. Author's interview with Tom Panza.

31. Board of Trustees minutes, December 3, 1970, March 23, 1971, June 5 and 9, 1972, June 30, 1972, September 25, 1972, and October 6, 1972; author's interviews with Abe Fischler and Ed Simco; Abe Fischler's interview with Tinsley Ellis.

32. Author's interview with Abe Fischler; *Self-Study University Private School*, 1972, NSU Archives; *The Report of the President on the Fifteenth Anniversary of Nova University*, NSU Archives; Board of Trustees minutes, December 3, 1970, March 23, 1971, and June 5 and 30, 1972.

33. Author's interviews with Robert Bogorff and Abe Fischler; Abe Fischler's interviews with Alex Schure and Tinsley Ellis; *Miami Herald*, August 6, 1972; *New Times Broward-Palm Beach*, November 22, 2001.

34. Mormino, *Land of Sunshine, State of Dreams: A Social History of Modern Florida*, 96; author's interview with Abe Fischler.

35. Abe Fischler's interviews with Robert Ellyson, Alex Schure, and Tinsley Ellis; author's interviews with Abe Fischler and Tinsley Ellis; Board of Trustees minutes, December 20, 1974.

36. *Western News*, September 3, 1974; *Hollywood Sun-Tattler*, December 13, 1973; *Fort Lauderdale News*, September 8 and December 13, 1974; author's interviews with Abe Fischler, Tinsley Ellis, and Ron Brown; Board of Trustees minutes, March 20, 1975.

37. *Hollywood Sun-Tattler*, February 14, 1975; Board of Trustees minutes, March 7 and May 23, 1975; author's interview with Ron Brown.

38. Board of Trustees minutes, September 26, 1975; *Fort Lauderdale News*, August 13 and 14, 1975.

39. *Hollywood Sun-Tattler*, June 11, 1975; *Fort Lauderdale News*, August 14, 1975.

40. Author's interviews with Ron Brown and Mark Dobson.

41. Laurance M. Hyde Jr. to Abe Fischler, March 17, 1976, and April 1, 1978, NSU Archives; Linda Yates, *Florida Bar Journal*, to Rosemary Jones, August 29, 1977, NSU Archives.

42. Board of Trustees minutes, March 22, 1978; author's interviews with Ovid Lewis and Tom Panza.

43. Summary of American Bar Association inspection team, January 14, 1981, NSU Archives.

44. Laurance M. Hyde to Abe Fischler, September 19, 1978, NSU Archives; author's interview with Ovid Lewis; Abe Fischler's interview with Hamilton Forman.

45. Author's interview with Ron Brown and Mark Dobson; *Fort Lauderdale News and Sun-Sentinel*, June 10, 1979; Board of Trustees minutes, June 10, 1979.

46. Author's interview with Ovid Lewis; *Hollywood Sun-Tattler*, November 21, 1979.

47. Law offices of Spear, Deuschle, and Curran, Fort Lauderdale, to Abe Fischler, February 26, 1979, NSU Archives; Abe Fischler's interviews with Hamilton Forman and A.D. Griffin; author's interviews with Abe Fischler, Ron Brown, Joel Berman, and Tom Panza; Board of Trustees minutes, February 28, 1979, and October 1, 1982.

48. Author's interview with John Santulli and Ron Brown.

49. Willard L. Boyd, ABA, to Ovid Lewis and Abe Fischler, July 16, 1981, NSU Archives; Board of Trustees minutes, September 13, 1982.

50. Author's interviews with John Santulli, Ovid Lewis, and Abe Fischler; Board of Trustees minutes, January 24, 1983, and April 6, 1984.

4. The Goodwin Trust and the Disappearance of the *Gulf Stream*

1. Board of Trustees of the Leo Goodwin Unitrust to the Board of Trustees of Nova University, May 3, 1976, NSU Archives.

2. *Fort Lauderdale News*, May 20, 1976; *Broward News*, May 26, 1976; Law Offices of Hogan and Hartson to "Unitrust Trustees," April 28, 1977.

3. Author's interview with Abe Fischler and Tinsley Ellis; Abe Fischler's interview with Robert Ellyson; *Fort Lauderdale News and Sun-Sentinel*, April 26, May 4 and 5, 1978.

4. Statement of Alex Schure, Board of Trustees minutes, April 25, 1978.

5. Board of Trustees minutes, April 17 and 25, 1978; author's interview with Abe Fischler; Abe Fischler's interview with Robert Ellyson and Tinsley Ellis; *Fort Lauderdale News*, June 22 and 26, 1978; *Miami Herald*, June 26, 1978.

6. *Fort Lauderdale News*, August 4 and 5, 1978; author's interview with Abe Fischler; Abe Fischler's interviews with Alex Schure and Ray Ferrero Jr.

7. *Broward Review*, March 4 and May 24, 1988; *Fort Lauderdale News*, February 24, 1988.

8. Florida Supreme Court decision, June 22, 1989, *Florida Bar vs. Alphonse Della-Donna*, case #69,324.

9. Board of Trustees minutes, November 17, 1980.

10. Author's interview with Abe Fischler; Leonard, *Nova University: Setting the Pace in Education for 25 Years*, 35–37.

11. *Fort Lauderdale News and Sun-Sentinel*, May 6, 1978.

12. Robert Bogorff, *The Leo Goodwin Institute for Cancer Research of Nova University, 1969–1980*, n.d., 8–11; Board of Trustees minutes, March 21, 1979, and June 11, 1980.

13. Author's interview with Abe Fischler; Leonard, *Nova University: Setting the Pace in Education for 25 Years*, 38–40.

14. Bogorff, *The Mysterious Disappearance of Nova University's Research Vessel* Gulf Stream.

15. Thoreau, *Cape Cod*, 114.

16. Bogorff, *The Mysterious Disappearance of Nova University's Research Vessel* Gulf Stream; author's interview with Robert Bogorff; Board of Trustees minutes, May 23, 1975.

17. Author's interview with Richard Dodge and Abe Fischler; *Fort Lauderdale News and Sun-Sentinel*, December 13, 1986.

18. Author's interview with Abe Fischler; Abe Fischler's interview with Phil DeTurk.

19. *Nova Knight*, November 6, 1984, n.d., 1986; *Hollywood Sun-Tattler*, n.d., NSU Archives; author's interviews with Frank DePiano and Brad Williams.

20. *Nova Knight*, November 21 and December 19, 1983; author's interview with Zeida Rodriguez.

21. *Nova Knight*, November 6, 1984, and March 6, 1985.

22. Ibid., October 30, 1984, and September 30, 1985.

23. Ibid., December 11, 1984, April 17 and 24, 1985, and November 10, 1986.

24. Abe Fischler's interview with Phil DeTurk; author's interview with Abe Fischler; Leonard, *Nova University: Setting the Pace in Education for 25 Years*, 56; *Nova University: Panama Center, 1987*, NSU Archives; *Fort Lauderdale News and Sun-Sentinel*, May 1, 1986.

25. Nova University Faculty handbook, January 15, 1975, NSU Archives; author's interview with Abe Fischler.

26. Author's interview with Abe Fischler.

27. Nova University news release, September 14, 1977; *Fort Lauderdale News*, September 26, 1977; *Nova University News*, vol. 3, no. 3, October, 1977.

28. *The Report of the President on the 15th Anniversary of Nova University*, NSU Archives; *Miami Herald*, undated newspaper clipping, NSU Archives.

29. *Miami Herald*, January 20, 1978, undated, 1978; *Hollywood Sun-Tattler*, February 23, 1970; *The Report of the President on the 15th Anniversary of Nova University*, NSU Archives; author's interview with Frank DePiano.

30. Author's interview with Robert Bogorff.

31. Abe Fischler's interview with John Scigliano, Phil DeTurk, and Al Mizell; author's interview with Ed Simco.

5. End to the NYIT Merger

1. Mrs. B.K. Dorsey to Abe Fischler, February 13, 1984, NSU Archives.

2. Board of Trustees minutes, September 12 and October 31, 1975.

3. *Nova University Approved Budget for 1976–1977 Fiscal and Academic Year*, NSU Archives.

4. Abe Fischler to Board of Trustees, June 18, 1979, NSU Archives.
5. *Miami Herald*, September 29, 1984; *Fort Lauderdale News*, September 27, 1984.
6. *Fort Lauderdale News*, July 5, 1978.
7. Ibid., May 3, 1978.
8. Board of Trustees minutes, March 29, 1976.
9. Board of Trustees minutes, April 25, 1978; Abe Fischler's interview with Alex Schure.
10. Abe Fischler to Ovid Lewis, September 10, 1985, NSU Archives; author's interview with Frank DePiano.
11. *Proposal for Nova/NYIT Agreement*, September 24, 1985, NSU Archives.
12. Board of Trustees minutes, September 12, 1985; author's interview with Abe Fischler.
13. Author's interviews with Abe Fischler, Tom Panza, Tinsley Ellis, and Frank DePiano; Abe Fischler's interview with Tinsley Ellis.
14. Abe Fischler's interviews with John Scigliano and Alex Schure; author's interviews with Abe Fischler, Frank DePiano, and Tom Panza.
15. Jay McCreary to Abe Fischler, May 7, 1985; Ed Simco to Abe Fischler, September 6, 1985, NSU Archives; author's interview with Ed Simco.
16. Terry Russell to Mary McCahill, September 11, 1985; *A draft of Nova University vs. New York Institute of Technology, in the Circuit Court of the Seventeenth Judicial District in and for Broward County, Florida, October 10, 1985*, NSU Archives.
17. Author's interview with Abe Fischler.
18. *Agreement*, October 31, 1985; Terry Russell to John A. Bond, January 9, 1986, NSU Archives.
19. Abe Fischler's interview with Tinsley Ellis.
20. Author's interview with Abe Fischler and Frank DePiano.

6. Stabilization and Expansion

1. Author's interview with Abe Fischler.
2. *Nova University, The Report of the President, 1988–1989*, NSU Archives.
3. *Fort Lauderdale Sun-Sentinel*, June 6, 9, 14, 28, and 30, and October 6, 1988; *Lakeland Ledger*, June 12, 1988; *Ocala Star Banner*, June 12, 1988; *Miami Herald*, June 6 and 9, and November 22, 1988; *Hollywood Sun-Tattler*, October 5, 1988.
4. *Nova University, The Report of the President, 1988–1989*, NSU Archives; *Fort Lauderdale Sun-Sentinel*, April 16 and December 3, 1989.
5. *Hollywood Sun-Tattler*, July 2, 1986, and June 9, 1987.
6. *Miami Herald*, November 16, 1988.
7. Author's interview with Ray Ferrero Jr.
8. *Fort Lauderdale Sun-Sentinel*, June 9, 1987.
9. Author's interview with Ron Chenail.

10. *Miami Herald*, July 2, 1989; *Hollywood Sun-Tattler*, July 4, 1989; author's interview with Abe Fischler, Ron Brown, John Santulli, and Ray Ferrero Jr.

11. Author's interviews with Abe Fischler and John Santulli.

12. Author's interview with Ron Chenail.

13. Author's interview with Abe Fischler and John Santulli; Board of Trustees minutes, April 6 and 30, 1984, November 25, 1985, July 28, 1986, and November 23, 1987; *Miami Herald*, February 1, 1986.

14. Author's interview with Abe Fischler, Tinsley Ellis, John Santulli, Stephen Feldman, and Ovid Lewis; dedication of the Horvitz Building, October 27, 1994, pamphlet in NSU Archives.

15. Author's interview with Frank DePiano, John Santulli, and Robert Bogorff; Robert Bogorff, *Dear Max, Dear Friend* pamphlet in NSU Archives.

16. Author's interview with John Santulli.

17. George H. Gore to Jack LaBonte, May 1, 1985, NSU Archives.

18. *Report of the SACS Inspection Team, May 25, 1989*, NSU Archives; Board of Trustees minutes, May 15, 1989.

19. Board of Trustees minutes, September 23, 1991; Bernice and Jack LaBonte to Abe Fischler, December 9, 1991, NSU Archives.

20. Board of Trustees minutes, May 22, September 22, and November 22, 1993, January 24, 1994, and September 18, 1995.

21. Board of Trustees minutes, May 24, 1994; author's interview with Nadine Barnes.

22. Author's interview with Jerry Chermak.

23. *Miami Herald*, August 22–30, 1992; *Fort Lauderdale Sun-Sentinel*, September 1 and 7, 1992; *Nova Knight*, September 1, 1992, vol. III, issue 2; author's interviews with Ron Brown, Elaine Poff, Ed Simco, Stephen Feldman, and Brad Williams.

24. Author's interview with Abe Fischler; Abe Fischler to the Board of Trustees, May 18, 1991, NSU Archives.

25. *Nova News*, vol. 1, issue 3, summer 1992.

26. *Nova News*, vol. 1, issue 3, summer 1992; author's interview with Ron Brown; *Fort Lauderdale Sun-Sentinel*, May 23 and 27, 1991; *Hollywood Sun-Tattler*, May 23, 1991; *Broward Review*, May 23, 1991.

27. Board of Trustees minutes, February 21, 1992; author's interviews with Stephen Feldman, Abe Fischler, Tinsley Ellis, and Ovid Lewis; itinerary of Stephen Feldman, February 24–25, 1992, NSU Archives.

28. Author's interview with Stephen Feldman; *Florida Trend*, summer 1992.

29. Stephen Feldman to Ovid Lewis, April 25, 1994, NSU Archives; author's interviews with Ovid Lewis and Stephen Feldman.

30. Author's interviews with Stephen Feldman, John Santulli, Frank DePiano, and Ray Ferrero Jr.

31. Abe Fischler's interview with Eddie Jones; author's interviews with Abe Fischler, Stephen Feldman, and John Santulli.

32. Jack LaBonte to Abe Fischler, February 12, 1992, NSU Archives.

33. Board of Trustees minutes, February 21 and May 30, 1992.

34. Miami Dolphins to Abe Fischler, May 20, 1992, NSU Archives; Abe Fischler to Miami Dolphins, Ltd., May 20, 1992, NSU Archives; author's interviews with Stephen Feldman, Abe Fischler, and John Santulli; Abe Fischler's interview with Eddie Jones; *Nova University Master Plan*, 1996.

35. *Nova University Master Plan*, 1996; Abe Fischler's interview with Eddie Jones; Board of Trustees minutes, May 20, 1996.

36. Abe Fischler's interview with Eddie Jones; author's interviews with Abe Fischler, John Santulli, and Stephen Feldman.

37. Ray Ferrero Jr. to Stephen Feldman, June 2, 1992, NSU Archives; Board of Trustees minutes, June 8, 1994.

38. Author's interviews with Stephen Feldman, Ray Ferrero Jr., Abe Fischler, Ovid Lewis, Ed Simco, and Charles Shirley.

39. Author's interviews with Ovid Lewis, Ray Ferrero Jr., Abe Fischler, and Tinsley Ellis; Board of Trustees minutes, June 8, 1994, and September 26, 1994.

40. Author's interview with Ovid Lewis.

41. Author's interviews with Ovid Lewis, Ron Chenail, Abe Fischler, and Frank DePiano; *Fort Lauderdale News*, October 28, 1987.

42. *Nova Southeastern University Sentinel*, summer 1994; author's interview with Ovid Lewis.

43. President's Statement, 1994, NSU Archives; author's interview with Ovid Lewis.

44. Author's interview with Ovid Lewis.

45. *Alumni Network*, vol. XIII, no. 1, April 1997.

46. Author's interview with Ovid Lewis.

47. Author's interview with Brad Williams.

48. Author's interviews with Brad Williams and Scott Chitoff.

49. *Athletics History*, NSU Department of Athletics, NSU Archives.

50. Author's interview with Ovid Lewis.

51. Author's interviews with Ovid Lewis, Abe Fischler, and Ed Simco; Board of Trustees minutes, May 21, 1994; *Alumni Network*, vol. XIV, no. 1, February 1998.

52. Author's interview with Ovid Lewis.

7. Merger with Southeastern University of the Health Sciences

1. Author's interview with Stanley Cohen.

2. *COM Outlook*, spring 2004, fall 2005; author's interview with Arnold Melnick.

3. Author's interviews with Fred Lippman and Arnold Melnick; *The Visionary*, fall 2009; *COM Outlook*, spring 2004.

4. *The Visionary*, fall 2009; *COM Outlook*, fall 2005; author's interviews with Arnold Melnick, Fred Lippman, and Stanley Cohen.

5. Author's interviews with Fred Lippman, Abe Fischler, Ray Ferrero Jr., and Arnold Melnick; *An Evaluation of the Desirability of Nova Univer-*

sity Acquiring the Southeastern University of the Health Sciences, NSU Archives.

6. Author's interviews with Stephen Feldman, Fred Lippman, Arnold Melnick, Stanley Cohen, John Santulli, and Joel Berman; Board of Trustees minutes, May 22 and September 27, 1993.

7. Author's interviews with Fred Lippman, Ray Ferrero Jr., and Arnold Melnick; *Dental Report*, n.d., NSU Archives; *COM Outlook*, spring 2004.

8. Board of Trustees minutes, September 26, 1994, January 23, 1995, June 24, 1996, and March 23, 1998; *The Record*, the official publication of the Broward County Medical Association, October 1996.

9. James T. Rogers, SACS, to Stephen Feldman, January 12, 1994, NSU Archives; Sandra L. Knight, SACS, to Stephen Feldman, March 11, 1994, NSU Archives.

10. Author's interviews with Fred Lippman, Arnold Melnick, Stephen Feldman, Stanley Cohen, and Tinsley Ellis.

11. "In Memoriam: Morton Terry," *COM Outlook*, spring 2004.

8. The Ray Ferrero Jr. Presidency

1. Author's interview with Ray Ferrero Jr.; Board of Trustees minutes, May 17 and December 1, 1997; *Alumni Magazine*, NSU, September 1997; *Miami Herald*, February 10, 1998.

2. *Miami Herald*, February 10, 1998.

3. Author's interview with Ray Ferrero Jr.; curriculum vitae of Ray Ferrero Jr., NSU Archives; *Celebration of Excellence, NSU, 1998*, NSU Archives.

4. *Alumni Magazine*, NSU, September 1997.

5. Board of Trustees minutes, January 26, 1998.

6. *Miami Herald*, February 10, 1998.

7. *Fort Lauderdale Sun-Sentinel*, December 13, 1998; *Celebration of Excellence, NSU, 1998*, NSU Archives.

8. Author's interview with Ray Ferrero Jr.

9. Author's interview with Brad Williams.

10. *Update, NSU*, summer 1989, vol. X, no. 2; *Celebration of Excellence, NSU, 1998*, NSU Archives.

11. Author's interview with Ray Ferrero Jr.

12. *Miami Herald*, February 5 and May 31, 1998; author's interview with Ray Ferrero Jr.

13. Author's interviews with Robert Bogorff, Ray Ferrero Jr., and Samuel Morrison.

14. Author's interviews with Frank DePiano, George Hanbury, Ray Ferrero Jr., Tinsley Ellis, and Tom Panza.

15. *Update, NSU*, winter 2000, vol. XII, no. 1; *Fort Lauderdale Sun-Sentinel*, August 1, 1999.

16. *Sarasota Herald-Tribune*, December 9, 2001; *Miami Herald*, December 9, 2001; *Chronicle of Higher Education*, December 10, 2001; *NSU Achievements*, Office of Public Affairs, winter 2001/spring 2002, vol. 3, no. 2.

17. *Miami Herald*, November 25, 1984; NSU News Release, September 17, 2003; author's interviews with Samuel Morrison, Ray Ferrero Jr., and Lydia Acosta.

18. Author's interviews with Samuel Morrison, Frank DePiano, Ray Ferrero Jr., and George Hanbury.

19. Board of Trustees minutes, March 25, 1991; Agreement between the Friedt Family Foundation and NSU, September 15, 1987, NSU Archives; Nova University Press Release, October 7, 1987; Leslie Brown to Theodore K. Friedt, July 27, 1988, NSU Archives.

20. *NSU Achievements*, spring 2001, vol. 3, no. 1; NSU News Release, August 6, 2009.

21. "Blockbuster Growth: How Wayne Huizenga Perfected the Art of Starting and Growing a Business," *Smart Business*, September 2005; "H. Wayne Huizenga," http://www.huizenga.nova.edu/About/HWayneHuizenga.cfm (accessed January 21, 2012).

22. *Fort Lauderdale Sun-Sentinel*, September 28, 1999; *Miami Herald*, September 28, 1999; *Update*, NSU, winter 2000, vol. XII, no. 1; author's interview with Ray Ferrero Jr.; NSU News Release, December 13, 2011.

23. *Fort Lauderdale Sun-Sentinel*, August 1, 1999, and March 23, 2000; *NSU Alumni Network*, fall 2000; *New York Times*, July 31, 2005.

24. NSU Media Alert, January 24, 2002; *Alumni News*, spring 2004, vol. XVIII, no. 2; *Fort Lauderdale Sun-Sentinel*, January 10, 2004.

25. Author's interview with Zeida Rodriguez.

26. Author's interview with Charles Shirley.

27. Author's interview with Paul Sallarulo.

28. *Sharkbytes*, August 30, 2010; "H. Wayne Huizenga School of Business and Entrepreneurship Vision/Mission Statement," http://www.huizenga.nova.edu/About/HWayneHuizenga.cfm (accessed January 21, 2012); NSU News Release, September 17, 2009.

29. Author's interview with Ray Ferrero Jr.; *NCAA Division II Mission statement*, NSU Archives; *Athletics History*, NSU Department of Athletics, NSU Archives.

30. Author's interviews with Brad Williams and Ray Ferrero Jr.

31. *Athletics History, Athletic Facilities*, NSU Department of Athletics, NSU Archives; *Horizons*, spring 2011.

32. Author's interviews with Ray Ferrero Jr., John Santulli, and Brad Williams; letter from the President, Ray Ferrero Jr., 2005, NSU Archives.

33. NSU News Release, February 11, 2009; *Fort Lauderdale Sun-Sentinel*, February 24, 2009.

34. "The Commons," http://www.nova.edu/studentlife/oncampus.html (accessed January 26, 2012); *Miami Herald*, August 26, 2007; author's interviews with John Santulli, Brad Williams, and Ray Ferrero Jr.

35. "Rolling Hills Graduate Residence Hall," http://www.nova.edu/studentlife/oncampus.html (accessed January 26, 2012); author's interviews with John Santulli, Joel Berman, and Brad Williams.

36. Author's interviews with Frank DePiano, Ray Ferrero Jr., Zeida Rodriguez, Ron Brown, and Sam Morrison; *Miami Herald*, August 25, 2001, and April 1, 2009.

37. Author's interviews with Zeida Rodriguez, George Hanbury, and Brad Williams; *Miami Herald*, October 8, 2000.

38. Author's interviews with Charles Shirley and Paul Sallarulo.

39. *NSU Fact Book, 2011*, 75; NSU News Release, June 14, 2011.

40. Author's interviews with Richard Dodge and Frank DePiano; *Fort Lauderdale Sun-Sentinel*, January 11 and 15, 2011.

41. *Horizons*, spring 2010; *Celebration of Excellence, 1998*, NSU Archives; author's interviews with Ron Brown, Phyllis Coleman, and Mark Dobson; NSU News Release, March 21, 1995; *Miami Herald*, February 28, 1999; *NSU Fact Book, 2011*.

42. *COM Outlook*, November 2000, vol. 1, no. 5; *COM Outlook*, August 2001, vol. 2, no. 4; author's interview with Fred Lippman.

43. *COM Outlook*, winter 2001–2002, winter 2006, summer 2007, spring 2011; *NSU Fact Book, 2011*, 42–48.

44. *NSU Fact Book, 2011*, 49–51.

45. *History of the Mailman Segal Institute*, white paper, in possession of the author; author's interviews with Ray Ferrero Jr., and Jamie Mayersohn; *Fort Lauderdale Sun-Sentinel*, March 27, 2001; Media Alert, NSU, March 26, 2001.

46. Author's interview with Ray Ferrero Jr.

47. Author's interview with Jerry Chermak; *Update, NSU*, winter 2000, vol. XII, no. 1.

48. Author's interview with Nadine Barnes.

49. *SharkBytes*, October 2009; author's interview with Anthony DeNapoli.

50. *NSU Fact Book, 2011*, 39–40.

51. *Fort Lauderdale Sun-Sentinel*, November 17, 2000; *Miami Herald*, September 16, 2003; author's interview with Ray Ferrero Jr.; Thomas W. MacFarland, *The History of Distance Education at NSU, Report 08–09, November 2008*, NSU Archives.

52. Media Alert, NSU Office of Public Affairs, May 31, 2001; MacFarland, *The History of Distance Education at NSU*.

53. Author's interviews with Ray Ferrero Jr. and George Hanbury; *Miami Herald*, May 21, 2008.

54. *NSUCommuniversity Outreach, 2000*, NSU Archives.

55. NSU News Release, January 13, 2010.

56. Author's interview with Tinsley Ellis.

57. NSU News Release, January 11, 2010.

58. Ibid., September 4, 2003.

59. *South Florida Business Journal*, December 7, 2009; *Miami Herald*, December 12, 2009.

60. *South Florida Sun-Sentinel*, June 8, 2008.

61. Author's interviews with Tinsley Ellis, Abe Fischler, Ron Brown, John Santulli, Dick Dodge, Stanley Cohen, Charles Shirley, Samuel Morrison, Tom Panza, Paul Sallarulo, Anthony DeNapoli, and Frank DePiano; *South Florida Sun-Sentinel*, January 26, 2003, January 10, 2004, and June 8, 2008; *Miami Today*, October 11, 2011.

62. *South Florida Sun-Sentinel*, June 8, 2008.

63. *Horizons*, spring 2011; author's interview with Ray Ferrero Jr.

9. The Hanbury Era

1. NSU News Release, December 8, 2010; author's interview with George Hanbury; Board of Trustees minutes, December 7, 2010.

2. Author's interview with George Hanbury and Ray Ferrero Jr.

3. Author's interview with George Hanbury; NSU News Release, April 7, 2011; *Estate Lifestyle*, August 2011.

4. NSU News Release, April 26, 2011; *SharkBytes*, April 26, 2011; *Estate Lifestyle*, August 2011.

5. Author's interview with George Hanbury.

6. Author's interviews with George Hanbury and Joel Berman; NSU 2010–2020 Business Plan, NSU Archives.

7. Author's interview with George Hanbury; *Who We Serve*, pamphlet by the Independent Colleges and Universities of Florida.

8. *SharkBytes*, August 26, 2011.

9. *SharkBytes*, September 6, 2011; author's interview with George Hanbury.

10. *SharkBytes*, January 24, 2011; author's interview with George Hanbury.

11. *SharkBytes*, October 19, 2011; author's interview with George Hanbury.

12. *SharkBytes,* July 18, 2011; author's interview with George Hanbury.

13. Author's interviews with George Hanbury, Ray Ferrero Jr., Frank DePiano, Brad Williams, Ron Chenail, John Santulli, and Anthony DeNapoli.

14. *New York Times*, December 19, 2011.

Bibliography

Newspapers/Periodicals/Magazines

Alumni Magazine
Alumni Network
Alumni News
Broward News
Broward Review
The Chronicle of Higher Education
The Cincinnati Enquirer
COM Outlook
Estate Lifestyle
The Florida Bar Journal
Florida Trend
Fort Lauderdale News and Sun-Sentinel
Fort Lauderdale Sun-Sentinel
Fort Lauderdale Tattler
Gold Coast Pictorial
Hollywood Sun-Tattler
Horizons
The Lakeland Ledger
The Miami Herald
Miami Today
New Times Broward-Palm Beach
The New York Times
The Novacrat
The Nova Knight
Nova Knights Newsletter
Nova Southeastern University Sentinel
Nova University News

Novatas
NovaTech
NSU Alumni Network
The Ocala Star Banner
Pictorial Life
The Record
Rocky Mountain News
Sarasota Herald Tribune
SharkBytes
South Florida Business Journal
South Florida Sun-Sentinel
Sun-Sentinel
Time
The Update
The Visionary
The Western News

Unpublished Papers

Bogorff, Robert. *The Leo Goodwin Institute for Cancer Research of Nova University, 1969–1980, 2010,* located in the NSU Archives.
History of Broward County Public Schools. (n.d., no author.), located in the NSU Archives.
Leonard, James Dwight. *Nova University: Setting the Pace in Education for 25 Years,* located in the NSU Archives.
MacFarland, Thomas W. *The History of Distance Education at NSU, Report 08–09,* November 2008, located in the NSU Archives.
Rushing, Joe. *Outline of South Florida Education Center for Science and Technology,* February 23, 1961, located in the NSU Archives.
Spivey, Herman E. *Nova University 1968,* located in the NSU Archives.
Synnestvedt, Stuart. *Education, Science, and Technology Center of South Florida,* February 24, 1961, located in the NSU Archives.

Interviews

2009–2010

Abraham Fischler, NSU president, 1970–1992
George Hanbury II, NSU president, 2010–present
Ovid Lewis, NSU president, 1994–1997
Ray Ferrero Jr., NSU president, 1998–2010, and chancellor, 2010–present
Stephen Feldman, NSU president, 1992–1994
W. Tinsley Ellis, NSU Board of Trustees

2010

Brad Williams, vice president for student affairs, NSU
Charles Shirley, alumnus; vice president, Comerica's Weston Banking Center

Cheryl Gotthelf, alumnus, licensed psychologist in private practice
Edward Simco, professor, Center for Psychological Studies, NSU
Frank DePiano, provost and executive vice president for academic affairs,
    NSU
G. Elaine Poff, director of university registrar's office for enrollment and
    student services, NSU
John Santulli, vice president for facilities management, NSU
Richard Dodge, professor and dean, NSU Oceanographic Center; executive
    director, National Coral Reef Institute, NSU
Robert Bogorff, university archivist, NSU
Ronald Brown, professor of law, Shepard Broad Law Center, NSU
Samuel Morrison, retired director of the Broward County Library System
Stanley Cohen, vice provost, Health Professions Division, NSU
Thomas Panza, general counsel and special assistant to the president, NSU

2011
Anthony DeNapoli, executive director, Office of International Affairs, NSU
Arnold Melnick, DO, retired, executive vice chancellor and provost, Health
    Professions Division, NSU
Frederick Lippman, chancellor, Health Professions Division, NSU
Jerome Chermak, headmaster, University School, NSU
Nadine Barnes, director of the Lower School, University School, NSU
Paul Sallarulo, alumnus; president, Nexera Medical; member, NSU Board of
    Trustees
Ronald Chenail, vice president for institutional effectiveness, NSU
Scott Chitoff, alumnus, practicing attorney
Susan Atherley, alumnus; adjunct professor, NSU; principal, Alexander
    Dreyfoos School of the Arts
Zeida Rodriguez, alumnus; associate director of enrollment services,
    H. Wayne Huizenga School of Business and Entrepreneurship, NSU

2012
George Hanbury II, NSU president, 2010–present
Joel Berman, vice president for legal affairs, NSU
John Santulli, vice president for facilities management, NSU
Mark Dobson, professor of law, Shepard Broad Law Center, NSU
Phyllis Coleman, professor of law, Shepard Broad Law Center, NSU

Abraham Fischler conducted several significant interviews with important
    individuals in the university's history who have since passed away. Their
    insights and comments are valuable additions to the story of NSU and
    would have been lost if not for Fischler's diligence.
Abe Fischler with Al Mizell and Philip DeTurk, February 4, 1999.
Abe Fischler with Alex Schure, Ovid Lewis, and Ray Ferrero Jr., October 9
    and November 6, 1997.
Abe Fischler with Charles Forman, July 3, 1997.

Abe Fischler with Eddie Jones, June 7, 1999.
Abe Fischler with Hamilton Forman and A.D. Griffin, November 13, 1997.
Abe Fischler with Helen Graham, June 14, 1997.
Abe Fischler with James Hartley and Tinsley Ellis, October 29, 1997.
Abe Fischler with Jim and Nan Farquhar, n.d.
Abe Fischler with John Scigliano, June 21, 1999.
Abe Fischler with Marilyn Segal and Richard Goldman, February 1998.
Abe Fischler with Robert Ellyson, May 1, 2001.

Books

Bogorff, Robert. *The Mysterious Disappearance of Nova University's Research Vessel* Gulf Stream. Fort Lauderdale: Department of Archives, Alvin Sherman Library, Research, and Information Technology Center, Nova Southeastern University, 2006.
Goldstein, Stephen L. *The Search for Nova University: An Essay on Its First Twenty-Five Years, 1964–1989*. Fort Lauderdale: Nova University, 1989.
Grunwald, Michael. *The Swamp: The Everglades, Florida, and the Politics of Paradise*. New York: Simon and Schuster, 2006.
Mormino, Gary. *Land of Sunshine, State of Dreams: A Social History of Modern Florida*. Gainesville: University Press of Florida, 2005.
Thoreau, Henry David. *Cape Cod*. Boston: Ticknor and Fields, 1866.
Wagner, Victoria. *The History of Davie and Its Dilemma*. Fort Lauderdale: Nova University/New York Institute of Technology Press, 1982.

Manuscript Collections

Presidential papers, NSU Archives
Minutes of the South Florida Education Center (SFEC)
Minutes of Nova Southeastern University Board of Trustees

Dr. Julian M. Pleasants is professor emeritus of history at the University of Florida (UF), where he taught for thirty-nine years. Pleasants served as director of the Samuel Proctor Oral History Program at UF from 1996 to 2008. He taught more than 11,000 students in his career at UF and was the recipient of more than a dozen teaching awards. He was chosen for inclusion in *Who's Who Among American Teachers*, *Who's Who in America*, and *Who's Who in the World*. He is the author and editor of eight books and numerous articles in various publications. His books on Florida include *Hanging Chads: The Inside Story of the 2000 Presidential Recount in Florida* (2004), *Orange Journalism: Voices from Florida Newspapers* (2003), *Gator Tales: An Oral History of the University of Florida* (2006), and *Seminole Voices: Reflections on Their Changing Society, 1970–2000* (2010) (with Harry A. Kersey). In 2010, the Florida Humanities Council awarded him the silver medal for nonfiction for the book on the Seminoles.

Index

Italic page numbers indicate material in figures. Color plates follow page 206.